# Why Humans Vary In Intelligence

# Books by Seymour W. Itzkoff

*Cultural Pluralism and American Education*   1969

*Ernst Cassirer: Scientific Knowledge and the Concept of Man*   1971

*A New Public Education*   1976

*Ernst Cassirer, Philosopher of Culture*   1977

*Emanuel Feuermann, Virtuoso*   1979

*How We Learn to Read*   1986


The Evolution of Human Intelligence
  A Theory in Four Parts

*The Form of Man, the evolutionary origins of human intelligence*   1983

*Triumph of the Intelligent, the creation of Homo sapiens sapiens*   1985

*Why Humans Vary in Intelligence*   1987

# WHY HUMANS VARY IN INTELLIGENCE

Seymour W. Itzkoff
Smith College

Paideia Publishers
Ashfield, Massachusetts

Published in the United States by

Paideia Publishers
P.O. Box 343
Ashfield, Massachusetts 01330

Library of Congress Cataloging-in-Publication Data

Itzkoff, Seymour W.
    Why humans vary in intelligence.

    (The Evolution of human intelligence ; 3)
    Bibliography: p.
    Includes index.
    1. Human evolution.    2. Intellect.    3. Genetic psychology.    4. Social
evolution.    I. Title.    II. Series:
Itzkoff, Seymour W. Evolution of human intelligence ; 3.
GN281.I87    1987    573.2    87-8861
ISBN: 0-913993-09-3

Dedicated to the memory of
Morris Lazerowitz
1907 - 1987

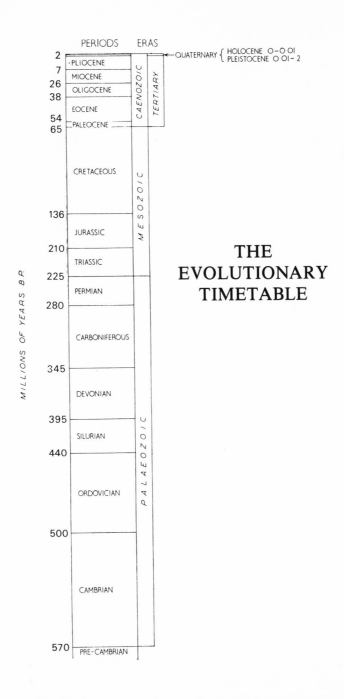

THE
EVOLUTIONARY
TIMETABLE

# TABLE OF CONTENTS

# FOREWORD

The first two books in this series had as their primary function setting forth the evolutionary evidence for the diversity of phyletic heritages in the human species. The evidence for differences in degrees of corticalization and endocranial capacity, together with some of the psychological and neurological data, was laid down in the first volume, *The Form of Man. Triumph of the Intelligent,* the second volume, shaped the evidence into a clearly-articulated evolutionary argument.

Inevitably, the ideological fears and superstitions of some of the critics of these two volumes read into the patently solid scientific facts all sorts of nefarious social intentions. It is natural to want to know the social implications of what can be quite abstract scientific evidence.

This was the sixteenth-century Church's fear about the acceptance of the Copernican hypothesis. What did such facts augur for the existing structure of theological belief and the position of the Church in a changing historical environment?

In the case of *Why Humans Vary In Intelligence,* it has therefore been necessary to jump the gun, so to speak, for, the issue of variable intelligence in humans is a far more volatile issue than was ever planetary motion in the sixteenth and seventeenth centuries. Adding to the integration of bio-evolutionary and psychological evidence in the first two parts is a third section on historical consequences, whose tentative conclusions may be surprising to some readers. Their dimension will need further explanation and elaboration.

The final volume in the series, *The Making of the Civilized Mind,* will close the theoretical circle. It will be more philosophical in orientation, concentrating on that ultimate sociobiological issue, the transformation of *Homo's* paradigmatic biological attribute, his intelligence, into the forms and institutions of cultural and civilizational behavior. I believe that it can be argued persuasively that the various levels of intelligence in differing ethnic groups give rise to the variable character of society and civilization.

This series of books, together with other academic writing commitments, could not have been completed without the committed support of various institutions and foundations. In addition, the moral support of that small group of stubborn warriors for truth has been of inestimable help in keeping me to this task at hand. Inevitably, at times it has been a lonely enterprise.

My Pat has, as always, been the strength and organization of this operation. No word of thanks can properly convey my feelings of dependence. For research assistance, Helen Kihmm started things off strongly, handing on the baton to Kristine Danowski, who supervised the major portion of the research and editorial work, putting it into manageable form, always with taskmaster attention to structure and schedules. Thank you, Kristine. Raji Pillai came on board during the final phase of manuscript shaping and for the index.

*Northampton, Massachusetts*
*March 1987*

# PART 1

---

# *OUR BIOLOGICAL HERITAGE*

*"Sit down before fact as a little child, be prepared
to give up every preconceived notion, follow humbly where
ever and to what ever abysses nature leads, or you shall
learn nothing."*

*Thomas H. Huxley*

# Chapter I

---

# INTRODUCTION: INTELLECTUAL RESPONSIBILITY

*Why Humans Vary in Intelligence* is the third book in a projected series of four on the evolution of human intelligence. It is transitional in that it summarizes the empirical and theoretical evidence in both the evolutionary and psychological domains of the origin and nature of variable human intelligence. It also takes the first steps toward understanding the contemporary results and meaning of the evolutionary evidence.

By the time the reader finishes this book, it will be clear why this issue of variable human intelligence cannot be swept under the rug as an embarrassment, as contradicting "reasonable" opinion. Many still do not see why we must delve into an issue that has excited such passion and that seems to bode ill for the common peace. There are some things about which we don't speak, so goes the truism.

Another belief hoary with establishment verities is that if scholars dredge up such problems, inevitably, evil human beings will turn the results to their own nefarious purposes. It is true, of course, that much pseudo evidence that was used to support the pernicious racist propaganda of the past will surface once more to promote such controversy.

My own view is this: important controversies must be aired openly and honestly. If not, terrible events will occur. As pointed out at the conclusion of this book, it is not so much that factual issues and controversies are exploited by those who would do evil. Rather it is that our unwillingness to face the realities, the evidence, and the truth creates a climate of hypocrisy. Such a situation becomes highly exploitable.

One untruth leads ultimately to more untruths until an intellectual climate heavy with mythology completely obscures reality, leaving us at the mercy of ideology. The great enemy of human progress is unreason. It is the supposedly good people of the world, the upholders of orthodoxy, who, in refusing to consider new ideas, even seemingly highly volatile concepts, become the great enemies of the peace. Simply, they will not fight for fact and truth.

What has happened is that as the power of persuasion that lies at the heart of the philosophical claims of the great religions has waned, humans have tended to invest similar kinds of emotional commitments in their more secular beliefs about the world. After all, the great monotheistic religions, including those of classical India and China, contain within themselves rich strains of intellectual content as well as the root cultural commitments that bind groups of social *Homo* together as ethnic beings.

Disturb the philosophical claims of these religions, show that they are only great and beautiful mythologies, and the intellect will search elsewhere for a more intelligible, more predictable description of the universe and human experience. With this search for fact, theory, and evidence must go the emotional valences that complement our minds, even our essence as human beings. So we endow our new philosophical commitment not merely with a hypothetical intellectual assent, as the secular scientific method requires of us, but also, as William James long ago described, with the "will to believe."

So it has been for well over one hundred years, as the industrial and scientific revolution has thrust before us experience that could not be explained or incorporated into the dominant Christian theology and philosophy of the western world. As the modern mind abandoned Christianity and indeed all the religions, the search for an encompassing philosophical substitute has shifted to Marxism and its various versions of environmental egalitarianism. This philosophy seemed to describe accurately the social meaning of evolving nineteenth- and twentieth-century experience, especially the social and educational thrust of European peoples. Modern science and its political offspring dissolved or proved irrelevant the older monarchical and aristocratic medieval social structure that had grown up around traditional Christian institutions.

The theme of this new ideology is of course the uniformity of human abilities to contribute to and share in the evolving institutions of western civilization. What began in principle as a theory of the equality of rights under constitutional law—equality of opportunity—has evolved into a claim for equality of condition. This means that wherever we find differences in education, wealth, or social class, the presumption is that the advantaged groups have somehow attained this privilege through the unlawful manipulation of the institutions of power.

This has led to an intergenerational war, tinged with a kind of classic Marxist revolutionary fervor, both to help the downtrodden and to nullify advantage. In the twentieth cen-

tury, this has often led to the *nullification of the advantaged.*
The intellectual pivot upon which these assumptions were
placed was the European experience which over several centuries had seen one disadvantaged group after another come
forth, energetically contributing to the prosperity and civilizational advance of the western nations.

What began as a trickle in the sixteenth and seventeenth
centuries was an inundation by the nineteenth when Marx
and the socialist movement were promulgating their revolutionary agenda. They expected this trend to be fulfilled
through a conflagration, and then finally stability, in the
communistic classless society. Here began the willful, conscious attempt to destroy elitism and aristocracy of any kind
not only in the institutional sense of power and authority, but
also in the individual's pretensions for personal integrity and
ambition. All innovation was to be vested in the Rousseauian
*volonté générale,* in the state as now represented by the com-
missars, the protectors of ideological truth having totalitarian
control over every aspect of social and cultural life (1).

At the very time that these ideas were gaining credence
among this vigorous group of progressive warriors against en-
trenched privilege, the European world was extending itself
voraciously. Inevitably this universal ideal was extrapolated
to include the historical experience of non-European peoples
now emerging from colonial control. That Marx himself had
great doubts about such a simple extrapolation, because of
his commitment to the philosophy that nations had to under-
go certain historical stages of economic development before
they were able to step into the ultimate postindustrial revolutionary stage, did not matter (2). The world was on the move
and philosophies to be at all persuasive had to argue in the
universal mode—everywhere, at all times.

After all, the Newtonian and the Einsteinian revolutions
in physical science did not suggest that principles describing
matter in motion behaved differently in Europe than in Asia.
A scientific law had to be universal. Thus even the historicism

of Karl Marx was relegated to a side track as we marched intellectually and inevitably into a phase of ideological thinking that was assured of certain social and cultural outcomes.

This sociological model of human nature and society has prevailed now for over a century. While many scientists in biology, psychology, and anthropology have accepted the evidence that human individuality and human differences are indeed real and have consequences for individual and social behavior, possibly even for national destiny, the heretofore undeveloped state of our knowledge has laid these lonely intellectual dissidents open to accusations of racism, elitism, and all the other rhetorical devices that can rob an individual and his arguments of dignity and intellectual worth.

The twentieth century thus has wreaked havoc with our expectations. The human toll, the price of such revolutionary commitments has been likewise horrific. Finally, at the close of this century, the inevitable falling away from dogmatic egalitarianism can be clearly discerned. People vote their attitudes with their feet, so to speak, despite the established dogma that purportedly still persuades. However, intellect requires that we make experience logical, ordered, rational. The lack of contrasting philosophical options has caused this arena of intellectual choice still to be forfeited to the now venerable and encrusted belief system of environmental amelioration.

The sociopolitical metaphor or myth of intellectual uniformity implies the rightness of the unlimited manipulability and control of individuals by those who can seize the reins of institutional authority. Throughout the world, notwithstanding the almost universal infatuation with the moral claims of this egalitarian socialism, the retreat from collectivism toward a more open society that now recognizes individual enterprise and productivity gains increasing impetus. In China, the abandonment of collectivism has led to a burst of energy that has revitalized the bureaucratically moribund Maoism of the past. The same can be said of India where individual talent and energy have seemingly shunted intractable historical cultural patterns into the past. Even in the Soviet bloc, the Hungarians, rich in creative intelligence, attempt to bypass a way of life that imprisons individual intelligence in the ideological vise.

It is one thing to study the world of the atom or the distant galaxies with dispassion. When it comes to the study of humans, however, the results of our theories in action have a way of becoming embedded in a complexity so difficult to penetrate, as compared with the physical sciences, that only time and events can illuminate clearly. It is this failure of a broad, rich, almost exhilarating intellectual paradigm—that of social, political, economic amelioration—that finally today is inspiring a rethinking of the issues of human nature and intelligence. One may be emotionally committed to the equality of humans as an ideal condition of social existence. It is another thing to argue concretely and factually that if only the reactionary institutions and policies of the leadership were dissolved, and new social relationships instituted, all would proceed smoothly toward this egalitarian dream.

When the results do not confirm our hopes and ideals, when we observe how societies once they have been corralled into the communist and socialist framework become culturally moribund, then politically and morally repressive, a reconsideration of such beliefs should become obligatory for all rational and thinking people.

Such a reconsideration, however, needs the support of deeper theoretical evidence, which is the underlying motivation for this series of books. This third volume attempts to summarize and integrate what has preceded it in the first two.

Here, the argument is made fuller in the sense that the theory is shown to be consistent with contemporary experience. The theory is triarchic, three large pieces of evidence that fall into place to enrich and confirm each other. The result will be a larger picture, the beginning shape to a new map of human nature in the context of the social and historical dynamics that sweep forth from this many-million-year-old process of becoming human.

The first part of the argument, here exemplified in Part 3, derives from the realities of our evolving contemporary experience. That the sociological model of human nature no longer predicts is simply because the slice of time that gave credence to those beliefs and the piece of geography upon which it was based were both highly circumscribed and unique. The theoretical position that I am presenting will likewise be tested in terms of the rational description of contemporary experience that flows from its assumptions as well as its predictions for the future. Subsequently it will also be tested by life and events.

The second part of the triad (Part 2 of this book) presents the evidence from psychological theory and experiment that leads also to predictions in the educational and vocational domains. I.Q. testing, which from the first has taken the brunt of the controversy concerning "nature vs. nurture," is only part of the story. Inevitably, in the early decades of the century there were errors born of ignorance and naivete, part of the growing pains of any infant scientific discipline.

Such polemics against this discipline as are contained in *The Mismeasure of Man,* by an acknowledged Marxist thinker, Stephen Gould, have constituted a travesty of intellectual criticism in their caricature of the discipline of psychometrics by concentrating their barbs on these early decades (3). It is like criticizing modern chemistry for the phlogiston theory of the sixteenth century, or damning physics for the nineteenth-century concept of the ether. Ironically, if a scientific discipline is to survive such criticism, it must remain useful, its predictions must carry themselves. If one examines the enormous investment in intelligence and aptitude testing in our own country and around the world it is clear that since World War II, and even before, the limited predictivity of I.Q. has been affirmed.

Even in the Soviet Union of the 1980s, I.Q. testing is not only heavily engaged in, but the results are liberally sprinkled in their scholarly journals (4). The Soviets are merely hush-hush about the implications of such research, especially as it contravenes everything Nikolai Lenin argued about bourgeoisie hereditarian bias. In fact the Russian psychologists have found variances in individual intelligence attributable to heredity at a seventy to eighty percent ratio, which is at the upper limit for anything found in the west. Finally, there seems to be in the Russian findings a close symmetry of I.Q. with the parents' social and vocational position, a fact to which only the bravest western psychometricians would dare to allude in the research organs.

When we add to the psychometric work of psychologists the genetic studies of human behavior in mental illness, criminality, alcoholism, learning disabilities, autism, the recent work in psycholinguistics, brain structure and function, psychoneurology, and a host of other allied and increasingly specialized disciplines, there can be no question that the nature/nurture controversy has been resolved, at least for this portion of historical time, on the side of nature. Now we can make myriad predictions about how humans behave on the basis of our psychobiological investigations. In contrast, a vast domain of assumptions about the environmental causes of certain behavior pathologies and psychosocial problems flowing out of the old paradigm have been dissolved by a lack of confirmation.

With regard to predictivity, the only problematic area of intelligence testing, at least to this writer, lies with that group of individuals having I.Q. scores from around two standard deviations above the norm, i.e., 130 I.Q. and above. One cannot obtain a clear relationship between quantitative measures of intelligence and the actual substance of significant creative achievements. In any number of longitudinal studies, the relationships between productive creativity of the rare sort and high I.Q. do not seem to be evident. It may be that so mysterious is that thing that we call "genius" that no test may reveal it in advance, even *ex post facto*.

Thus in this second triad of empirical evidence, the psychological domain, there is a general consensus within the community of scientists involved in such research that a genetic/hereditarian explanation seems now mandated (5). We are the products of our personal individualities. This individuality is explained to a great extent by our genetic structure as it interacts with the external environment. Of course the nature of this interaction still remains to be more fully clarified.

What is regrettable is how little the general public has been informed by the public media about the evolving turn of scientific opinion. There can be little doubt that the ideological control of sources of information has warped the public understanding of one of the central social-policy-sensitive issues of our time (6).

It is fair to say that in general the hereditarian hypothesis in human intelligence variability has been confirmed. However, there is yet another and perhaps deeper question that has developed in this changing experiential situation. Differences between individuals are in some sense differences in quantitative intelligence. The tests as they have evolved from the traditional correlational I.Q. testing to the newer, more experimental reaction time (RT) testing give rise to real educational, practical, or intellectual predictive distinctions. The RT tests, further, are information-processing experiments that require little schooling or cultural enrichment in the test subject.

These tests are all predictive of what individuals will be

able to achieve given the requirements of modern civilized life. They tell us that high intelligence requires the application of variably complex symbolic intellectual skills. The correlation between individual I.Q., education, and the outside world patently exists. But I.Q. differences are also revealed between identifiable social, ethnic, and racial groups in our ever-intertwined world community.

This is where the friction begins. These differences, especially the so-called racial differences, point to real historical, geographical, and indeed civilizational separateness of backgrounds and heritage. Is there any correlation between this heritage of difference and the very uneven results both in the psychological as well as the social arenas, the first two elements in our theoretical triad?

The psychological, or microscopic explanation now points to a macroscopic domain of analysis, the evidence of peoples and their heritage, indeed the broader picture of evolutionary origins (Part 1). The dominant assumption about this question has been absorbed into what is called in this book the myth of the post-Neanderthal diaspora. This means that, in theory, the unity of mankind existed up until the very end of human evolution. It was at the ultimate moment in the evolution of sapient human beings, hardly 50,000 years ago, when modern cranial morphologies had already been achieved, when their correlated cultural material artifacts had likewise taken on their final form, that the human species began to separate and divide itself into what we now experience as the various racial and ethnic groups of our world.

According to the accepted wisdom, what intellectual, cultural, and personal differences now exist are a product of relatively recent geographical and ecological separations experienced by the various subgroups of our human race. It is the validity of this proposition that constitutes the basic underlying motive for this series of books on the evolution of human intelligence. Of course, the proposition itself did not directly lead to the intention to write about these matters. Rather it was the rapid discovery, after intensive delving into the recent biological, evolutionary, and anthropological literature, that this "just-so story" was just "not so."

The two other aspects of our triad: (1) contemporary social experience and (2) the microscope of psychological and neurobiological research, can show us what exists as a contemporary reality. They cannot explain *why* this is so. It is this writer's view that until the *why,* the historical evolutionary explanation, is added, our understanding of human nature will be bereft of root knowledge. What we see today can be ephemeral, as partisans of the sociopolitical causation school argue. That is why their manipulations of man and society have no surcease. We are all supposedly infinitely malleable, subject to social conditioning. So, they argue, the only solution to our seemingly intractable cultural problems is more of the same, inventing an endless progression of "bourgeois," "racist," "sexist" demons that ostensibly stand in the way of their ever-receding utopia.

The purpose, thus, of this third volume in the series on the evolution of human intelligence is to bring together the biological and psychological evidence into a coherent perspective and to make the first attempt to show the consequences of our billion-year-old heritage of biological evolution for the dynamic realities of today. The subject is too vast to encompass briefly. Inevitably many unanswered questions will remain after a reading of what here follows, as there were in the case of the first two books in this series, *The Form of Man* and *Triumph of the Intelligent.*

What is happening as one researches these matters is that a totally new map of historical and contemporary experience seems to be revealed by radically revising the existing theoretical opinion concerning the facts and implications of human intellectual variability. In fact I would venture to argue that the issue of intelligence differences, both quantitative and qualitative, writ large among the ethnic communities of our earth constitutes the great "Copernican" theoretical issue of our time.

This is why so many millions of people have been destroyed in brutal genocidal explosions in our century. That is likewise why in our western world of secular, rational, dispassionate scientific study, some 350 to 400 years after the great persecutions, inquisitions, and heresy burnings that ushered in the modern era, we see so much hysteria and hatred expressed against those dissidents from the established orthodoxy of intellectual uniformity. This helps to explain the twentieth-century crusade for the environmental obliteration of such human differences.

Let me affirm in the strongest terms possible that a book whose subject matter is an explanation from the standpoint of human evolution of why humans vary in intelligence *does not* have as its purpose to exacerbate the pain or to promote conflict. My belief is that the longer the rational, wise, educated people refuse to face the truth, continue to live in a world of smug, complacent, incense-filled sureties about our own species, the longer the hatred and the destruction of our civilizational goals will continue.

Is it naive to argue still in this day of ideology-ridden contentions that there are truths that can be objectively established? Is it likewise childlike to think that fact and truth can have no preestablished moral valence of good or evil? Can it really be that we can anchor a moral, egalitarian society on the quicksand of illusion and dream?

If we want to promote peace and harmony within the human community; if we want to build a world in which this greater human community can live under the rule of equity and law, not only equality before the law, but eventually equality of social condition—Karl Marx' ever-elusive classless society—we will have to argue about facts and evidence. No longer can we afford, as has been the case so many times in the past, to persecute the weatherman for the storm.

# Chapter II

---

# HUMANITY'S UNFINISHED JOURNEY

## The Lifetime of a Species

The estimate given was one million years. This number stood for the average length of time that a species maintained its taxonomic integrity. Because a number is speculated—this one million years—does not necessarily imply that a form of life dies off after so many years (1). This figure was derived from mainline forms of life, but there are those rare recidivists who have remained on the periphery for sometimes hundreds of millions of years. This estimate has long preyed on my mind. We humans are from an extremely volatile line, thus the figure for the life expectancy of a species such as ours might in theory be quite a bit less (2).

Our categories of race, species, genus constitute the conventional lines of demarcation that we like to think generally mirror the real world of evolutionary change. At this point in the study of *Homo* (the genus), Hominidae (the order), there is a tendency to push back the species lines of *Homo sapiens* to at least 250,000 years ago, often to 500,000 B.P. (3). There are some thinkers who believe that the demarcation of *Homo sapiens* from *Homo erectus* is truly an artificial taxonomic division. *Homo sapiens* types and *Homo erectus* would have probably been interfertile (4). Indeed, there is a distinct possibility that such differing forms of *Homo* lived simultaneously on our earth as recently as 50,000 years ago (5). Is it possible that we could have been interfertile with *Homo habilis,* our primal linear ancestor, two to four million years ago?

All these speculations are preparatory to considering our own position today in the flux of evolutionary change. For, in a way, the entire rationale for a study of human intelligence lies in its significance for our destiny over the many millennia in which we humans still expect to inhabit the planet as a viable form of life. It would seem necessary on occasion to take this larger view of events. What biological/evolutionary message lies embedded in our past that could alert us to the changes that will affect our long-distance future?

## Dilemma of Human Intelligence

It has been the argument of this series of books that we humans are the evolutionary inheritors as well as the carriers of one of the great adaptive mechanisms of biological existence, intelligence. Our impact on the natural world around us should testify to the awesome power of man's brain. The question that we must entertain is that considering the nature of this biological phenomenon and considering the relatively short period of time that intelligence in an anthropoid—*Homo*—has become a powerful element in the equations of living things, where do we start, where are we going?

As this book, *Why Humans Vary in Intelligence,* proceeds to spell out its message of variable intelligence, and the still uncompleted expression of human intelligence in this large, wandering, interfertile, superspecies, *Homo sapiens,* it will be clear that we are presented with a number of great dilemmas and challenges. It will also be clear that the day-to-day, even decade-to-decade flow of political events is but a ripple in a slow tidal surge that represents the dynamic expression of larger evolutionary events working their way through the human species into the face of our planet and beyond.

It is the variability in human intelligence, and thus in human culture, that is the key to understanding the problem of our destiny. Like every great adaptive breakthrough in the history of life, the first probings in the advance of a line of animals or plants into a new ecological plateau is like a trickle eroding its way through the dike of environmental encapsulement. The trickle, having undermined the defense, then becomes a torrent. As with the primal advance of the ancient mammals to secure their new ecological niche, the transformation of the original prototype is quick and revolutionary (6). What was an initial foothold is rapidly transformed into many niches as the breadth and openness of this ecological opportunity is exploited. Variability becomes the rule, often from a narrow lineage (7). Through the natural processes of mutation, many forms of the primeval line develop and go their separate ways until they meet their own inevitable constraints, either biological or ecological.

In man, the splintering seems to have been restricted to two basic forms, the australopithecine man-ape and *Homo.* Because of the interfertility of *Homo,* his adaptability to many climes, his wandering and interbreeding, extreme variability and speciation were restricted. Instead, because of the lack of constraints as these intelligent creatures outpaced their opponents, variability became intercultural, a competition of intelligence between human groups, with the selective advantage of higher intelligence becoming the supercharged engine of human change.

However, as we shall point out in Chapters XVII to XIX, while the great proportion of *Homo's* tenure upon earth has been characterized by fatal internecine encounters, with ever more intelligent forms pressuring less evolved populations, there has been a reciprocal process of miscegenation. Thus the elimination of weaker, more primitive, forms of *Homo* has been paralleled by a smoothing of the major distinctions between the evolved north and the more stagnant south, even while sharp and ancient racial distinctions fade into the background. As we tend ever more through interbreeding to become a vast panmictic species, our excess intellectual capacity enables us to veer from the raw ethnic and linguistic exclusivity that ends in competition and war. We become philosophical and humanitarian. Our ethical intellectual sense begins to override the older limbic system and we strive to behave on the basis of law and reason toward all mankind.

Reason and philosophy, however, are more subtle forms of human interaction. They can lead mankind in many directions, both forward and backward. Blind sociopolitical and economic ideologies that are guided by erroneous philosophies can practically destroy a society. Ethnic hatred undergirded by a theory that equates high social or economic achievement by individuals and groups with conspiratorial negation of the equality principle can lead to genocide. It has happened over and over again in the twentieth century (Chapter XX).

Each period in history has its pivotal point of decision making, that fulcrum from which flow the subtle, assumed errors produced by ignorance and self-delusion. We win one small battle for reality and reason only to lose one somewhere down the line. I have no great expectations that knowing the evolutionary facts can permanently free us of the myths that have clouded our minds.

What is truly new is the reality of our international context. The sober Romans only had to plan for a universal empire over more or less their own kind, and in a day of far less volatile change than ours. They were supreme for an impressive array of generations. Eventually, they eliminated their best minds, and the incense of myth and religion undercut their game plan, eventually to dissolve, and give Europe another chance with history.

Our circumstance today is far more difficult, for the intelligence is distributed so variably from continent to continent, people to people. Intelligence is a qualitatively complex entity. In its undeveloped form, it is more or less the hostage of lower mammalian emotions and visions. Blind ethnic hatreds, magical solutions, susceptibility to pseudo-gods and causes make it difficult to persuade, teach, reason with any sort of success. Can we teach the truth and the real options for choice, decisions, national and international policies when the finger of analysis points directly at us, at our own dignity, self-knowledge, pride?

Remember, too, how sophisticated, highly intelligent peoples, the Germans and Japanese, became so enmeshed in their own twentieth-century hallucinations that they set out to conquer the world, in the case of the Germans actually to engage in a genocide against the Jews and others who were at least their equals and possibly intellectually superior as a group. If these peoples could not withstand the seductions of myth, how can we expect that the peoples of the twenty-first century will reject the soothsayers who promise nirvana but deliver disaster?

## Mankind's Adaptive Direction

Still, the evolutionary facts do offer us a truer perspective on the heritage of humanity than we now have available to us. Thus we must explore and mine the facts even if current ideology refuses to recognize them. Every great evolutionary breakthrough—and the exploding intelligence in the hominids is certainly one of the most epochal developments in the history of life on earth—has gone through a progression of stages. In each case, whether it be land-living, air-breathing amphibians, amniotic-egg-laying reptiles, birds defying gravity, seals and whales emigrating from the land to the sea, a combination of fortuitous structures has made possible the basic evolutionary thrust, and the gradual modification, perfection, or specialization of other secondary adaptations to fit the ecological niche (8). This is what we might describe as the stepwise perfection of the form inherent in the basic model. After the perfection of fitness, however, the evolutionary tale continues.

Soon comes ultraspecialization, oddly perverse distinctions, as, for example, occurred in the late reptiles, possibly even among the birds, a breakdown of the line into minute races, extreme articulations of adaptive function and its causal selective honing. Then new challenges arrive to bring opportunity to some forms, ultimate dislocation to others. Sometimes the challenges signal the disappearance of the species.

*Homo* has an evolutionary perfectable form. His greatest adaptation is intelligence itself, one of the oldest, if necessary, patterns of adaptability in animals (9). In addition, it is one of the slowest patterns of adaptation to reveal itself in all lines. Intelligence is nascent in animal organic existence. The world and nature bring it gradually to the fore. As a species, how long have we been around? Certainly *Homo habilis* was on the scene from five million years ago. Whether we would have been interfertile, we and they, is a good question. In the case of *Homo* this particular aspect of our evolutionary progression is not critical.

What is more important is that by about three million years ago *Homo habilis* had advanced enough in deadliness and intelligence to begin to harry his australopithecine hominid cousins into oblivion. Henceforth began the steady incremental advance of intelligent humans, spreading, proliferating, and separating around the world, coming into contact or conflict as they do today, interbreeding, without surcease. The outcome, until most recently, has been the steady shaping of an ever more intelligent and thus specialized hominid leading to *Homo sapiens sapiens.*

On the basis of those past four or five million years in the "public" appearance of *Homo,* and the gradual transformation of not only his physical being but the product of his intelligence—culture—we can argue that the form of man has been shaped and honed. The question is what does it portend for *Homo's* physical, intellectual or cultural outlook. We can glean only a partial lesson from the human experience. Therefore, let us refer to others who have taken similar journeys: the birds, the whales, for example.

In each case the initial breakthrough was followed by a multiplication of variants, then their specialization and stasis. It took the birds about 100 million years from the foetal pulsations of *Archaeopteryx,* the earliest bird (150 million years B.P.), to reach their plateau of brain growth in the Eocene period about fifty million years ago (10). Since then, the relative size of the bird's brain as compared to its reptilian ancestors has grown from seven to eight times. This represents a small advance in fifty million years, and that mostly as a result of fine-tuning competition with other birds. Thus we can hypothesize that for the last fifty million years the birds have "perfected" their form within their established ecological niche. Recently and suddenly, literally thousands of bird species have "disappeared" as a result of man's explosive impact on the environment. Today only a certain kind of adaptable bird intelligence, that of seagulls, starlings, sparrows, for example, seems likely to survive, even flourish.

The case of the cetaceans—dolphins, whales, porpoises—is also instructive. They reentered the seas during a time of great mammalian expansion and competition about fifty-five million years ago, the late Paleocene, early Eocene. Within thirty million years they had perfected their form and have since barely changed. This process included the growth and establishment of a unique intelligence, one somewhat comparable in its specialization to man's, and which serious scholars have analyzed with awe (11).

Like the birds, they have developed an extremely specialized exemplification of intelligence, now subject to the depredation of that bipedal predator of the land surfaces, *Homo*. It is interesting to note how vulnerable are those lines of animals that have developed sharply articulated expressions of intelligence, reflected in finely-honed adaptive patterns within delineated ecologies—the skies, the seas—compared to the more flexible and relatively unspecialized bodily structures and ecological refinements of land-based humans.

However, we too are and will be vulnerable, because we can't go home again. We have destroyed too much of our homeland, our bridges are gone—leaving only the stench of chemical or other pollution. This vast upheaval of cultural detritus, the material and technological consequence of our spontaneous intelligence hovers over us like a smokescreen, confusing and blurring our sense of direction.

Forward, however, is the only direction we can go. That direction demands that we perfect our intelligence as a species. This perfection requires that a new form of inbreeding take place. In must take place among the most able in our worldwide community of races and ethnic groups. Caution, we still require the genetic adaptive reserves and the variability that are necessary for protection against disease, emotional hysteria, or any other challenge that would render a completely blended population susceptible. Humanity's march forward can only be built from the ultimate cause of progress, intelligence.

Clearly, higher intelligence, in general, not a qualitatively uniform kind of intelligence, will be required. This is an intelligence that is probably as fully realized as possible in the cultures of Cro-Magnon, classical Greece, the Renaissance, of Europe generally up to the first decades of the twentieth century, when the genocidal episodes began with the Armenians. I do not mean here to ignore either the great achievements of classical Chinese or Indian civilization or the powerful civilizational thrust of the northeastern-Asiatics—the Chinese, Koreans, Japanese—that is culminating the twentieth century.

There are morphological constraints on the unlimited advance of intelligence. The size of the *sapiens* neonate skull was shaped to the limits of the female pelvis (12). Certainly the unique surge of growth of the infant's skull in the weeks after birth testifies to natural selection's ability to mine the store of genetic variation in our ancestors that allowed for this special postnatal advance. What is interesting is that the growth of the infant's brain, or the concomitant suppression of relative growth in the foetus, subsequently requires an extremely specialized, attentive, intelligent, caring mother to ease the helpless infant over its crucial months of dependency (13).

not
father?

## Ultimate Biocultural Heritage

It is unlikely that nature will make available to any existing inbreeding human population a new structural opportunity for the further growth of the cortical brain. What we will need is the garden-like cultivation of existing high intelligence throughout the various populations of the world, so that through this crucial adaptive dimension of *Homo* we can survive. At least in the area of instrumental and practical challenges of social adaptation, we would hope that cultural/intellectual differences would fade away and that mankind could ultimately truly participate in a United Nations of reasoned behavior.

What is our model, and how does it express itself in society? In *The Making of the Civilized Mind,* the final volume of this series, these critical issues will be discussed. It will be argued that, indeed, there is a form toward which *Homo* is advancing. The evolutionary argument will be set forth there in its full cultural meaning. Biological intelligence in its human transformation will be seen to exemplify itself in a certain kind of individual civilizational behavior and symbolic capabilities. Bring together a population of qualitatively related and high capacity intelligence and, like the critical mass needed for an atomic explosion, it will spontaneously produce a civilization in the full sense that we all admire and aspire toward.

Can one argue that this completion and fulfillment of the human form of intelligence, whether it be a homogeneous intelligence worldwide or many variants in one, a pluralistic joining of diversities of equal intellectual power, are inevitable? Certainly the selective dynamics have worked continuously to iron out the racial differences of state and grade within the human community. It is also clear what intellectually advanced humans can do. Their power of intelligence over competing forms of life is well demonstrated. The guidance systems of philosophy, however, are still needed to discipline and shape this power. While one is tempted to be dialectical and deterministic, with Hegel and Marx, for example, that it has to happen and it will, this philosopher can not believe that outside conditions alone will selectively encourage the emergence of a universal civilizational level of intelligence within the entire human race.

We have recently experienced the impact of philosophically based acts of institutional genocide, the premeditated, systematic, often bureaucratized rounding up of highly intelligent minority populations within national boundaries, people wiped from the face of the earth by gas chamber, execution squad, or starvation. It is possible, indeed it has occurred a number of times in the twentieth century, that we will again retreat from our supposedly inevitable evolutionary goal.

If intelligence is ever to fulfill its expression as the form of man, it must be consciously cultivated. We must wage a war against domination by lower mammalian forms of human thought. The educated classes need to stimulate the suzerainty of a genotype among humans capable of winning this battle against superstition. They must seek the instrumental means for such a victory that will harmonize with all that is best in ethical expression among humans. The historical determinists may have been right. There is a destiny to be fulfilled, built out of millions of years of evolutionary dynamics. We can assist the process or be prematurely destroyed in misguided resistance.

The succeeding chapters in *Why Humans Vary in Intelligence* will attempt to give flesh to the argument placed before the reader here: that we are still only partially evolved as a species in terms of the fulfillment of a larger evolutionary commitment, the perfection of animal intelligence. This partially completed stage in our history leaves us with a world population of extremely variable levels of intelligence. The result of this state in our passage through time has become manifest with the arrival of the twentieth century. It has inaugurated a phase of turmoil and tragedy.

The roads that mankind travels are no longer one-way highways from the advanced into the less progressive yet receptive southern tier. The context of progress will now have to take place on a geographically neutral human stage. Everywhere the process of corticalization and intellectual advance will have to find its historic means of expression, if not now or soon, then with even greater travail later on.

Certainly there are racial and ethnic differences that today complicate the task and create a heavy emotional cloud. As pointed out below, however, high intelligence has a universal morphological character that transcends race and ethnicity. On the other hand, less advanced forms of human intelligence will mimic, in their closeness to the physical, the personal, those ancient mammalian biological sources, revealing sharper differences in human beings that existed at an earlier stage, developing from the time when we parted, moving out of the primeval African homeland, over a million years ago.

Progress toward a more uniformly high level of intelligence may not eradicate cultural, psychological, and ethnic differences in personal expression, but it will enable mankind to speak the same language, manipulate the same symbols of knowledge and social competency. Out of this process may yet come the solution for which we have long dreamed, *e pluribus unum*.

# Chapter III

---

# THE MEANING OF BIOLOGICAL INTELLIGENCE

## Origins of Variable Life

First let us agree that there is something that we can call intelligence in the biological world. Then let us agree that, of all the creatures that have existed and exist today, humans powerfully display that biological attribute that we call intelligent behavior. Finally we have to ask why does intelligence as an adaptation of living things exist, alongside fecundity, great size, ferocity, speed, inconspicuousness, and countless other characteristics, all of which seem to have something to do with creatures' ability to survive?

For the answer, let us go back to some of the fundamental forces in nature that produced intelligence. In the process, we will confront the issue of variability within nature itself. For there, in all living things, the question of variability is as big as the question of life itself.

For that question of life and its origins, the reader may refer to the first book in this series, *The Form of Man, the evolutionary origins of human intelligence* (1). The argument in the present book is limited to those evolutionary questions about intelligence that will help to explain the issue of variability within our species, nay, even within our own families.

The issues of biochemical variability in its evolutionary adaptive function and intelligence variability are closely intertwined, for they are the broad adaptive products of life on earth. If all had been perfectly stable in those early eons as our planet solidified and cooled there would have been no life. In a sense the very existence of life reflects the dynamics of change in that early biochemical cauldron. Living things in their own random, inchoate, unselfconscious ways stumbled onto the means to acquire and metabolize other organic compounds, to grow, give off useless organic residues and survive in a dynamic and varying environment. In sum, it is an outside world that is in varying states of flux that creates conditions for the existence and energetic struggle of life.

Variability itself, as we look out on the plethora of solutions to the challenge of life, constitutes one important result of those random biochemical changes that time and experience have imprinted on the history of living things. So many of these biochemical alterations or even stabilities have failed. Only the winners of wars write histories. So, too, only the survivors of evolutionary history can testify to the successful experiments of nature's game of biochemical roulette.

Somewhere along the line certain biochemical changes in organic compounds were by chance found to be useful and thus some organic forms survived. Other biochemical combinations that did not change found that their environments *had* changed; their stubborness and fixity disappeared with them. Only the changeable ones who succeeded left their mark, not merely their biochemical mark, but perhaps even more important, their propensity to change. As it turned out, as surely as our earth turns, the environment has changed.

Variability in living creatures stands as the evolutionary monument to the chance quality in those early organic compounds to change systematically and sequentially, even if at first randomly, and then to fit the survival requirements of our changing planet. Thus it was that in a fan-like expansion, the equation of random biochemical changes, shaped by the conditions of the environment, produced ever wider varieties of living forms, in a sense exploring the possibilities of survival. Other compounds, such as those amino acids that rotated light to the right in their molecular structure, were quickly gone, disappearing with the evaporating opportunities like countless other life possibilities. We will never know them. We know only the survivors.

## Variability in Space and Time

Variability in space of course is part of life's great opportunistic gambit. All God's creatures eke out their livelihood in almost an infinity of guises, structures, behaviors. Variability in time sifts each of these approaches in space. How do creatures handle the changes that come their way, as the universe itself turns? Here the relationships are more delicate, for, to maintain its basic structural integrity, every animal line has to balance both stability and change. The successful solution through natural selection has resulted in a structural distinction. The exterior of the organism may remain stable, relatively impervious to outside impact; the possibility for change will be centered in the genoplasm itself which is protected from random outside changes.

The survivors thus institutionalize the fact that change itself in the outside environment on average occurs predictably. Some parts of the environment change more slowly, others more dynamically. Thus the snails at the sea bottom mutate rarely, because it is in their survival interest not to disturb their equilibrium.

Creatures who have survived in more febrile environments have a successful heritage of many changes that have been selected positively in the past. This success is imprinted as an impetus for their inner genetic variability. Thus, over time, we see played out a game of probabilities. To those placid ones on the fringes, environmental cataclysms often lead to massive exterminations. Such creatures have not produced the reservoir of variability over time and thus possess few inner genetic differences in their spatial distributions to help them over the rough periods. Periodically in the past, scientists have noted vast decimations of lines of creatures, for example, in the Permian period 250 million years ago when the amphibians were struggling onto the lands. Great extinctions of more primitive invertebrates then took place. Again, such cataclysms took place at the time of the dinosaur extinctions at the end of the Mesozoic, sixty to seventy million years ago.

For those highly dynamic animal lines, a time of stability can lead to enormous attrition rates; as the mutant forms can go nowhere, they are maladapted in place. Thus we often note that most mutations are negatively selective; they don't work out. In a period of great dynamic alterations, however, those life forms that have a tradition of change, given some time allowance for their mutations to show up, may survive.

So, too, highly dynamic creatures usually carve out for themselves a wide spatial dispersal range in the environment. Thus they are positioned for changes not merely by a reservoir and tradition of constant mutations, but they are variable throughout their life range (in space as with the teleost fish 400 million years ago, or the mammals seventy million years ago). A great disaster at one point in space will allow some to survive because they do vary and carry a reservoir of preadaptations.

Our planet and the life that was created on it are part of one system. Some forms of life, such as unicellular creatures, have probably changed very little over time. They have opted for the possibility of remaining one with their primeval conditions. As the earth has matured, other options, differing relationships with mother earth's evolving destiny, have become available. Plant and animal life in a kaleidoscopic melange of possibilities has come forth (2).

Still, the basic laws of life must be obeyed. The opportunities for variation are created from the basic conditions of our environment. There would not be variability either in space or time had not the lessons of survival and extinction etched themselves into the evolutionary record. No one can predict when this fandango of stimulus and response will end. To be sure, one or two billion or years to the contrary, the message of life, change, and evolution is one of youth. At some point, the evolutionary possibilities of the earth, inorganic and organic, will have fulfilled themselves. Even the inert cosmic gases go through their repertoire of possibilities.

It is all out of our and thus life's control. Our words may be anthropomorphic, or teleological, heavy with purposeful metaphor, but the process is random, and mechanical in the *opinion* working out of the possibilities as with the metal ball in the pinball machine that bounces its way among the pins and depressions finally to find its resting place.

## Intelligence as an Adaptation

In itself intelligence is one of the possibilities for survival in a variable environment. A bit more efficient in handling change than the well-guarded genes and their rhythmic sequencing of the biochemical possibilities, intelligence is even more sensitive to external challenge. In a sense those with intelligence have less opportunity to fall back on the time and tested. There is less automated programming here. Nature's pulse of change has provided the opportunity for intelligence. There is a price, however. Here, it is the necessity for eternal vigilance. The safety net of the ancient response system is scarred by great gaps. One misstep and the fall through is to eternity.

*So dramatic*

Intelligence deepens with animal life and the roaming disposition. Fixed solutions were the other fork. Biochemical versatility in the handling of one's digestive needs had been abandoned for the search for the perfect, if specialized, meal. If one roams, however, behavior must be substituted for structure. Sensory organs—eyes, ears, nose—to absorb information—fins, feet, arms, wings for movement, and above all the possibility for learning. These are the elements out of which intelligent behavior becomes possible.

Moving around is fine, but it can be blind if every movement, every sensory input remains wholly novel information. The knowledge built in through instinct, located in the genes would have to be enormous. The genetic structure to accommodate the proper guidance system that would deal with every adventurous situation would inevitably overwhelm. An example is the Irish elk, needing to renew yearly its glorious bony carriage. So a shift begins. Behaviors within limits are allowed to develop adventitiously, and, as in imprinting on the young, by the events arising out of the environment. Here behavior will be shaped by the ability of the creature to organize life's experiences.

We learn so as to be able to anticipate. The biochemistry of learning is now switched from an automatic guidance system rooted in the genes to a looser arrangement where the individual has some choice superintended by the nervous system and the brain. The variable environment now is met not by rapid genetic changes in time or dispersed variations in space. Rather a prowling, curious creature adjusts to a changing environment by absorbing information about this environment through its sense organs, thence organized by the brain within the broader parameters of behavior and physical structures, possibilities that are, of course, set by the genes.

The trip wire of instinct is loosened and the animal increasingly can withhold automatic reaction responses by searching for meaning in its memory store heritage. The more growth is directed to learning, manipulating, experimenting, the more the final behavior of the mature individual will be laden with appropriateness and optimum survival possibilities.

In short, intelligence serves its life preserving function as a complex biochemical response system. Instead of growing new and more specialized organs for specific physical response—arms, legs, horns, wings, teeth—intelligence, concentrated in the bundles of nerves, synapses, integrating sensory organs with basic physical response structures, serves as a malleable, flexible adaptive counter to a world in change. The brain, gradually centered forward and topside seeks inputs that will allow it to organize outside information, anticipate events so as to adapt to the momentary changing state of external challenges and opportunities.

Gradually, time and the selective shaping of these appropriate response structures will allow for the growth of intelligence in certain animals so that they can begin to free themselves from the rigid stereotyping of behavior. *Instinct is safe and sure. Intelligent learning behavior takes its chances with a dynamic, changing world.* Those genetic patterns that allow for a wide latitude of behavior before tripping the response wires of predetermined reactions took many more millions of years to be worked into a system of learned, intelligent behavior. Easier to grow wings and hooves than a complex brain.

Moving up the phylogenetic scale of higher intelligence, creatures have ever more room to explore, freedom to react or not, before the imperatives of survival require an automatic response. Behavior is increasingly centered in the phenotype, the external individual. The objective of intelligence as an adaptation is to move into ever wider concentric circles of experiences and new environments, to keep one step ahead of nature's alterations, never to be left behind with that always growing number of "almost" survivors.

From the beginning, right into our own time, intelligent learning behavior has remained a means of predicting one's way through experience, seeing the world as orderly, organized, and likely to repeat certain basic events, challenges. Learning, remembering, and organizing this information into law-like anticipations of events become the key to successful reproduction, thence bringing one's offspring to reproductive maturity, i.e., survival.

The intelligent forms of life more often give rise to subsequent generations that may be slightly different from their immediate progenitors. Here the often-mutating genes allow for the development of increasingly malleable forms of life living ever different patterns of existence. Nature is not reinforcing highly specialized structures of response to small ecological environments, such as a specialized predator feeding on a unique prey. Rather it is saying: "intelligent ones live in many worlds, for we don't know what tomorrow will bring" (3).

We can understand why intelligence is perhaps the great and central adaptation for animal life. Just as we contrast the animal with the plant, the former being motile, surviving by feeding on a wide variety of organic food sources (heterotrophic energy production), so too intelligence becomes the paradigm of animal adaptation in that it furthers this primal directionality of animal life. If human individuals are limited to a more restricted diet of foods than dogs, they do have available to them a much wider variety of such edible foods from a much wider variety of environments.

Any opportunity for further learning, adaptability, movement, or for freedom from a rigid response system that roots us securely to one ecology, such as a specific food source, is quickly latched onto by preadapted intelligent creatures. Once the adaptive choice has been made, and natural selection has rejected the laggards in this one crucial shift, an evolutionary mark has been made. The variations in one direction will have been noted in our chromosomes and genes, other possibilities thereby excluded. The new trend will continue as long as external circumstance reinforces positively the flowering of the particular adaptation. These carriers are both phenotype (the behaving individual) and genotype (the reservoir of possibilities) waiting to manifest themselves in the event of the occurrence of great changes or deviations from the normal circumstance of life.

Think of the difference in function between the learning phenotype, the individual animal representative of the species in question, and the genotype, the reservoir of variations in the interbreeding species as a whole, as follows: The learner provides for the opportunity of adapting to changing variable environments by changes in behavior. The learner is the living actor, the existing representation of the possible genetic model.

The genotype meets nature's challenge for possible variability of adaptive behaviors in the depth of time. Mutations occur at different rates for different lines of animals and plants. More dynamic lines will mutate more often and always at the leading edge of selective opportunity. These mutations showing themselves at various places in the population are often detrimental, sometimes fatally so, at other moments mildly disabling. However, in time, this existing variability in the line of creatures can provide opportunities for wholly new adaptive shifts.

Naturally, difference within any species allows for some members to show their individual characteristics to better advantage. If their variable structural and behavioral talents were to be selected favorably as compared with other members of the species, one particular genetic exemplification of the species could present wholly new lines of adaptive variability and thus represent a new element of evolutionary "progress."

## Intelligence, Specialized and General

Psychologists today still debate the question as to the nature of human intelligence. Is there a so-called unitary factor that brings together all the diverse behaviors of man into an overall picture of his capacity? Or, is our intelligence merely a composite of a variety of relatively independent skills and abilities somehow brought together as a complex unity located in the brain and nervous system (4)? (See Chapters IX and XII.)

The evolution of intelligence gives us a hint as to how we might solve this dilemma. This insight derives from the selective demands placed on intelligent behavior in animals by nature. As noted above, intelligence serves as a means of anticipating challenges and opportunities well before they occur, thus allowing for the preadaptation of behavior in the individual member. The purer the manifestation of intelligence as behavior, adaptability, or decision making, before instinctual reactions determine the case, the less this intelligence can be rooted in a highly defined instinctual behavioral system.

Thus, the horse, the cat, the elephant, the starling are all highly intelligent creatures. However, to a greater or lesser extent, these intelligences serve some very clear-cut adaptive behavior and some important specialized organs that define behavior, whether it is galloping over the plains or lying in wait for prey.

The more intelligence approaches the limit or the fulfillment of its underlying adaptive strategy, the less physiologically, morphologically, and behaviorally specialized is the animal bearer of this intelligence. Outside of man it is clear that the primates, from the time of the evasive tree shrew of the Eocene period some forty-five million years ago, have inherited this adaptive and thus selective role among the mammals.

One reason we see the chimpanzee as the great ape most closely related to *Homo* is that while the orangutan and the gorilla are highly intelligent creatures, their intelligence seems oriented toward a more specialized behavior. The chimpanzee seems to us to be a generalist, often playful, a wanderer of no unique skills, even dietary predilections.

With *Homo,* this characteristic of the adaptive placement of the primates has been honed by natural selection to its ultimate refinement. Even our sensory organs have a receptivity of no special acuity. Our taste, touch, and olfactory sensitivities are recidivistic. Our hearing is limited as to range of sound; even our ability to distinguish these sounds qualitatively is limited. Our vision while excellent is not especially keen in comparion with birds or mammal predators. If we have color and binocular skills, they are an inheritance from our primate ancestors (5).

On the other hand, our intelligence takes this limited fund of sensory information gathering and creates complex structures of meaning that give us enormous amounts of information and the ability to organize the sounds and smells of our world. We create mechanical devices to extend our sensory abilities far beyond their natural scope. In every area of structure and behavior, man's intelligence vastly enhances his behavioral capacities. It is precisely because humans were bereft of the close allegiances of intelligence with specialized organic adaptive functions that we have gone so far.

The only exception here is our linguistic ability, a highly specialized skill that even while giving new powers to the mind beyond that which other animals have been able to gain with their signal-sound communications, does at the same time mask and condition the raw mental prowess of our intelligence. We will discuss this dilemma and paradox of human *he's teleological?*

intelligence later in Chapter XII. Beyond this, the answer to the questions of "g" or general intelligence seems to be fairly clear.

To the extent that our major behavioral activities as a species are freed of instinctual regulation and determination of behavior, our intelligence ought to be purely relational or meaningful. Intelligence geared to sensory or automatic calculations, or praeternatural pitch identifications, or skills in reproducing three-dimensional landscapes or figures, parallels the specialized and basically instinctually guided intelligence of all higher mammals.

In the billions-year-old behavioral and adaptive sense of what intelligence has served to procure vis à vis survival, intelligence must in some sense be unitary and increasingly abstract in that it serves no permanent practical objective or function.


# The Direction and Limits of Human Intelligence

Big creatures get bigger, fecund animals reproduce more prolifically. All forms of life push their adaptive specialty to the limit, the carrying capacity of the environment, the tolerance and borders of competing forms. So, too, intelligence as an adaptive play of life inevitably will crowd the limits of environmental toleration. In that sense intelligence pursues its inner necessity to exploit and expand through the particular creatures (species) that carry it along through space and time.

It is important to remember, however, that there is no secret internal mechanism that guides animal adaptation to the fulfillment of its ultimate end (telos). The conditions of a varying environment and the indifferent acquiescence of nature to the sorting machine of natural selection alone determine the direction and pace of the expansive power of intelligent behavior. Were the environment to stagnate, were automatic instinctual mechanisms to uncover new adaptive functions, then the special advantage acquired by intelligence over the eons would be lost, and intelligent forms of life would gradually wither into oblivion.

Intelligence always works against certain environmental barriers—animals or ecology. This is its test. Also, it comes to the fore in animals that do not develop early on physical means for adaptation. It is a hidden adaptation usually of the slowly evolving, half failing—for the slow growth of the complex neurological feedback structures takes time, as slowly as it takes our own neurology to heal after a wound or operation compared with our physical bodies. Intelligent creatures in a line of animals usually develop last, but usually are sharply articulated by their identifying characteristics, for example, the stealthy panther or the broadly roaming wild dog of the African plains. Even the whales and dolphins traversing vast ocean domains, using echolocation to find each other and the shape of their environment, denote an articulated intelligence both of body structure needs, and a response to what is still a demanding adaptive environment.

Only man is an exception to specialized attack or defense, an unspecialized primate, also late and slow to develop. Intelligence in man has here surpassed nature's first line of ecological or biological defenses. Man may be on a very long leash, but he still has a leash. His way of momentarily surpassing nature is culture, and it is within the confines of his ethnic membrane (Chapter XIX) that the final dynamics of intelligence have catapulted him. He progresses through culture; within its confines he is king. Outside he is frail.

How do the primeval selective rules that control the evolutionary advance of intelligence bear on this thing we call culture? We see humans immobilized in primitive ritualized patterns, left behind in the recesses of our world. Even at the frontiers we see a fraying at the edges within the great civilizations, in the panmictic urban technological world, itself frozen, unable to advance because a cloud of intellectual prohibitions obscures reality and the possible.

The truth then, as odd as it may seem, is that though culture is in many ways a suprabiological creation of the human mind—it has no apparent biologically restrictive limits— culture can become a surrogate arm or eye, almost a bodily structure. Because of the spontaneous manner by which mankind creates culture, it itself can restrict the flow of intelligence over wider and ever more adaptable modalities of behavior. It is freed of close biological/genetic determinism, ready to flow and be altered within and between the generations. There is now a created capacity for intelligence itself to fail, to violate the ancient laws of growth, change, adaptability, experimentation, prediction.

This is why civilizations have died. This is also how mankind's intelligence can create its very own antinomies and violate its own basic biological principles. Eventually culture and civilization must obey the laws of the leash. As long as mankind was dispersed and divided into subspecies, even small ethnic groups, the condition of variability in space was met for intelligence to flourish as an adaptation. Thus the stagnated primitive in his jungle redoubt remained a source of variability, a reservoir of difference to bail us out in case humanity stumbled elsewhere.

Now, as all the one-time primitives have been blended into a world culture, increasingly homogenized intellectually and culturally, the danger arises that *Homo* may not be able to substitute new cultural mutations in time as a means of constantly changing and thus adapting. Intelligence as a tool of adaptation will be sucked into the quicksand of myth, ideology, dogmatic religious tradition. We may for a while remain sophisticated in certain material, literate ways, yet be just as stagnated, rigid, thus vulnerable to change. No real differences may remain within the species to bail us out.

# Chapter IV

---

# THE VARIABILITY OF HOMO

## The Neanderthal Myth

The reeducation of our citizens might best begin with the Neanderthal myth. The commonsense perception of human intellectual homogeneity rests on the belief that we are all descendants of some *post*-Neanderthal form of human who arose, seemingly from nowhere, some 35,000 years ago. Having appeared upon this earth in a veritable immaculate conception, we proceeded to push our Neanderthal and other primitive ancestral brethren into oblivion, then to spread out to the four corners of the earth, diversified into the races and ethnic groups of historical times (1).

The danger in such an erroneous view is that it inevitably will run counter to contemporary facts, thus causing confusion, counterproductive actions intended to ameliorate the consequences of the past and thus the very diverse conditions under which we humans live. The truth is not that far off.

There are some crucial facts, however, that give us a completely different perspective on the transition to a post-Neanderthal stage of human evolution.

The details of the truth of human variability lie fairly close at hand in our Paleolithic past. This story has been told in earlier volumes of the series. However, I feel that the issues of *Homo's* inheritance of the evolutionary mantle as the carrier of intelligence are important enough to be retold. It can give perspective to the more concrete details of *Homo's* breakup and subsequent intellectual and cultural diversification.

# In Search of Protoman

Intelligence needs time to evolve. For a creature like *Homo sapiens* to evolve, a creature who has burst all bounds, subsequently to ravage the world, takes much time also. That is why we must consider origins. The placement of the adaptation of intelligence in *Homo* is an accident of structures and events, mammal events. That intelligence has risen to dominance is an evolutionary denouement that this writer sees as almost inevitable on an earth that was still relatively young and undergoing constant geological, climatic, topographical, and ecological changes.

*Homo's* ancestors, like the mammals of the Mesozoic (the age of the dinosaur), lay low for a long time. For almost 150 million years, under the very noses of the dinosaurs, the mammals slowly developed their complex set of adaptations—mammary glands, warmbloodedness, fur, a triangular integrated sensory system (nose, eyes, ears coordinated by a large brain situated at the front in the skull)—all as defenses by a small animal form trying to avoid the reach of its more obvious and numerous reptile neighbors (2). Given great environmental changes at the end of the Cretaceous, about seventy million years ago, they were able to emerge from their encapsulement and triumph over the dinosaurs, now highly specialized and somewhat senescent (3).

Just as the mammals can trace their lineage to ancient and maladapted reptiles such as the synapsid and therapsid lines, the primates were of an undistinguished line of mammals. The root primate—the tree shrew—was a very conservative mammal, who remained cautiously in the trees during the great mammalian expansion seventy to sixty million years ago (4). Some thirty million years later when the primates were emerging as forest living generalists, of a higher than average intelligence, the ancestors of *Homo* then were still probably conservatives. Otherwise they would not have retained that ability to walk upright on the land surfaces as they did. Rather they would have specialized, as did their monkey and ape cousins. I have postulated a crisis in the evolutionary history of the primates that may have precipitated the shaping and concrete morphological determination of intelligence's direction as it lodged itself in these primates (5).

We can not know for sure what happened twenty-five to thirty million years ago. The evidence is understandably meagre. Yet the results of these unknown events are here to be seen, in the monkeys, the apes, even in the remnant lemurs and tarsiers. Especially, the results are to be seen in contemporary *Homo,* and those eons are not too far removed that contributed the first fossil remains that gave us tangible proof of these events (6).

For our argument, these mysterious events point to an ancient breakout, first by the apes and then by the Old World monkeys, about thirty million years ago. The Old World monkeys, too, evolved up to and beyond their Rubicon, then, suddenly plunged forward. The ape and monkey fossils attest to it. Yet we don't see evidence for a proto-bipedal hominid for another twenty or so million years.

Certainly our ancestors were there, but no fossil that we

have yet found seems to be a likely candidate. Owen Lovejoy of Kent State University recently has made one of the most cogent hypotheses about the events and characteristics that could have shaped proto-*Homo* (7). Certainly similar to his therapsid protomammal and tree shrew primate ancestors, he was a defensive and out-classed creature. Probably he had evolved far beyond the prosimian lemurs and perhaps contained an amalgam of ancient monkey and ape traits. Today, we have both. He was thus a candidate for the anthropoid breakout of the Oligocene thirty million years ago, but he lost and was shunted to the sidelines.

How else do we explain our relatively quiet language, compared to the shrieking of the apes, the tender familial care of the young, the bonding of male and female, the latter continuously sexually receptive? This latter trait is also characteristic of gibbons, who in their monogamy share a similar family makeup with proto-*Homo*. Interestingly, the gibbon, of all the great apes, is the one on the periphery, a virtuoso brachiator at the very edge of the forest canopy (8).

Inconspicuous on the forest floor, proto-*Homo* walked on two feet, at least part of the time, partly to stay unobtrusive, and probably in defense, and developed its so-called paedomorphic characteristics—small facial features, infant-like gracile bones, in its postnatal state needing extended care because it was born helpless, with a large brain-to-body ratio as it developed after birth. These were all characteristics that announced its defensive adaptive needs: stay small, quiet, smart, protective. Thus proto-*Homo* survived, as his larger competitors went off after easier pickings.

It is important to emphasize these paedomorphic qualities of man; they represent a delay in the development of traditionally adult characteristics (9). Grown-up humans look and act like the young of their earlier more successful ape and monkey cousins. Much later, long after proto-*Homo* had developed into *Homo,* another crisis extruded this memory of paedomorphic defensiveness from *Homo's* genetic reservoir, and once more it saved *Homo,* but this time the results were more immediate and cataclysmic. This occurred 250,000 to 150,000 years ago.

Our hypothesis about this first crisis and the consequent creation of the basic form of *Homo* is built not from any tangible physical or historical facts, rather it is the result of intellectual detective work. The unknown ancestors of *Homo,* the lack of subsequent fossil indicators, imply the existence of a peripheral creature of no great number or consequence; then, the burst of expansion by other anthropoids—apes and monkeys—but still no hominid precursor twenty to twenty-five million years ago. Finally, many millions of years later (about five million years ago) we see *Homo* and *Australopithecus* well ensconced on the plains. *Australopithecus* was a still incomplete hominid, not fully bipedal, with many ape characteristics and a small brain (10). *Homo habilis* was more fully evolved, with a delicate physiognomy and the basic apparatus of human adaptation—except for the final and full growth of an unusual primate brain.

In addition to the great morphological reconstruction of the basic primate form that arose from this jungle womb of creation, there was another even deeper dimension to *Homo's* primeval heritage. This was a highly volatile genotype with an intense rate of mutations, especially for brain size. Obviously, with all the structural alterations that fixed themselves in the frantically adapting prototype, the key element in the harmonizing of these physical and social changes, making them work for our protohominid creatures, had to be this powerful, defensive brain. Here, evasion and family protection were given their key selective impetus, and, ultimately, the tradition for positive selective feedback of an ever expanding brain, within a relatively delicate and malleable facial and skull container, rooted itself deeply in our basic makeup. That is, until the present point in our evolutionary journey, when the advance in brain size seemingly has been blocked, intelligence has been taking on a new characteristic of intensive neurological "densification."

## Crisis and Biological Memory

Let us go forward many millions of years in time to the Upper Paleolithic, late in the Ice Ages, perhaps no more than 250,000 years ago. This is a jump of at least fifteen million years. During this time man had come out of the forests onto the plains, utilizing his large brain and his bipedal potentialities with great selective success. The mark of this success lies in his bone structure. The ancient delicacy had retreated; the primate-like heaviness of jaw, brow ridges, and general thickness of bones, whether below the neck or above, testify to *Homo's* success. We had become widely dispersed and seemingly fixed in our various ecologies (11). Then, once more, crisis.

Again, the actual events are unknown. The human product, however, was as radical a reconstruction of the now well-established millions-of-years-old hominid model as was proto-*Homo* of the then existing Oligocene thirty-million-years ago primate model. From a five-foot, stooping, heavy, plodding tool user, *Homo erectus,* arose a tall, baby-faced, gracile creature with a skull of eggshell delicacy, a bleached and relatively hairless creature, whom we now call Cro-Magnon.

Of course, we do not find the actual bones of this Eurasian product of the glacial tides until much later. Such miracles of discovery cannot be counted on. Yet, though 200,000 or so years are but a moment in evolutionary history, the evidence argues for the probability of such a physical reconstruction. The event had to have begun to take place, at the latest, a quarter of a million years ago, a product of vicious selective pressures. Such pressures most probably were exerted not by the primate host, as had occurred so many million years earlier in the forests, to create a similarly paedomorphic reconstruction (rate gene mutations to retard the development of the adult features even past the sexual maturity of the individuals in the line undergoing such mutations). Rather, given the evidence and the probabilities, weather changes, and thus changes in the economy of making a living and surviving were now at the root.

The product of this revolution was an enormous brain that literally forced itself into the ever expanding cranium, no bony blockades in this long, energy-riven infant. Had Cro-Magnon not been extruded from the evolutionary ice-basin of creation, we would not be discussing the problem of variable intelligence. *Homo* would still be plodding about the continents not too far behind the development of our most primitive cousins, those that anthropologists since the nineteenth century have doted upon.

I have alluded above to the fact that Cro-Magnon had a vastly enlarged cranium, upward of 1600 cm$^3$. Cro-Magnon was the culmination of a long tradition of purely physical enlargements of the brain, not to mention its reorganization in structure. The great difficulty that modern women still have in giving birth to these great-headed infants, as compared to the ease of the birthing process of anthropoids, testifies to a dangerous heritage in the evolution of the female. Here the success of hominid women in rearing what really are foetuses reminiscent of the marsupial mammalian solutions, almost became the modern female's undoing (12).

Since the passing of that ice-encased era, the average endocranial capacity of humankind has decreased, even among the Eurasian descendants of Cro-Magnon (13). Perhaps the limit of the female pelvis has forced the process of progressive encephalization and higher intelligence into some new pathway. Could it be that a purely neurological process, what above, metaphorically, was called "densification," meaning the expansion of blood supply to the more complex branches of the dendrites that interconnect the brain cells, could have made up in complexity and quantity of brain matter what formerly had expressed itself in purely metrical capacity?

The sum of the significance of this revolutionary super-*sapiens, Homo sapiens sapiens,* or Cro-Magnon, is that here was merely one unique representative of the human race who had come to live among us, certainly by 50,000 B.P. Many other human types existed at that time, ranging from transitional *sapiens* types such as Neanderthal man in the north, with a large but yet unreconstructed cranium, to more transitional *Homo erectus/sapiens* types in Africa and southeastern Asia. In the far east, existing in what seems to be a very restricted geographical domain, were the descendants of *Homo erectus pekinensis,* making step-like progress toward sapiency, but seemingly awaiting a genetic infusion from the west to precipitate their own revolutionary dynamics of reconstruction and advance (14). We will discuss this issue further in Chapter XVII.

## Variability—Breaking the Mold

How can we explain the possibility for such an unlikely event occurring, the precipitation of Cro-Magnon, *Homo sapiens sapiens,* within such a diverse population of humans throughout the eastern hemisphere, yet generally set within the now millions-years-old mold of bony *Homo erectus?* For, to be sure, *Homo erectus* was a successful inheritor of the mantle of primate intelligence, modest though it be from our standpoint.

*Homo erectus,* by the middle Pleistocene 500,000 years ago, was well grooved into ever deeper specializations that separated this species into a number of discrete racial forms. Could man have also ultimately divided himself up into diverse species? Probably not, for the basic model leading from protoman of the Oligocene thirty to thirty-five million years ago was probably genetically imprinted in the form, such that the movements back and forth of the various *Homo erectus* types would have amounted to a genetic separation, even at a distance, of no more than a few thousand years.

However, knowing the migratory character of mainline mammalian forms, including the biped, *Homo,* there probably would be some genetic contact at the fringes that would radiate into the mainstream racial forms and thus maintain the interfertility of the line even over the vast continental distances (15). The key element in the problem of human variability is that, even given the enormous phenotypic (surface) differences arising from a genetically unstable form of life, the great mammalian rule of the wandering flexible animal types be maintained.

Look at dogs, cattle, cats and other higher mammal types. They interbreed even as their genetic variability has created many different, often extreme types. Even at the seeming periphery of diversity, no inhibitions exist that could inhibit complete mongrelization. We do not ordinarily see this kind of interfertility among highly variable phenotypic and specialized life forms rigidly fixed (adapted) to their environment.

When protoman appeared in the Miocene some fifteen million years ago and gradually was shaped into the final form of *Homo,* he experienced an important breakthrough. There on the plains he found himself virtually without animal enemies. He was making a sharp transition from a variable bipedal ground or tree climbing life-style into this new ecology. His sharper intelligence and his unique presence had placed him beyond the reach of the traditional predator/prey dependencies. As the existentialists would say, man was alone in the world.

At this stage in human evolution, the puzzling problem of man's biosocial nature came to the fore; it still bedevils us. Not only did this tiny defensive ape/monkey now lose those forest qualities of evasion in exchange for the larger vistas of the wandering plains, but he began to exhibit a deadly aggressiveness (16).

Also, we note that *Homo,* as he began to establish his unique prototype, departing more and more from the typical biosocial forms of primate adaptive behavior, set off on the plains toward his own personal inner biological realization. The reason that the usual adaptive constraints in the behavior of man no longer held arose in part from the character of his genetic heritage. The highly intensive mutational rate that had proved positively selective, for defense, within the forest, could not in one short evolutionary moment on the plains be short-circuited, especially now that *Homo* lived in an even more dynamic ecology.

If a high mutational rate, especially where it concerned brain growth and its accompanying facets of structure and behavior—such as language use and intense family bonding—was adaptive in the forest, it became even more useful on the plains. This was because while the hominids had no direct competitors on the plains—except for their own fellow beings and perhaps the cousinly contending australopithecines—life was still difficult. One glance at our primitive brothers of a century or so ago with their hunting and gathering ways of life will show that while man survived, making a living with ever fewer direct instinctual skills was just as difficult.

That is the point. The heritage of the past had freed protoman from much specific behavioral and morphological specialization. The purpose and utility of a large brain and the concomitant behavioral character of evasion were here fully realized rather than the specific instinctually guided morphological talents such as existed in the high flying gibbon, out of reach at the very treetops. The gibbon is an extremely specialized ape. Without the dense forest mantle to accommodate him, he is quickly maladaptive.

What happened with *Homo* on the plains, as we can perceive from the fossil evidence of three to five million years ago, was that of a continuously growing relatively unspecialized primate brain. The only specialization worth noting is *Homo's* unique bicameral structure—left and right hemispheres, with a set of associated language areas usually located in the left hemisphere (17). The impetus of the heritage of genetic instability in the brain was now continued, this because his family and social linguistic structure had become firmly rooted, now positively, in the new ecology. Natural selection probably quickly culled out any laggard semi-bipedal atavists. The selectivity of the growing brain and man's increasing competence at making a living and defending his family from other hominid predators was thus given a great stimulus. The actual mutations had to have come by themselves, randomly, so goes the theory, but highly selected in one direction—"orthoselection" (selection in a straight line)—for always more and greater human intelligence, with all that that fact connoted for society and culture (18).

The biology of *Homo* now took on the coloration of his hominid brain. This heritage of brain growth was rooted deeply in the morphological capacity for malleability of behavior, helped to a certain extent by man's upright posture. It all bred a keen awareness of the world, and was positively selected for by *Homo's* success in rearing his helpless young.

We know how predatory birds try to raid the nests of other more vulnerable birds, and how predatory animals try to separate their prey's young from its parents. Obviously humans for a long time into the past have had to be invulnerable from all but other human predators. The lack of instinctual control of newly born human babies reflects the fact that this set of behaviors did not work counterproductively in insuring the survival of this helpless creature. Devoid of the instinctual restraints imposed on other forms of animal life, the neonate human could cry to its heart's content and still be protected from any other nonhuman predator.

# Cultural Selection

If the brain with its consequent shapings of human mentation and cultural life now developed by its own inner laws, this did not mean that the rate of expansion and the character of brain mutations were everywhere the same. It only meant that wherever humans moved, the laws of human variability—the centrifugality of those minute mutations—would themselves be shaped through social selection. Each human group would set its own laws for shaping and fixing these evolving variations, and practically along a 180-degree spread of differences.

Inbreeding in small groups could make each migrating tribe its own measure of the cultural character of the social group it was willing to become. The group could dictate the rate and nature of its own unique variability as it became distributed throughout the group. Thus each social group could voluntarily shape this variability by eliminating certain structures, patterns, and behavior from the social unit. This could be done merely by excluding those individual carriers from the breeding unit, giving greater emphasis to other types of characteristics by allowing these carriers to bring more young to reproductive maturity than others. Thus the cultural/psychological character of the group would be tilted in one structural/behavioral direction rather than another.

What this meant for intelligence and its evolutionary significance was that the growth of the brain and intelligence in the hominids became quite variable, often a by-product of other random structural mutations—for heavy brow ridges, for extra skull bones, for particular relationships in the formation of connecting bone structures of the face, and a host of other seemingly nonselective characteristics that could very well have been accompanied by hidden alterations in the myriad neurological components of the brain (19).

In the last century, A. R. Wallace raised the question why such an enlarged brain was necessary for a human line, which in *Homo erectus* was already so far beyond the necessity for animal competition (20). The answer lies in the facts. *Homo's* present range of variation in brain size and structure (from 950 to 1900 cm³) is so vast that it boggles the imagination (21). The reason for the great variation is that the selective barriers existing outside the human band's social and cultural reach were dissolved some ten to five million years ago. Since then, like Topsy, the brain just grew (22).

## Brains and Tools

Let us be clear about one crucial relationship between purely morphological/structural characteristics in the evolution of *Homo* and his cultural development. From the very earliest dated fossils of *Homo habilis,* three to four million years ago, we find a strictly parallel development in endocranial capacity and the products, e.g., stone tools, of peoples having that particular endocranial capacity. As a corollary, as *Homo's* skull, and thus his brain, grew larger, so, too, do the cultural remains available to us from that stratum of time show a development in complexity and in intensity of intentional shaping (23).

However, it is fair to say that there is also a qualitative element added to the dependent variable character of the brains = tools argument. First, the scraper tools of highly evolved *Homo sapiens* from northeastern Asia 30,000-20,000

B.P. show a relatively regressive character given the highly advanced skulls with which we find them associated. Also, the southern African Boskopoids, at about the same period of time, if not more recently, had enormously expanded brain cases. Yet the so-called Wilton stone tool technology that is associated with these people, even given the dramatic and colorful rock wall paintings attributed to them, was not anywhere nearly as sophisticated as the northern Cro-Magnon culture of their contemporaries, or even antecedents (24).

Another interesting and perhaps mysterious aspect of the relationship of brain size and structure to stone tool technology is given in a comparison of the so-called Acheulean culture as compared with the Neanderthal Mousterian tortoise-core flint chips. We can trace this Acheulean culture with its faceted hand axes and granite choppers back to the earliest phases of *Homo erectus.* In fact the Acheulean is a worldwide technology found everywhere with the remains of the erectines, with one exception. The isolated northeastern *Homo erectus pekinensis* never seemed to have utilized this laborious, often loving method of shaping and faceting their tools (25).

At the very end of the trail of *Homo erectus,* the Acheulean culture evolved a truly remarkable and beautiful variety of such stone tools, in many shapes and sizes. The esthetics of the tools in their design—tear drop, oval, sword, dagger-like, often extremely artfully faceted—testify to a real sense of beauty as well as practicality. It should be said that some of the more monstrously large hand axes, though beautiful and awesome, could not possibly have been utilitarian. Only a giant could have wielded them. The fossil remains have never suggested (Richard Leakey in 1985 claimed to have found leg bones of an African erectine that would make him *very* tall) that *Homo erectus* was more than about five feet tall.

Some of the beautiful tools from the end of the period of erectine culture have been found that are not associated with any fossil remains, so we do not know the exact evolutionary stage of these final purveyors of Acheulean culture. Soon afterward, however, the Neanderthals came on the scene (about 100,000 B.P.). They seem to have spontaneously developed their own culture—the so-called Mousterian (from the French site where their tools and bones were first discovered in the nineteenth century) with a tortoise-shell technique of fracturing a multitude of flint chips from a rock core (26).

The Neanderthals had a skull structure, which while in its endocranial capacity was quite large (generally more capacious than the worldwide average of our own contemporary *Homo sapiens*) was different in formation as compared with the model of *Homo erectus,* and also with Cro-Magnon, *Homo sapiens sapiens,* his European successor. It thus seems clear that in general we do see a correlation between brain size and brain structure and its cultural accompaniment up until the end of the Pleistocene (8000 B.C.) (27). Also, if one dares to assert it, there seems to be a causal relationship as well. *NB*

So we state it: The level of cultural complexity, sophistication, control over the environment in the economic and military sense is directly related to the state of intellectual advance, whether this be calculated by endocranial capacity, excess neurons, interneuronic dendritic connections, or richness and quantity of blood supply to the arteries of the brain. This *Imp.* relationship has arisen in nature not as a result of a direct external shaping by the environment or by interspecies competition. The hominid brain, with its cultural exudation, has been shaped by genetic, even biochemical, factors over which external circumstances have had little control. The shaping of these external features, the product of that inner genetic reality, of which we are scarcely aware, has taken place in the interaction of the human groups themselves as they struggled to survive over the last several million years.

Since Cro-Magnon's sudden appearance on the world scene, nature once more dipped into her grab bag of "curves" and threw at *Homo* a whole new environmental and climatic scene. The Ice Age "hair shirt" that had disciplined man selectively could now be shed. As horrific as it was, it had allowed for an entirely new human demography and ecology.

Even before the end of the Pleistocene, what began as a rare and freakish creative event in a tiny subpopulation of northern, Caucasoid erectines, had developed over hundreds of thousands of years into a large subdivided population that spread from central Spain to the Ural mountains at the borders of Russian Siberia. Already these populations had been and were on the move worldwide.

In addition, the mutational buildup in variations had produced a more gracile type than the tall, broad-faced northern types. Living around the Mediterranean littoral, as the ice retreated north after 8000 B.C., these so-called "old Europeans" were creating a new post-Ice Age civilization along the Adriatic, in Yugoslavia, in Crete, probably mixing with the Cro-Magnon Moullians in their migrations into Egypt, northern Africa, and beyond. We may discover in the skulls of Cretan Minoans, in the Greeks, Sumerians, Hittites, and others, somewhat less capacious skulls than the Cro-Magnon ancestors, but these peoples were also somewhat shorter in stature (28).

However, when we examine those Holocene (since the Ice Ages) cultural expressions, do we see reflected an intelligence that even in potentiality was less than those awesome Cro-Magnons? This is the puzzle of high human intelligence that faces us in our more interbred world of great and rapid migrations of peoples who derive from vastly different intellectual and cultural patterns and histories.

Recently a reproduction of the Lascaux cave in France was opened near its original. The original paintings were in danger because of alterations in climate caused by bacterial factors. The reproduction could give tourists a sense of the art works without degrading the originals. Talented artists were hired to reproduce the Cro-Magnon Gravettian murals, but to dispassionate observers, the results were pitifully poor compared to the spontaneous originals of these ancient, supposedly barbaric peoples.

Again, in the not too distant past in northern Italy, a people arose, a blend of the original Roman-Celtic populations little noted for their artistic imagination and the Gothic and Lombard Germanic invaders of the early medieval seventh and eighth centuries A.D. Less than a thousand years later, these now Renaissance Italians presented mankind with an artistic civilization which if not superior in creativity, imagination, and technical realization to anything in the ancient world, was certainly on a level sufficient to stir any human heart or mind.

We do not really know the external analyzable combinations that signal great intelligence and creative insight. In our mixed populations of today, endocranial capacity is only roughly correlated with high intelligence achievements (29). As Alice Brues states, you measure between the ears to get the best sense of human differentiation (30). As for intellectual capacity, you still can not be sure.

## Modernizing Mankind

As part of the progressive hybridization and population expansion of the human race, another element meets our consciousness. Good evidence exists for the probability that miscegenation has always taken place when distant peoples meet, even in war. It probably took place as well during the late Ice Age expansion of *Homo sapiens sapiens.* We have found skulls that hint at a Cro-Magnon/Neanderthal hybridization in Israel and the Near East (31). There is a strong possibility that a whole range of progressive erectine skeletons that appears suddenly in the African fossil finds, 125,000 to 75,000 B.P., was probably the result of the mixing of the retrogressive indigenous populations and small numbers of people from the north (32).

The point that needs to be made here is that the demographic pattern has tilted toward a worldwide explosion of peoples over the last two to three millennia, increasing enormously in the last two centuries. It is probable that hidden within all populations that expand in numbers is a reservoir of quite variable intelligence that could not express itself significantly over time in periods of duress when the small populations were held in relative check by the selective winnowing that accompanies scarcity. With the recent exploitation of our ecology, the expansion of the economic base, and thus the possibility for larger populations being able to survive, we today see a vastly variable population living under conditions of plenitude. The creation of this plenitude, sad to state, the resultant mass populations have had little or nothing to do with. The billions that are on our earth today survive by virtue of the achievement, the productivity, and the genius of a relative few, the products of our recent Ice Age heritage.

who grows the food you eat? who created your leisure?

## Chapter V

# SOCIOBIOLOGY: SELECTION AND SURVIVAL

## The Unity of Knowledge

For over one hundred years now, the search for the means to unify the sciences of life and behavior with the social and cultural disciplines of the world of *Homo sapiens* has proved a most intriguing, if baffling, challenge. Ever since Darwin's work was accepted into the circle of knowledge, thinkers have rightly thought: if we humans are biological creatures, and if there are scientific principles that seem to unify the structure and behavior of living things in general, ought not these self-same principles apply to the world of humans?

The catch is to identify those principles and endow them with a causal elegance sufficiently broad and detailed that they will penetrate the realm of cultural behavior and illuminate its deeper biological stratum. This has yet to happen. But the logical necessity of the fact that our universe is whole, and that science and philosophy are committed to the search for unitary principles and laws that bring all aspects of experience into the great system, still goads us to give the problem one more try.

Someday, the enigma will be penetrated and we will have a predictive theory. At that moment, humanity may very well gain some real control over its destiny, no longer to be subjected to the occasional and often premeditated horrors that, for example, we dwellers in the twentieth century have experienced.

As early as the mid-nineteenth century of Herbert Spencer and Francis Galton, the latter Darwin's cousin, there were attempts to understand and develop theories about man's varying biological qualities, given the hereditarian basis of illness and defect (1). Further along, into the twentieth century, behavioristic psychology, under the impetus of John Watson, then Leonard Bloomfield and B. F. Skinner, utilized a biological model of adaptive animal behavior as a guide in developing a model of human thought consonant with man's deeper biological motivations (2). The experimentalist orientation of those researchers seemed to argue that below the surface of value, cultural pretensions, and verbiage, humans were really behaving like the drive-ridden animal forms of the biological world. What we humans experienced in culture were merely the surface trappings of a very complex animal.

Looking deeper, one would find that the aboriginal stimuli were similar to those motivating all animals, the basic satisfactions of food, procreative, and other survival needs. Indeed, although Freudian psychology seemed a far more sophisticated concession to the unique qualities and facts of human mentation, the Darwinian biological model, in the purest embodiment of Freud's theories, was always lurking in the background (3).

We are animals. To become adapted and survive in the process of natural selection, animals must satisfy these basic biological needs. Beneath all the folderol of dreams, pathological mental states, neuroses of emotional behavior, even psychosomatic diseases, lie a few basic biological needs that beg for satisfaction.

In all, from the complex receptions to such approaches by the knowledgeable public, one can note a sense of receptivity to the basic logical intuition as to our biological selves. Yet as each of these theories overcame the inertia of the past and surged to a certain prominence, one can note the gradual ebbing in public acceptance, due to the lack of predictive fulfillment of its particular version of the biosocial connective theoretical tissue. Simply, the theories didn't predict well enough, and what they were able to explain that was not clarified from other scientific, philosophical, or even religious approaches was too complicated and artificial to generate a real consensus and thus inevitably the kind of research that would have continually fructified those theories.

In anthropology too, we have seen the waves of sentiment go back and forth from theories using the biological model, starting with the so-called evolutionary approach to culture of Morgan and Tylor in the nineteenth century, which rightly or wrongly utilized western culture as the model and goal of evolutionary cultural development (4). The reaction to this quasi-Darwinian modeling of *Homo's* social and historical evolution is to be found in the powerful work of Franz Boas and the relativistic school of cultural anthropology, which rejected the evolutionary model for culture (5).

The beginning of the twentieth century saw many social and political movements that ostensibly argued against any extrapolation from biology to social theory, such as the so-called social-Darwinist survival-of-the-fittest view of social, economic class structure, i.e., the most successful people in the contemporary world were the ablest, most competent, intelligent, and they met the fitness test of natural selection.

The socialist and communist movement, utilizing the socio-economic model of Karl Marx, certainly believed in an equal-ity of man and a conventionality to the nature of society that removed biological factors from any explanation for what had gone on in human history. However, Marx himself, deeply impressed by Darwin's work, wanted to dedicate to Darwin part of *Das Kapital* because he felt that his own work contained in it the same scientific pattern of inquiry that in-fected Darwin's *Origin of Species* (6).

If cultural anthropology has since accepted a relativistic nonbiological or antiselectivist approach to the study of cul-ture, physical anthropologists were not constrained by the same sociological ideal. As pointed out in Chapter V, "Selec-tion and Survival" of *The Form of Man,* the first volume in this series, the search for an explanation of the various struc-tural and behavioral uniquenesses of the evolving hominids in terms of adaptive fitness has been a dominating theme for over half a century.

Recently, the work of S. L. Washburn led many anthro-pologists onto the road of practicality in analyzing man's bi-pedal gait and posture, frontal coitus, language, tool-mak-ing, and innumerable other human structures and behaviors (7). The argument here was that if the theory of evolution was to apply also to the coming of *Homo,* then we should be able to show the selective advantage and usefulness of those uni-que characteristics of *Homo* that distinguish him from other primates and the animal world in general.

As argued in Chapter I of this book, the test of any theory about man is how it meshes with what we now know about humans. If we believe in the continuity of nature—and all of these bioselectionist theorists obviously do, because they want to connect the biological world with our cultural world—then they have to play the game to the end. There-fore, they have to pursue their explanations about the evolu-tionary factors that produced *Homo* in the first place through to the supposed evolutionary factors that still undergird his existence and functioning in historical times.

We cannot stop at the point where man appears historically and involve supranatural creationist factors that would separate in theory and fact the two worlds, the biological—man in process of becoming *Homo sapiens sapiens*—and the sociological—cultural *Homo sapiens sapiens* himself. The anthropological theory that explains man's uniqueness must be relevant today in logical content and be somewhat predictive about man's contemporary behavior. At the very least, it must explain why the two do not mesh, perhaps invoking the coming of agriculture, as some have done. (The argument here is that the transition from migratory hunting to sedentary agricultural settlements in some way created new forces, dynamics, and cultural relationships that changed man's destiny (8)). The age-old question of children from five to seventy-five is, why. Why did such a change come about, and how and why did it change millions-of-years-old patterns of behavior?

## The Sociobiological Argument

The modern controversy over sociobiology arises from such traditionally befuddling roots. It is once more a new attempt, albeit using a quite different theoretical biological model, to explain contemporary human behavior and institutions in natural selectionist terms, in a theory that reconnects these two disparate realms of intellectual discourse, the biological and the sociological.

The sociobiological controversy that has developed in the 1970s and 80s derives from a gradual sophistication in the mathematical treatment of population genetics. It has been concerned with problems of natural selection and how we must view the changes that take place within species and between species in terms of their evolving fitness (9).

Certain forms of life seem more closely drawn together socially and selectively than others. From swarms of insects to herds of buffalo the evolutionary interactions involve relationships of the individual with its group, as, for example, the different functions of subpopulations of bees, ants, and termites, all genetically programmed in their social behavior. Do we see natural selection operating on individuals within the group or on the group as a totality (10)?

Darwin originally had thought of natural selection as operative on relative individual fitness. His instincts about the competition of life forms, drawn from his wide travels and observations, came well before the concept of the gene, the mechanism for the transmission of characteristics of individuals and species. The inevitable alterations (later mutations) that form the structure for change become the grist upon which adaptation and natural selection work in the passage of time (11).

In the 1960s a number of theorists—J. Maynard Smith, William Hamilton, and Robert Trivers—working through the mathematics of kin selection, revealed that many ostensibly group factors in natural selection could be absorbed by concepts such as "inclusive fitness" (Hamilton) and "optimality" (Trivers) that precisely related the genetic relationships and interactions between members of a group who actually shared a family of genes (12). What was thought to be group selection on the purely phenotypic level (structural or behavioral) could now be seen as a surface reflection of a deeper consanguineous genetic affiliation. We were really seeing, as J. Maynard Smith revealed to us, a process of kin selection, in which genetic relationships were being more directly acted on by the sorting forces of evolution (13).

In the struggle to survive, individual or group members made what often seemed like choices in their behavior to pass on their genes in one direction rather than another. Mathematical calculus would show that the "decisions" were always made in the direction of the optimal distribution of affected members' genes (14). The total result of this dispersal of kinship relationships leading to a positive evolutionary result for the group was called by Hamilton "inclusive fitness."

Edward O. Wilson's comprehensive *Sociobiology* (1975) and Richard Dawkins popularization, *The Selfish Gene* (1976), quickly brought this more technical discussion to public attention (15). A drama was here presented in which the individual gene now marched to front and center stage as the core element in the evolutionary selective process. The phenotype, what we observed with our senses, was now a mere surface decoy for a more dramatic struggle that was taking place between the germ plasm of individuals, each striving for immortality.

The theme of this first phase of sociobiology, at least in its more radical expression, can be expressed by E. O. Wilson, writing in *On Human Nature* (1978): "Because the brain can be guided by rational calculation only to a limited degree, it must fall back on the nuances of pleasure and pain mediated by the limbic system and other lower centers of the brain" (16). While E. O. Wilson was not especially concerned about priorities, whether it was the individual or the group that bore the burden of natural selection and survival, he did clearly state that it was the distribution and redistribution of certain genetic patterns that determined individual or group behavior regardless of first cause.

It was Dawkins' pithy book, *The Selfish Gene,* even more than Wilson's own discussion of implications, that focused on the almost mechanical and deterministic character that surface behavior assumed when under the guidance and suzerainty of the selfish gene. Intraspecific behavior that we could describe as cooperative, altruistic, aggressive, competitive, as important as it was for the resulting success or failure of a species in the evolutionary sweepstakes, was really a manifestation of deeper genetic dynamics. The individual genes were engaged in a fundamental selective race all the while using surface social behavior as a pawn in their rush to reproductive immortality (17).

The supposed independent laws by which we understand social relationships are shown to be chimerical by this wing of sociobiology. Underneath the apparently autonomous workings of nations is a deeper reality of genetic interactions wherein the individual and his close genetic relations work to extend themselves into the next generation by maintaining surface conditions—status, economic wealth, power, charisma—that will translate into reproductive success. The individual, his children, aunts, uncles, cousins form a cohort of affiliated genes that reflect this deeper bond.

The altriusm of parents for children is made understandable when we reflect on the genetic heritage that children represent. Parents who give up their lives to rescue the three children in their blazing home are in reality saving that one hundred and fifty percent of themselves. Each child is constituted of fifty percent of each parent's genetic makeup. Upon death, the parent is more than preserved. The sociobiologists go further. They claim that a whole series of human relationships can be illuminated by a consideration of the subtle genetic dynamics of each individual genotype utilizing surface means to maintain its potential immortality: promiscuity versus puritanism; jealousy versus indifference; cooperativeness versus competition all have their deeper translatable survivalistic strategies (18).

## Dominating Gene

The apparent drive of a species to maintain itself as an inbreeding unity, often seeming to allow individuals to be sacrificed for the greater good, is argued to be social mythology. Dawkins, in his later book *The Extended Phenotype,* argued passionately that no matter how much it may appear that social interaction is the arena in which natural selective processes take place, the fundamental unity of evolutionary processes in animals is the gene, the replicator; never of necessity can it be the surface phenomena, the so-called vehicles of the replicator. It must be, then, that although complex phenotypic interactions seem to constitute the playing field on which population dynamics are being worked out, closer analysis will eventually reveal that they really emanate from the genetic level (19).

This train of argument had been developed by William Hamilton, John Maynard Smith, and George C. Williams (20). In Hamilton's approach to the individual/group problem, "evolutionary change is change in gene frequencies in populations, and, for a population under individual selection, the direction and magnitude of the change will be determined by the relations among the inclusive fitnesses of the organisms in the population. When a phenotype that appears to reduce fitness persists in a population, we may sometimes be able to resolve the puzzle by considering the inclusive fitness of the phenotype . . . . " (21)

In general, G. C. Williams argued that when one observes adaptations apparently beneficial to group members and disadvantageous to individuals, an argument tending toward inclusive fitness may be invoked. However, most such examples are in reality misinterpretations of the facts, fortuitous effects rather than products of natural selection: "Results of physically inevitable events, misplaced forms of kin-altruism spilled over to benefit unrelated individuals, or even sheer statistical artifacts, i.e., summations of some instances of individually advantageous behavior . . . no group-selectionist explanation was to be preferred to any individual-selectionist alternative, which in addition was . . . much more parsimonious." (22)

Of course there was tremendous opposition to such a decidedly genetic determinism. It punctured our accepted and

conventional wisdom about the well-nigh infinite malleability
of humans through their social processes. Even such a committed sociobiologist as Daniel Freedman writes in his book
*Human Sociobiology,* ". . . Dawkins talks about genes for
coyness and genes for fastness (female sexual behavior) entering the population at different rates depending upon the
genes' relative success. I simply do not think in this way. Such
traits are obviously *not* determined by single genes, and the
model is wrong at its inception. Those traits are, rather,
almost certainly polygenic and each of us is a unique blend of
opposed tendencies. To my mind, the selection of complex
traits is best regarded as a multiply caused process, a response
to simultaneous pressures at all levels of selection." (23)

Clearly this is merely a plea for a holding off of the all
too quick and simple solution in favor of the slow consideration of the interaction of complex genetic combinations giving rise at a more unobtrusive distance to the social behavior
in question. Freedman by no means would accept a purely
social or cultural source of such behavior. The biological
paradigm must be correct. What about the Shakers in nineteenth-century America? Here was a religiosocial group that
abstained from sexual relations of any kind; it had to resort
to a continual infusion of recruits from the outside in order to
maintain its existence. Eventually, the supply of recruits dried
up and the Shakers disappeared. How can sociobiology explain such behavior, even through a model of "inclusive fitness"? (24)

Apply the test once more from the study of the biological sources of human behavior. Does it fit with anything that
we know about the workings of human culture? When the
opponents of the sociobiological model went to work on the
various extrapolations from animal behavior and population
genetics to the world of man, all hell broke loose. In 1981,
E. O. Wilson, ever resourceful in responding to the critiques
of clean-cut selectivist interpretations of human behavior, institutions, and cultural modeling, co-authored, with Charles

Lumsden, an important response, *Genes, Mind, and Culture* ✓ (25).

While the genetic leash on human behavior and culture still exists, as Wilson and Lumsden claim, it is obviously a bit longer than previously postulated. Nevertheless the biological restrictions that do exist shape the forms of culture that we devise. Behind the process of culture building and cultural dynamics in history lie many channels of individual development. Coming together, these create institutions that serve the basic selective requirements of humans.

The differences in cultures, and in the history of cultures, to the extent that they arise through the competitiveness of rival individuals and groups, argue for the existence of genetic differences. Indeed the ebb and flow of social patterns, political dominance constitute the surface manifestation of deeper dynamics in shifting population genetics. There are limitations on the extent to which purely social manipulations in populations can modify behavior. Examples of persistent traditional gender behavior, as on the Israeli kibbutz and indeed eventually in all societies going through violent social changes, represent one aspect of the sociobiologist leash represented in society and in interpersonal behaviors (26).

The core of Lumsden and Wilson's model is a concept they call "culturgen." These are units of cultures: taboos, cuisines, personality types, tools, religious beliefs, kinship patterns. By conceptualizing culture in terms of such units, one can attempt to understand the patterns by which the genes create what the authors call the epigenetic rules that guide the development of the culturgens and their possible conscious social modifications. Lumsden and Wilson really do believe that a close analysis of the interaction and alteration of these culturgens over time will allow for a phenotypic mapping of the inner genetic malleability in the populations, much as we would map the physical and behavioral characteristics of lower animals in a rapidly changing external environment. Not only do we see a certain amount of phenotypic malleability, for example, changes in the size of animals given more or less food, but also changes in average size as a measure of the dominance of certain genes in the population given more or less food over a series of generations (27).

Naturally Lumsden and Wilson believe that with humans the range of purely social and cultural manipulations of behavior is much smaller than cultural or sociological determinists would have it. However, even given the many changes which the authors see as blatantly occurring in all cultures, they view this process as a manifestation of what they call "gene-culture coevolution." The most common examples, to which they bring a rather formidable mathematical analysis to bear, are incest rules, the village social structure of simple agricultural societies, and changes in women's fashion over the years (28).

## Self-Knowledge and Predictability

Philip Kitcher has summarized the main critiques of E. O. Wilson's various programs. This included Wilson's gene-culture coevolutionary theory, which was brought to a conclusion in his highly provocative *Promethean Fire* (1983). 1. A theory of atoms of culture (culturgens), whether mental or material artifacts, cannot constitute the primordial grist for a theory of what culture is or how it acts dynamically. What Wilson is doing is taking our verbal descriptions of such "atoms" at face value, whereas, in reality what they are and how they interact might or might not be completely at odds with our commonsense verbal descriptions of these matters.

2. Lumsden and Wilson's supposed mathematical mapping of these interactions does little to reveal instrumentally

any new predictive possibilities that are not obtained in the usual kinds of analysis of ethnographic data used by anthropologists. Kitcher forcefully argues that at best the mathematics utilized by Wilson simplifies the issues of human preference: "In sum, we have an implausible solution for a problem about a social expression of human preferences, in a case where there are no detailed results that could be used to distinguish the solution from the most elementary quantitative analysis of the situation." (29)

There are other criticisms of the more elaborate theoretical programs of Wilson and an associated theoretician Richard Alexander whose book *Darwin and Human Affairs* (1979) puts forward a more modest program, yet one that seems to give greater recognition to human choice and knowledge. Following on Hamilton's arguments for inclusive fitness as a concept that will harmonize individual and group genetic interest, Alexander states: "When the abilities of potential recipients of nepotistic benefits to translate such benefits into reproduction are equal, then closer relatives will be favored over more distant relatives . . . ." (30) "The single environment in which all that I have just said can become irrelevant, of course, is that in which the interactants have become consciously aware of their natural history . . . ." (31) "Individuals and groups least bound by history are those who best understand it." (32)

It is on the above issue of "knowledge of" that sociobiology begins to fall apart. The issues that the sociobiologists wish to analyze from the standpoint of fitness or natural selection are really at the periphery of human culture: homosexuality, incest, primogeniture, the rise and fall of hemlines, gender/behavior correlations, status and reproductive potency. Naturally, all these issues are important to understanding human behavior. However, no evidence has been shown to argue that these so-called culturgens interrelate in any lawlike or predictive manner, that one can find reliable stabilities in either their interaction with other culturgens or make predictions about other and large events on the basis of such seeming biologically rooted interests, e.g., promiscuity, primogeniture. Alexander makes twenty-five predictions on the basis of the inclusive fitness theories. Alexander himself notes that they are either circular or trivial (33).

As Kitcher notes, much of what Lumsden and Wilson have claimed to prove through mathematical analysis of the expression of so-called epigenetic rules for mapping out genetic predispositions into cultural instrumentalities is really reworded, or reconceptualized from what can be gleaned either from folk traditions or field observations of anthropologists (34). A good theory might do this more efficiently but only as a prolegomenon to offering greater predictive power in wholly unexpected realms of individual behavior or the dynamics of social institutions.

The great power of mathematics has lain in regularizing within an unequivocal symbolic system of relations, facts that heretofore existed in the scattered and fuzzy area of human observation, discourse, and emotional prejudice. Most importantly, following Occam's *"essentia non sunt multiplicanda praeter necessitatem"* (a plurality must not be asserted without necessity), mathematics helps us to reshape a theory, guiding it toward a new heuristic program. At some point in the deductive mathematical chain, this theory must reveal new observable and predictable consequences.

At the present point in sociobiology, we have no unitary structure of behavior to which we can trace, even at a distance, strict selective advantages in culture—from individuals, and then likewise enhancing the inclusive fitness of groups. Surely, we can point to many behaviors that give some of us an advantage most of the time, but there is never any close genetic correlation to be found to these discrete cultural behaviors. Statements about the advantages of specific child-rearing practices in certain primitive societies or supposedly adaptive but blindly-held taboos still lie in the realm of folk wisdom.

The sociobiological model throws some interesting light onto this tradition. However, because you can always point to counter examples, to behavior that does not necessarily lead to a lessening of individual or inclusive fitness, these sociobiological claims loose credence. In sum, both the cultural relativists and the sociobiological determinists may have their intellectual day in the sun someday. At this stage, however, the failures of these particular models of man derive from experience and fact.

## Our Biological Selves

There does seem to be a human nature out there that proves resistant to the tampering of political tyrants, whether fascists or Marxists. What the actual theoretical components to this stubbornness in human behavior are, no one yet has discovered. Of one thing we can be sure. Over one hundred years of theories of biological determinism have failed to produce the theoretical or practical fruits that would persuade. So, too, have the one hundred years of sociological determinism or cultural relativism failed to illuminate or equate with human propensities. The attempts to enclose us in social and political prisons and to persuade us, Orwell-like, that we ought to be happy in these settings, should assure us that there is something out there we can call human nature.

The nub of all of this is that both extremes miss, both in theory and practice—the sociobiological determinist and the cultural relativist. Each has eschewed or ignored the essential sociobiological mechanism that defines our animal social essence, the unique character of and the variability in human intelligence. You simply do not get to the core of mankind's paradigmatic nature by studying the dynamics of incest taboos. Nor do you see the core of human relationships arising from the momentary economic class structures of a society.

The physical anthropologists have become bogged down in their search for a selective grail that would reveal the evolutionary mechanism for the ascent of man, in such peripheral territorial, sexual, bipedal behaviors. So, too, the sociobiologists have been overawed by the intriguing equations of population genetics and the interactions of kin selection in such interbreeding groups. Of course a deeper truth lies with the biological vision, because our heritage arises from this source. Out of the evolutionary matrix will come a revivified sociobiological, anthropological, even psychological perspective on human learning more akin to man's true animal nature (35).

The sociological egalitarians and the cultural relativists know that they are climbing a tree about to be severed from its roots. There can be no sociology, politics, cultural anthropology without giving man's biological heritage its due. The other way points toward "creationism." Indeed contemporary Marxist ideology has taken a long step in that direction. That is why it is incumbent upon all philosophical liberals to hold off giving assent to any particular representation of the facts of the case.

Kitcher, a committed opponent of the current state of sociobiological discourse and a borderline ideologist for the "other" side still concedes that ". . . a serious human sociobiology needs help from many fields. If it is to be achieved, it will have to draw on the work of evolutionary theorists, behavior geneticists, developmental biologists and psychologists, sociologists and historians, cognitive psychologists and anthropologists. Any resultant discipline would be a real synthesis. But it is hard to synthesize when some of the contributions to the union are yet unformed." (36)

In the next chapter, a model will be set forth of a possible sociobiology of man, modest though it may be in terms of reduced expectations of direct linkages with preprogrammed genetic constellations for cultural behavior.

# Chapter VI

# TOWARD A SOCIOBIOLOGY OF MAN

## Humans Are Different Animals

To discuss the sociobiology of humans, one must understand the special nature of man's biological heritage, his evolutionary past. One just cannot assume that we are two-legged hyenas with a number of unique peculiarities—language, culture, etc. It is puzzling why so few of those who study the character of sociobiological interactions have dipped into the mysteries of man's journey into the present in order to distill those factors in man's biology that render his behavior different. One ought to return, as Richard Alexander does, to the beginning of man's cultural achievements rather than merely commenting on the impact of knowledge and self-awareness on biologically adaptive behavior (1).

In the earlier books in this series, special reference was made to that little-noticed evolutionary process, orthoselection, first outlined by G. G. Simpson and now much discussed in evolutionary theory in rehabilitating Richard Gold-schmidt's works on "hopeful monsters"—now called "punctuated equilibrium" by Niles Eldridge and Steven Gould (2). The recognition that the evolutionary record in general cannot reveal to us a smooth process of minute mutational changes in various lines of creatures and that gaps in the record can sometimes be interpreted as true saltations, structural breakthroughs that allow members of a line to move beyond the slow incremental changes that classical Darwinism proposed, has opened a new awareness of variable evolutionary avenues.

When protohominids entered the expanding savannahs of Africa, for possible better pickings, little could they expect that in that one short step they would have crossed a selective boundary. Such an occurrence in evolutionary history is rare. But when it did occur it produced the amphibians, reptiles, birds, even, if more slowly, the mammals. It would not be overbold to argue that that one short step into the world of extended vistas constituted one of the great evolutionary breakthroughs in the history of life.

We must therefore be careful in comparing the human sociobiological situation with that of man's neighbors as he vaulted forward in time to our own puzzling era. Humans are *sui generis,* as anthropologist Leslie White of Michigan once claimed (3). Yet we are still mammals and primates. The great breakthrough by *Homo,* once he had completely put his bipedal act together on the plains, was in brain size and structure.

It is the growth of the cerebral cortex that has revised man's relations with his biological neighbors, even broken with his own biological past. From a size only slightly larger than a chimpanzee (although man was smaller in stature), four or five million years ago, man's brain exploded in size and structure. What we are as human animals owes itself to more than the cortical accretions, vast as they may be, in the frontal and temporal/parietal areas. The interconnectivity of this new brain (isocortex) with the older primate allocortical areas, themselves subject to enormous enlargement, thence with the lower brain, has created a very complicated thinking creature (4).

Chapter III contained the discussion of the evolving relationship between learning and intelligence and the genetic control system. The point of that discussion was that the growth of intelligence in all animal lines augurs a loosening of the strict genetic behavioral controls that we denote in instinctual patterns of animal behavior. The loosening of these ties is characterized by a greater freedom of action and reaction for the animal before triggers of instinctive behavior are pulled, forcing its hand, so to speak. As animals climb the ladder of intellectual advance, the genetic controls over behavior allow them increasingly greater latitude for investigation, adaptation to new geographies, etc., before the boundaries of restriction are overstepped and the instinctual trigger released.

Since it is the cortex from which the investigative behavior emanates to learn, memorize, or relate, the growth of the cortex will inevitably restructure the entire behavioral repertoire so that the sensory and neurological patterns that oversee the pathways of instinctual responses are increasingly interdicted, as if an insulating material were placed between input and output. This insulating factor of delayed response allows for the storage of impressions, for the evaluation and organization of information, and then, for the mobilization of behavior on the basis of new circumstances and not necessarily the knee-jerk instinctual repertoire that would be the inevitable response from a genetic and thus a purely physical storing of past histories.

By the time Cro-Magnon *(Homo sapiens sapiens)* arrived on the glacial scene about 35,000 years ago, (certainly this form of man had existed for some time before this moment), he arrived with an evolving culture equal to the best of civilized humans in the subsequent historical period (5). Cro-

Magnon's endocranial capacity of 1600 cm³ together with a delicate paedomorphic construction, marks the culmination of man's biological shaping into a wholly new type of primate, but also sporting a wholly new level of adaptive behavior.

Considering the relationship between brain size and structure during the entirety of man's visible evolutionary "progress," we can argue that morphological changes issue in behavioral changes. An aspect of these behavioral changes lies in the cultural artifacts and institutions that man spontaneously produces.

*NB uni-directionality*

It is thus a serious mistake in any sociobiological calculus not to take into account the alterations that have been made in the Darwinian trinity of equations for mutation, adaptation, and natural selection. There are here concrete facts that have become part of any real evaluation of the human species' sociobiological heritage. Of utmost importance, the revolutionary nature of the adaptive and selective impact that *Homo sapiens sapiens'* brain has made on general contemporary evolutionary conditions must also be evaluated.

Can there be any doubt that on the basis of *Homo sapiens sapiens'* tenure upon the earth for let us say the last 50,000 years we have seen the palpable, visible consequences of the creation of an animal form that is hardly less revolutionary than was the development of the vertebrate spinal chord for the subsequent history of life on our planet?

## Our Brain Creates a New Biology

A dual evolutionary set of processes accompanied *Homo's* increasingly successful sojourn on the plains, perhaps from ten million years B.P. One was the tremendously increasing inertial dynamic of mutations for increased brain size—at various points of crisis and renewal in man's evolution—and the consequent reconstruction of this primate's brain. The second was that from a very early phase of his arrival on the expanding savannahs of Africa man needed to have selected out for him no special offensive or defensive physical structures to maintain his ecological niche against nonhóminid competition. The term is orthoselection, or evolution in a straight line (6).

This is not orthogenesis of the metaphysical sort argued by C. H. Waddington, E. S. Russell, P. T. de Chardin (7). Orthogenesis argues for an inner directionality that aims at a fixed point of arrival. Indeed, we could not, nor could nature predict at any point in this evolving scenario what man would look like a million years down the road even given prior trends in mutation, adaptation, and natural selection.

This breakout quality in the evolution of *Homo,* his early freedom from the close modeling that natural selection finally imposes on all creatures caught in the nexus of competition is exemplified in a familiar fact about the human family. Incident after incident has been told, relating especially to the holocaust that enveloped the Jews in World War II. A family or group of families, including infants, hiding from the Nazis is on the point of being discovered. An infant begins to cry uncontrollably. A rag or other material is shoved over the infant's mouth and nose; often the result is the death of the young one. Most animals have built into the instinctual structure of their young a freeze reaction which at least for a moment can make the young invisible or unheard by the enemy.

We humans have given birth to young so undeveloped that they can be considered foetuses not unlike those of the monotremes (8). Yet the young, so defenseless, are not gifted by nature with the ability to respond to a parental sign to freeze in protective reaction. How long back in man's evolutionary history did abandonment of such a crucial adaptation go? How long ago did it signal man's freedom from competition, from indifference to the announcement of public presence revealed by the infant's cries?

The above example is symptomatic of the systematic lifting of man beyond the existing selective net from the late Miocene (twenty to twelve million years ago) to our own time. The tradition of mutational instability in brain size and structure continued to move spontaneously in this one direction leading to ever higher intelligence in humans. Below the surface of events, a process of selection indeed had taken place for frequency of mutations in those phenotypic functions undergoing positive selection. Certainly, unstable genes that had proved malfunctional were relegated to the evolutionary ash heap. Simply, those genes disappeared from the species' pool because they had proved selectively counterproductive.

A larger cranium and a bigger brain, however, continued on their own without special external pressure. The Darwinian theory only requires that a creature be generally successful, and is certainly lenient about other phenotypic developments riding piggyback, so to speak, linked with the more successful gene and chromosome packet. Thus, we humans, in addition to a highly sensitive defensive intelligence, have language, a social family structure, sexual habits that all can be seen as more or less adaptive.

Humans are not alone in having constellations of behavior that are not adaptive at all points. Birds are often careless with their young, and it is not always the runt that falls out of the nest or gets picked off by a predator. Lions too display behavior often unexplainable in strictly adaptive terms—females who out of laxity do not care for or feed their young. Chimpanzees are notorious, sometimes baboons also, for the casual care and feeding of their young. In their ecological position in the phylogeny of their lines, they apparently have surged beyond the close selective culling that occurs in creatures that have been subject to fine competitive jousting for many millions of years.

There is also an ancient selective truth in not having evolutionary frontiersmen too closely meshed with their environment. The explorers need room to follow new trails, to meet the challenge of changing climates, geography, even the challenge from new points in the animal sweepstakes. This partially explains the exploratory behavior of young mammals—gorillas, orangutans, cats, dogs. While young, they are malleable. Thus, changes that have occurred in the circumstances outside the species or race within the past generation or two might be adapted to by a still flexible, learning creature.

Human paedomorphs that we are, we remain playful, learning, to the end, because intelligent adaptability is our key to survival. So long as we are able to bring our young to reproductive maturity by utilizing this unique adaptation, malleable, intelligent behavior in meeting the unknown, we will have fulfilled nature's test. It is no matter that we have a host of stupid counterproductive behaviors: superstition, shamanism, cannibalism, genocide, ecological depredation, fratricide, incest. These are by-products that have issued from a brain along with an enormous expansion in complexity of structure, density of neurological connections, and sheer volume. They have also catapulted man's reptilian, mammalian, and primate brain structures into a prominence not seen in the original prototype, but which in man have grown somewhat proportionally to the growth of the cerebral cortex.

## Signals and Symbols

The resultant alteration in behavior away from the primate norm is reflected in the new level of communication that is exhibited by *Homo sapiens*. The theory of signs attempts to order the differing logical patterns of communication inputs and expression in animals as they receive information through their sensory organs (9). Animal behavior in response to sensory information received, organized, and then repatterned into overt actions is usually aborbed intellectually into a theory of signs. Roughly speaking, a sign is the meaning, significance of the input, in terms of the values for behavior that are expressed in, let us say, the evasive action of the chipmunk when he perceives the signal—shadow, screech—of the hawk.

In most animals, such signs become signals, automatically invoking preprogrammed repertoires of behavior: flight, freeze, defense, attack. The word signal argues for an overt physical reaction by the receptor individual. If the sensory information happens to be ignored, it obviously has no meaning; it is a sign of nothing, and no signal behavior is invoked (10).

In man, the signs that we receive and respond to rarely release selective behavioral actions or reactions. The smells that we smell disgust some, invite others, leave some indifferent. Few sensory inputs are channeled from sense organs to the automatic behavioral system of the "instinctual" brain. Signs for humans have become symbols, not signals.

Symbols are the meanings, largely conventional, that we attach to all sorts of experiences in our social existence, from perceptual inputs to purely social and cultural relationships. Human symbolic behavior is evident in anything from the magic dances around a bonfire in which tribes attempt to invoke the gods of rain, to the game of chess. As Ernst Cassirer put it, man is "animal symbolicum," having left the safe animal world of signal/sign behavior to the more evanescent domain of created meanings (11).

It is quite probable that as man entered the Miocene plain some fifteen to ten million years ago, he gradually left behind what still was an unformed and malleable instinctual system of responses, a system that was parallel to the rich, adaptive, unspecialized world of mammals that then still existed. Just as the specialization of mammals has in general culled many lines of those creatures since then, so, too, hominid evolution has seen the increasing specialization and inevitable deadliness of *Homo's* advance. While the great advance in sign/symbol use has derived from man's major organ of specialization, speech, the overall behavioral pattern in all species and races of *Homo* has been reshaped, to the symbolic.

The selective power and success of the growth of the brain, man's intelligence, and the efficacy of symbolic communication have had their impact in eliminating the less fully evolved hominids and humans over the course of these millions of years. The result, as was pointed out in Chapter IV, is a creature who has left behind one adaptive level (instinct, sign/signal behavior), and is well on the route toward distilling his intellectual/symbolic abilities and their consequences in the world of social and cultural meanings.

What is most puzzling about the biological meaning of symbolic behavior, which obviously has to arise from man's unique social bonds, is the fact that these symbols are a spontaneous exudation of man's brain, both from the cortical and the subcortical elements. We dream, fantasize, envision future possibilities, mixed with all the various tendencies of thought, emotion, fantasy, hallucination, and express these spontaneous symbolic wellings in social and cultural patterns.

What does it mean from the standpoint of inclusive fitness? It could lead to behaviors both practical and efficient in the matter of survival, but we know that often it does not. Human beings within their very complex cultural/symbolic world, often exhibit stupidity, ignorance, counterproductive enthusiasm. We see little of the nitty-gritty of practical, clearcut adaptive animal behavior when we examine the prodigious effluent given off by the new and complex brain structure of *Homo*.

The kinds of human behavior to which sociobiologists

have tended to apply their analytical tools mostly involve those that *are* at the core of our most basic biological qualities of thought and action: gender personality differences, racial differences in infant behavior, cannibalism, incest prohibitions, status groupings in males. It would be difficult to make a strong case for these matters either involving truly deterministic or thus predictive outcomes—gender, race, status alignments (12). Each of these matters reveals countless variations in how humans treat them, and has few clear adaptive or selective consequences for the individual or group.

So what if, as Daniel Freedman has shown, infants of different racial backgrounds react differently to irritants, such as a thin handkerchief, being lightly placed over their faces (13). Does it signify consequential differences in personality and behavior structure as the infants grow to maturity in social settings where they receive equivalent and roughly similar education? Are we not dealing here with reactions that are closer to the limbic structure of our behavioral patterns? Are not these structures, as a consequence of individual maturation and social enculturation, soon to be overwhelmed by the symbolic shapings that arise from an education that is cortically assimilated?

Even the issue of incest might be argued from the standpoint of a cognitive interpretation of human behavior. Whenever children are brought up together, such as brother and sister, but regardless of blood relationship, they tend to act like brother and sister, avoiding sexual involvements. (Yet we know that under certain conditions, certain groups would push aside the incest prohibition in order to preserve their power, to keep it within the family.) (14)

Would it not be possible to make a case for a rational rather than a biological source of the prohibition? All enculturated peoples are aware that the sexual drives of humans are powerful eruptions from below, akin to the animal world of biological power. They have enveloped their own kind in a net of prohibitions to discipline these biological fires so that they do not undermine the network of rational institutions and behavior. So, too, do humans act in their interpersonal relationships. The need to control ourselves in a host of day-to-day relationships, even to eschew violence for the distant and abstract conceptual benefits of law, motivates us to separate our mental from our biological activities.

Thus we all avoid engaging in sex with our close blood relations or with those with whom we have grown up in a socially nonsexual relationship, not for considerations of biological fitness but rather for intellectual, symbolic, and thus cultural considerations. The incest taboo lies at the border of our awareness of the difference between the biological and the cultural, an awareness that is rooted in the perceptual or intellectual rather than in the instinctual or preconscious domain. That intellect or bizarre symbolic mentation can move us to violate this universal *sapiens* prohibition argues for its conventional, symbolic character.

The relationship of *Homo sapiens* to the biological world is now vastly different from that of the various phyla. Certainly, man, having broken through the environmental constraints that limited other primates, is still governed by the principles involved in the Darwinian trinity: mutation, adaptation, natural selection. For the moment, however, the principles of natural selection lie within the sociocultural world of man and not in the traditional selective categories of mammalian life.

Think of this change as being reminiscent of the relationship of life with the temporal course of thermodynamic exchanges in the physical environments of our solar system and galaxy. Life is a counterentropic phenomenon. While the free energy levels of our galaxy are slowly dissipated from intensive exchanges of heat toward the uniform coolness of eternity, here and there in our universe little eddies of energy can be building up over time. These enclaves of counterentropy take free energy from the environment, from other living forms, the plants, the energy-laden atmosphere, and create concentrations of free energy—but only for a time (15).

In the end, life on this earth will also be subject to the second law of thermodynamics and we all will be merged in stillness. Life does not disobey this law, because, the second law is descriptive of events over an indeterminate span of time. Within this time frame, "the mice can play."

So, too, man, being in a world of biological phenomena and biological principles, has for the moment surmounted the traditional restraints. Why do we need a brain of 1600 cm³ rather than one of 600 or 900 cm³, as Alfred Wallace asked (16)? The answer is that we do not. Nature itself created the inner sociobiological dynamics that sent the brain and its carrier, the skull, into an explosive expansion. Suddenly we found ourselves standing on a new plateau seemingly guided by highly different principles and laws of social, individual, even biological interactions.

This does not mean that no patterns, principles, or regulations can be observed in our biosocial world. Quite the contrary, the human brain, subject to the laws of physics and chemistry, has issued in its symbolic effusion a new panorama of effects. What we see in the cultural expression of man, from the very moment that man leaves the world of inchoate instinctive signal behavior to carve his first stone scrapers, is the creation of a new set of principles. However, even culture is not necessarily *sui generis,* for this behavior issues from the billions of interconnecting neurons in that biochemical mass of blood, glial matter, dendrites, axons, that constitutes our ordinary animal brain. At this point in our knowledge, the relationship between its structure and its function is too complex for us, perhaps even for our ingenious computers, to fathom fully.

So we create new social laws and principles parallel to, perhaps mirroring in some mysterious way, the workings of the brain. All that we can ever know of this is through our own symbols, our words, our equations. When we speak in cultural terms—politics, society, history—we create a grammar of meaning. As scientists in psychology and neurology create their own particular models of mental activity, they do the same. Finally, the sociobiologists will themselves create a symbolic version of man's unique biosocial behavior. All these symbolic pictures will of necessity have to fit together both in their concrete predictions of events on different symbolic levels of discourse as well as in the translation of rules from one structure of ideas to another. This is the most problematic aspect of all, as we try to mine each others' symbolic worlds of discourse and meaning both to confirm what is being argued on each level of knowledge and to create a newer, more comprehensive, picture that we could then propose as being somewhere nearer the truth than before.

## A Sociobiology of Culture

What are these dynamics of human sociobiology going to be like? Let us tentatively propose that the sociobiology of *Homo sapiens* arises directly from man's intelligent behavior, itself formed from the growing brain. It is the brain alone that determines the levels of cultural expression in *Homo*. It is the brain that creates the kinds of social structures that have accompanied and undergirded its variable expression of intelligence.

If the elimination of related species and more closely derived hominid types has been a by-product of the selective power of intelligence, then we must probe the meaning in culture of this expanding intelligence. We cannot claim that the intrageneric and intraspecific forms of competition have been explicitly selective. After all, humans have subsequently destroyed much of the heritage of fauna and flora that accompanied *Homo* into the present. It does not appear that such a selective advantage was an unequivocal gift to mankind.

The archeological history of human progress both morphologically and culturally reveals patterns in the growth of both brain and intelligence. Even while man has been eliminating so many of his comrades in transition—call them intermediate types—he has remained extremely variable himself. This variability in brain structure and intelligence is revealed in culture, education, and every other comparative measure that we would adduce.

It is, however, not a variability indifferent to selective factors of fitness in the competitive cultural scheme. In the past, more intelligent ethnic groups have destroyed less evolved humans. In our own century, ideology has led to the genocide of the intelligent. Nevertheless, for many thousands of years the cultural and demographic power of the intelligent has been too amply demonstrated for us to allow the events of one or two centuries of countercultural civilizational trends to interdict this basic premise about human fitness in the setting of culture.

What we are arguing for, then, is a view of man's sociobiological nature that focuses on the power of human intelligence in culture, the total configuration of a social group's intellectual stamp on its symbolic meaning structure. This is what a culture is in the first place, an interrelated nexus of meanings arising from one people's experiences and values in language, religion, art, and government, in its economic and technological skills, moral and educational interests. Here is where the sociobiological analysis will have to begin, to see cultures as varying representations of the brain's spontaneous though educated expression of symbolic meanings.

We will see man's social nature arising not necessarily out of individual physical weakness—the need to cooperate to survive—but from that primeval mammalian emotional glue that binds a group, now transformed from the limbic system to a shared cognitive/diencephalon, intellectual/emotional symbolic world of meanings. Individual human beings cannot be human without this social immersion. Indeed, in the cognitive depths of the culture, in its capacity to create from the environment ever new instrumentalities of power—political, military, and technological structures—it is assured of at least a momentary immortality, not against inchoate nature or the animal world about man, but against the competitors of man's own species, sometimes and even possibly, his own brothers.

Chapter VII

---

# HUMAN AGGRESSION: A MODEST CLARIFICATION

## Not Simply Biological

By now it is clear that comparing wolves and monkeys with humans as regards what can be called aggressive behavior throws little light on how humans may and will act. Also, to look at the remnant primitive societies in the world and to draw conclusions about supposed territorial triggers for aggressive behavior, or even to attempt to find recurrent cultural patterns, the so-called formalized aggression of headhunting groups for example, will not do (1).

These models cannot predict for us events in the context of more dynamic historical civilizations. The name of the game, biological aggression, seems to change in the transition to so-called advanced civilizations. Konrad Lorenz at one point suggested "cold showers" and active sports competitions to "drive discharge" aggressive tendencies in men (2). More recently, Richard Sipes has concluded that "the practice of war is accompanied by a greater development of combatant sports and other lesser forms of violent aggression." (3)

Certainly, the ancient Greeks were completely immersed in their recurring olympiad competitions; and it is quite true that their decline can be in part attributed to their suicidal/fratricidal conflicts, in which their finest young men were destroyed. Yet certainly the Romans were not especially active in competitive sports. Their warlike aggressive dispositions were not thus inhibited. Also, the various Near Eastern dynasties—Persians, Chaldeans and Assyrians—were not noted for their athletic involvements. Yet war and aggression suffused their cultural history. How does this theory square with the United States and Europe in the 1980s as compared with the warlike turmoil of the Arab world?

*How indeed!*

Unfortunately there is no simple calculus that we can abstract from our biological heritage, mammalian or anthropoid, to do the trick for us: (1) predict when certain conditions or circumstances are likely to trigger massive aggressive responses, (2) allow us to take preventative actions that would short-circuit the environmental/genetic pathway leading individuals and societies into aggressive undertakings.

# Origins of Human Aggression

In this chapter, a brief evolutionary hypothesis will be presented that will explain why certain simple and overly reductive sociobiological explanations cannot be found useful. At the same time, it will be argued, preparatory to the next section, on the human mind, why the problem of human aggression is so difficult, and how the variability of human intelligence, from the standpoint of our evolutionary heritage, has become a clue to solving this contemporary mystery.

Let us first probe the evolutionary meaning of biological aggression. In the beginning, the earliest living molecules, the so-called heterotrophs, distinguished themselves as a form of life from the other basic biochemical alternatives for capturing free energy and metabolizing it. The heterotrophs existed on organic molecules while the autotrophs took their nourishment from the inorganic clays or the sun. The autotrophs became the plants, the free-moving heterotrophs, the cannibalistic animals.

At a certain stage, of course, some heterotrophs specialized in eating plants (autotrophs), but the origin of life itself was constituted by the aggressive searching out, if not pursuit of more vulnerable organic foods. Just as we have categorized intelligent creatures as living on the edge of motility, variability, sensitive to innovations and change, almost in tune with the turnings of the earth in its vagrant course through the universe, so, too, accompanying intelligence has come the tradition of aggression and exploitation of the environment.

Aggressive creatures in all the phyla of animal evolution have stayed at the top of the food chain. In their exploitation of fellow creatures, they live the chancy life. They are limited in behavior by genetic restraints born of the selective requirements of sustaining their prey, thus insuring themselves that they will be provided with a steady meal ticket. In a sense, as other more placid creatures solve their adaptive problems by falling into steady, secure ways of earning a living, or else multiplying en masse, the predators, because they must be bigger, more ferocious, energy expending, and mobile in seeking out their food supply, are necessarily fewer in number (4).

We humans today are predators, meat eaters, the scourge of our environment. Yet we are unaccountably numerous as compared with the lion or tiger. Close at hand, our surviving close relations, the apes and monkeys, are by and large frugivorous. Even though they will eat meat, they are not adapted to a life of killing and eating. Somewhere along the line, the hominids, *Homo* at least, departed from the forest model of primate existence, a small, timid, insectivore-like creature of the Paleocene, sixty-five million years ago, turned into two-legged killers of both animals and humans, often without the survivalistic rationale of turning the kill into food for themselves and kin.

Nature, however, has a peculiar way of rationalizing life's past experiences by embedding them into our genetic memory. Thus an ancient history of aggression within the mammalian experience has many millions of years later the possibility of being extracted from the repertoire of recessive reserves, to be recalled into action by newly adaptive circumstances.

The mammals did not become dominant without the energetic expression of aggression. They elbowed aside their therapsid reptile competitors of the Mesozoic era, and then probably administered the coup de grace to the dinosaurian hosts. While the mainline mammalian aggressors became specialized creatures, for the others—herbivores and general vegetarians—this aggressive tradition was still there, if latent. Like the killer whales who evolved from what was essentially a refugee movement of mammal losers entering "safe" waters, the primates could have and did generate other aggressive lines, besides man.

Perhaps the key to understanding *Homo's* transition from a creature with myriad defensive adaptations—a large, split hemisphere brain; language (whispers); foetus-like dependency in the infant young; continuous oestrus in females, who are limited in mobility and thus in need of constant protection; small size; few aggressive aids such as fangs and claws—lies in a comparison with those other few aggressive primates. The Japanese macaque, Patas monkey, baboon (Himadraha), Ceylonese langur all are at least partially terrestrial and highly aggressive, truculent animals (5). Some, such as the baboons, have become terrestrial only recently (several million years ago), in part probably due to the disappearance of the wide variety of apes that once existed on the plains in the Miocene and Pliocene fifteen to five million years ago (6).

When one considers that the adaptive relationships on the plains, for example, the sharp predator/prey symbiosis, are far clearer and more dramatic than in the forest, one can appreciate the appearance of aggressor mammalian forms. The distances are long, the food sources widely scattered. Just as we find high intelligence in the elephant and the horses and indeed an additional specialized adaptability that has allowed cows, sheep, goats, horses, to be domesticated, so, too, the plains predators, hyenas, lions, leopards, pumas, wild dogs all are extremely intelligent, sensitive, and ferociously energized animals.

Possibly, in the process of the great ecological changes produced by the eruption of great mountain ranges and the formation of the late Miocene (fifteen million years ago) savannahs, a new set of relationships in animal adaptations was introduced onto the African scene. When the more adaptable of the previously repressed anthropoid forms moved through this new window of opportunity, these new selective conditions became manifest. Many if not most of these experimenters failed. The ramapithecine apes were probably part of this equation. Neither powerful in forest nor competitive on the plains, they disappeared, leaving only one descendant, who retreated into the Southeast Asian jungle and reappeared as the orangutan (7).

What worked for *Homo* was a high intelligence that would be made malleable and useful in the distances of open country. Then, protoman needed to have the skills to make a living with this intelligence. He simply could not at that stage of his evolution turn around and become a sixty-mile-per-hour bounding cheetah. His walking pace never went beyond the chicken stage (8). I suspect that during this early phase, perhaps fifteen to ten million years ago, a series of powerful selective rolls of the mutational dice took place.

The resulting creature, however, was one who had gone through the selective mill before. Nature in the first place would never have come up with that concatenation of characteristics that constitute the forest armory of adaptations that originally resulted in a protohominid rather than an ape. Environmental pressure and a high mutation rate along with that probabilistic edge of extra intelligence gradually created *Homo*.

Now, some fifteen or so million years after man's forest separation from the proto-apes and monkeys, the mutations bubbled forth, the selective sieve passing the majority of these evolutionary products into oblivion. Eventually a wholly new version of primate intelligence came forth. Except for the subsequent explosion of incremental cortical growth and intelligence that took place throughout the Pleistocene (1.75 million years ago until 8000 B.C.) this creation of an aggressive open-country living, bipedal primate was the penultimate agonizing revolution in the history of our kind.

We have the results in our basic human structure, both brain and body. Perhaps, one of these days, we will understand more causally the physiological relationships that have recreated the meaning of animal aggression as it now expresses itself in *Homo*. Let us discuss these changes.


## The Human Re-creation

First of all, aggression has become, even more so than in the mammal world, a paradigmatically male characteristic. We no longer see a division of labor as in the lions, where the female does the dirty work of the kill, the male calmly awaiting the outcome to gorge himself on her labors. The human male through millions of years on the hunt, the human female forever involved in pregnancies, surrounded by a fragile brood of miniature vulnerable young, reflects this sharp sexual dimorphism. The large size and strength of the human male reflect a common characteristic of open-country primates, indeed, of all mammals.

Our weak backs reflect the probability that we were only partially preadapted for bipedalism when we emerged from the forests about fifteen million years ago. Ultimately the plains created a new kind of aggressive creature. We did not specialize, as did the robust australopithecines in eating tough roots and vegetation. Or if we did specialize, it was the extreme concentration of our adaptive thrust for survival in honing our intelligence.

Over these fifteen or ten or even seven million years of life on the plains our anthropoid shift in aggressive behavior was away from limbic system, instinctual signals: it evinced a reactivity to ever more cognitive/cultural controls. This great shift in so many basic parts of brain function, the amygdala (supposedly regulating aggressive behavior), the hippocampus (regulating sexual activity, the flow of testosterone, pituitary and thyroid functions), reflects a complex series of neurological and enzymatic interactions that had to be sharply realigned in function. My hypothesis is that some of this deviation from the ape and monkey norm had probably taken place earlier, in the forest, as part of a defensive complex of adaptations that probably required in addition to a proto-verbal intelligence a certain amount of male fierceness in defense.

Defensive evasiveness, quietude, occasional fierce combativeness at the threshold of hearth and home is one thing. What caused the sudden shift to the genocidal mode that can envelop a human group, even to act against its own brethren? How can we understand this radical transition? In all likelihood, this great penultimate selective crisis, the second in the three moments of *Homo,* occurred here on the plains.

The first had taken place in the Oligocene jungles (thirty-five to thirty million years ago) as each of the many lines of proliferating apes staked out territorial claims. At first proto-*Homo* was a loser here. Slowly, paedomorphism, the rate gene changes in individual development that protected the family, and its stock of odd but ultimately adaptive defensive characteristics eventually won proto-*Homo* an undistinguished place in the tropical forests. That is probably why his fossils have been unavailable to us as yet. Too few proto-humans existed then, and until now we have not been lucky, the probabilities for discovering such rare creatures being extremely slim.

The second phase was the one here in question, the shift to a complex of adaptive behaviors required for existence on the migratory plains ecology. Here too the protohumans were few in number, at least for many millions of years. This late in our evolutionary development, they could not develop the defensive adaptations of the ungulate browsers and grazers. The ancient heritage of mammalian aggression here became a premier selective characteristic for these evolving mutating human creatures, now cataclysmically vulnerable. No more the subtle nudging and edging for forest survival. The cats were powerful, the dogs numerous, the food distant, yet temptingly beckoning. It had to be that the inevitable variability produced by the mutations, among many possibilities, a family of creatures capable of mustering the aggressive energies in an outgoing extroverted, offensive manner. It is to this distant time that we probably should point as the moment of separation of the hominids into proto-*Homo* and the more rapidly evolving and adaptively specialized australo-pithecines.

The first thing that had to occur in protoman was the realignment of diencephalon/limbic system functions. This happened later in the similar transition of terrestrial monkeys, but in man it was more voluntary, less instinctual. This aspect of man's shift seems to confirm Bernard Campbell's view of man as deriving from a line of primates that was partially monkey in heritage, a truly intermediate hominoid form (9).

Heinz Stephan has noted that our so-called allocortex, the limbic and other precortical elements under the brain mantle show enormous enlargement in man, almost as much as with the cortex (10). This was for man a new mammalian brain. The result is evident in the emotional, passionate, even violent nature of man, no matter what the character of his intelligence, no matter what cultural ambience he has developed with his peers. This emotionality, often terroristic, warlike, sometimes religious, messianic, is certainly different from any other of his primate relatives, suffused as it is by the symbolic-cultural-linguistic elements that define our human nature. Consider for a moment the many verbal expressions of aggression, from the screams of exasperation to the disciplined paean of the advancing Greek phalanx.

This second phase of the evolution of human aggression is reflected in the gradual domination of the human limbic system by the more cognitive, thinking areas of the brain. Increasingly, the limbic responses were intercepted and transferred into more conscious, instrumental, and effective areas, in war, in the hunt, in the general protection of the social group.

We note that as *Homo* climbed the phylogenetic intellectual scale and made the transition to *Homo sapiens sapiens* in terms of advanced brain size and structure there was diminishing evidence of cannibalism. Ritual cannibalistic feasts usually involved tearing out areas of the skull at the point where the spinal chord enters it (the foramen magnum), ostensibly to get at the brain. Certainly *Homo sapiens sapiens* is not less aggressive than *Homo habilis* or *Homo erectus,* his collateral ancestors. It is just that the direction of human aggressive energies was directed otherwise, often fatally so for competing human types and their social groups. Indeed

*Homo* has been bad news for a vast array of living forms that he has eliminated from our earth.

## Brain Structure and Aggression

As with so many aspects of man's peculiar nature, there is a paradox in this shift of the so-called "aggressive" dimension. Aggression seems to have a general morphological locus in the brain. The brain's frontal areas have been traditionally identified with the powerful, willful activities of human beings. During the 1940s and 1950s, several varieties of mental illness, some of which showed pathological expressions of an aggressive sort were resolved by so-called prefrontal lobotomies which severed the connection between the parts of the brain—front and rear.

These operations often resulted in the diminution of the traumas, the headaches, the seizures, the uncontrollable rages. The side effects, however, were often grievous, a human being without will power, sense of purpose, ability to plan, imagine a future. Even when intelligence was unaffected, the utilization of this intelligence was often lacking (11).

It seemed as if the wiring that released the deeper mammalian passions of the older brain and the behavior that was controlled in the frontal areas of the brain, especially in the right hemisphere, were closely related. These millions of years of evolution had left their trace. The puzzle was that along with the aggressive power that seemed to be channeled deeply into the human nervous system, then to the surfaces of behavior, the frontal areas acted both as conduit and censor.

For it is to the frontal areas that we look in identifying the so-called "P" or postponement factor that Ward Halstead and David Stenhouse have described as a crucial evolutionary component of intelligence (12). This issue will *define agressive behavior ?*

be discussed more fully in Chapter XI. However, let it be said here that our paradox arises from the tremendous development of the frontal areas and their capacity to inhibit drive expression or instinctual signal behavior in the human animal. The frontal areas of the human brain, as A. R. Luria and Roman Jakobson have discovered with regard to language, are the enactive, grammatically-sensitive areas of linguistic expression (13). They also serve to discipline—postpone, practice, premeditate, plan—all those elements that one might see as antagonistic to the rage of aggressive behavior.

These two elements, aggression and inhibition, seem to coexist in one area of the human brain, the frontal lobes as they are wired to the lower limbic areas. No doubt the range of variation between individuals is very great. The genes involved in the creation of the brain and the various related morphological elements of human intelligence must number in the dozens, and in their interactions give rise to an almost infinite variation of human types, in emotionality, energy, intelligence, discipline, spontaneity—all factors that seem to emanate from this frontal area of the cortex and its connections to the lower brain and our primeval inheritance (14).

What we noted above with regard to the gradual transference of aggression from a special kind of human cultural and ethnic energy toward ever more cognitive, intellectual controls and channeling akin to the relationship of the libido, ego, and superego of Freudian psychology can be noted as well in the area of human sexuality. There is no question that the end of sexual periodicity in the hominids and the ensuing unceasing roar of sexual energies constitute a paradigmatically human element.

*what stereotypes.*

On the primitive cultural level, human sexuality must be controlled by a powerful symbolic discipline lest it destroy a society with its rampant aggressive demands for satisfaction. At the same time, we note its cultural origins in the sense that so much has to be taught to humans about sex. It is clearly

*cf. the Muria gonds*

enveloped in socialization even at the most primitive human levels of culture. Thus, human sexuality, like the first phase of human aggression, reveals biosocial qualities that hark back far in time to that mysterious era of protoman's separation from his monkey and ape relatives.

To civilized humans, sexuality is sublimated into love, disciplined by the mind, turned on or off depending on voluntary decision, sometimes with "Freudian" consequences. Many view a person's development, intelligence, civilized state by the ability to postpone sexual gratification in favor of conscious and ethical decision making. So here, too, certain powerful human energies, rooted in ancient mammalian structures (the amygdala) are in highly developed peoples, corticalized; they are placed under the discipline of conscious, rational, cultural, and personal decisions.

*[handwritten margin note: but primitives don't love?]*

Finally, one should note the price we occasionally pay for having evolved beyond the traditional behavioral patterns of our primate relatives. As Hans Selye, P. MacLean, and A. T. W. Simeons (in his *Man's Presumptuous Brain)* have noted, a wide variety of psychosomatic diseases—ulcers, acne, tics, heart palpitations—can be shown to derive from this odd and paradoxical opposition between our powerful drives and the accompanying cognitive censors that inhibit their expression in the daily course of good social behavior (15). The stresses come about because individuals are unable to balance these drives, the powerful libidinal imperatives that give tone to our personalities, with the necessity to restrain these drives in order to be able to live among men.

Here, too, the variation between individuals can be enormous given even a certain measure of intellectual equality: the discipline and creativity of celibates such as John Locke and Isaac Newton; the rampaging infantilism of a J. J. Rousseau and W. A. Mozart. George Bataille, making an interesting connection, suggests that the saintly ascetic nun and the lascivious Catherine the Great are not really far apart, each resolving the human dilemma of ecstatic passion at the extremes of personal expression (16). Yet there is room for each under the canopy of cultural acceptance.

So here it is, a picture of human aggression that departs from the typical sociobiological models. Obviously such a powerful, energizing presence in the human condition must have carried great selective advantage. For *Homo sapiens sapiens,* it now exists both as terror and sublimity. Whatever selective message it carries with it from the past, as *Homo* became increasingly corticalized, human aggression underwent a final transition. Its evolutionary message is far more complex and epiphenomenal. To extirpate the aggressive urge, even with cold showers and athletic activity, could, as Sigmund Freud noted, cauterize the creative drives that make civilization not merely possible but worthwhile. The fictionalized picture of the pathetic, inexpressive lobotomized hero of *One Flew Over the Cuckoo's Nest* ought to forewarn us about easy answers or solutions.

# Chapter VIII

---

# THE BIOLOGICAL PERSPECTIVE

## A Revolution in Life

In this chapter, let us summarize the biological perspective on the evolution of variable intelligence in humans. It is difficult to perceive the biological element in our destiny as well as our heritage because of the overwhelming nature of the biological transformation that *Homo* has experienced.

How does one judge revolutions, critical turning points in the history of a phenomenon? One of the best ways would be to judge them by the consequences that they throw off. In the history of life, there have been many revolutionary transformations, pivotal constructions, biochemical, morphological, behavioral. Certainly the creation of a form of life able to metabolize its energy requirements without cannibalizing other organic forms, using only the rays of the sun to meet its needs, made possible the existence of a vast array of complex, high-energy requiring animals. Plants made it possible.

Later the notochord and the spinal chord allowed a new form of animal life to explore the middepths of water and develop the mobility that subsequently gave rise to fish, amphibians, reptiles, birds, and mammals, in short the higher forms of exploratory, intelligent animals. Other revolutions, such as the lung, enabled the teleost fish to filter oxygen through their gills from the water without rising periodically for gulps of air; it created a new world of life in the depths. The air-breathing lung made life possible for the amphibians and their descendants on land; the wing created a new adaptive world for insects as well as for reptiles and mammals (1).

Finally, intelligence, one of the basic adaptive techniques in the repertoire of mobile exploratory life, found its paradigm in man. It was revolutionary because of what *Homo* did and is doing to our planet. Man gives no quarter. Thus the rat, starling, dog, cat, seagull, myriads of insects, all "socialized" creatures, flourish, and the rest are destined for oblivion as we boil over in numbers beyond our planet's capacity, or even its geography (2).

So revolutionary has been the impact of human intelligence that we have effectively destroyed our heritage. Only a few decrepit chimpanzees, gorillas, and orangutans remain to remind us of our long anthropoid journey to the present (3). There is, however, another remnant, and this exists within our own walls. We still have the residue of the most recent transformation of this human host. This residue, massive in numbers, still exists beside us as brothers and sisters, coexisting with those who are still creating the revolution. The power to engulf our planet earth, to obliterate our upward path has emanated from a small subspecies of our human line. This subspecies, arising suddenly in the north less than a quarter of a million years ago, endowed with a phenomenally large cortical hominid brain, has in effect transformed the life equation (4).

Certainly primitive peoples, those whom the explorers discovered throughout the continents in the last five hundred years, did not touch or alter this basic and preexisting equation. It is true that a few species, the emu, the mammoth in North America, the Irish elk, and others had disappeared, but mostly as a consequence of the massive hunting depredation of those revolutionary Cro-Magnons of Eurasia (5).

For the most part, even as transformed into evolving *sapiens* by the migrating Eurasians thousands of years ago and on, those peoples of Africa, North and South America, Southeast Asia would not have turned the earth on its nose. The revolutionary impact of this new intelligence—on technology, medicine, agriculture—has achieved this end. Further, now that the migratory highways lead in all directions, it is clear that we are dealing with what has been called a panmictic species, one in which it is doubtful that genetic isolation, even on a subspecies level, can be maintained, no less can it develop and evolve into the future. We are soon to be highly interbred.

What still remains, however, is that variability in intelligence in all mankind. Instead of being encapsulated in unbreachable jungles, on islands in the Pacific, in northern mountain villages, the variability is around us in our megalopoli for all to see. At its height, human intelligence can create an Athens or a Florence. At its depth, it hovers within our decaying cities, in the chaos and degradation of a world teeming with people, now only partially able to digest, internalize, and productively amplify on the possibilities for man and nature of the true powers of intelligence in *Homo.*

Put it this way. Has anything made such an impact on the earth since the formation of the spinal chord in animals? Does it necessitate that a revolution in the history of life of such magnitude create vast new lines of living things? Is it not possible at least in its first stage of this particular evolutionary revolution, which might very well culminate in the senescence and extinction of *Homo,* that the first consequence might be the pseudodominance of one form of life, a superintelligent animal, man?

If so, the biological perspective ought to gain our attention. We should abandon those childish assumptions of omnipotence that create fantasies such as cultural relativism in which we assume that something called "culture" creates the substance of individual and social existence (6). Indeed, if this thing we call culture creates or determines our behavior in any sense, it is because it is in reality and in concept an arm of the biological forces that are working through human intelligence. In the short as well as the long term, these forces will tell us where we are going.

## Origins of Human Variable Intelligence

It is important to explain why such enormous variability in intelligence can lodge itself within an interbreeding, intermixing species such as *Homo sapiens*. We have already spoken in Chapter IV about the unique ecologically selective conditions in the northern Ice Age Eurasian latitudes that created *Homo sapiens sapiens* who then expanded and intermixed with the rest of mankind, by small degrees at first, but recently in ever greater proportion.

It is my purpose here to reiterate the meaning of this variability in its biological sources. Once that is established, then the fact that the old Neanderthal myth of *sapiens* origins has been punctured need not disturb. We will understand the general context in which the human line became fragmented, how that was possible in evolutionary terms, and why this fragmentation—variability in intelligence—now constitutes the great dilemma and challenge of this present era in human biocultural evolution.

The tradition in evolution whereby a line of animals enters a new ecology, masters its adaptive requirements, then proliferates into a variety of forms, is an old one. For example, the ancient crossopterygian fish, ancestors of the amphibians, flopping from one dessicating water hole to another, finally, through dint of their recidivistic air sac, to survive in the warm muddiness of the ventilated outdoors, gave rise to a rich diversity of creatures, first frogs and salamanders, then the reptiles and mammals (7). Each new line presented an ensuing possibility for advance and branching.

Mammals, the survivors of an ancient conservative synapsid/therapsid line of reptiles, were not that diverse a form until they burst through the dinosaurian bottleneck seventy to sixty-five million years ago (8). With the disappearance of these giants, the mammals then proliferated into a vast panoply of types, that is, until man arrived on the scene (9). Remember, each of these lurches forward in new structures and behaviors came at an increasingly later and maturing period in the history of life.

With the aging of the earth and this maturing of nature's reservoir of genetic possibilities for adaptive life—the present denizens blocking the free flow of morphological and ecological possibilities—each new development ran into a new equation both of competition and possibility. This aging process in the history of life explains the fact that when man entered the savannahs of Africa at a relatively late stage in the adaptive flux of living things he was virtually alone. He was now adaptively beyond the reach of mammal predators, lions, leopards, even dogs. Thus while his aggressive intelligence made short shrift of his closest competitor, rival hominids like *Australopithecus,* and other plains living anthropoids of that era, he was able to travel the plains uncoerced by external selective pressures (10). Since, however, he was a product of earlier and intensive selection in the forest, to have been able to survive by his wits, family, intelligence, obscurity, he had to have had a history, a rapidly evolving tradition of mutating regularly and with some marginally positive results.

On the plains, the selective advantage of high intelligence, utilizing his long-distance sensory organs, eyes and ears, a preadaptive product of his forest intelligence, was enormous. This tradition of spontaneous mutations seems to have continued orthoselectively (in one direction) in the organ under greatest selective pressure—the brain. Man's intelligence, now literally exploded in growth, was also somewhat linked to the growth in the size of *Homo*. Thus *Homo* covered great distances hunting for meat to satisfy the oxygenating requirements of his insatiable brain and its roaming, predatory intelligence.

Because of the numerous genetic elements that went into the creation of the brain cortex, the subcortical limbic system, the entire neurology of reaction and response, it was inevitable that as the cortex grew, the other associative parts of the brain would expand and also vary in the same measure as the cortex. It is inconceivable that these small groups of humans traversing the continents as they did from about 1.5 million years ago, not meeting other humans for generations at a time, would not take on a unique biogenetic character, that their mutations for brain and personality would not be bred into their social groups. Other groups would diversify in slightly differing directions.

Thus came into effect the racial differences that developed around the world, spontaneous variations fixing themselves with diverse selective implications, e.g., skin color, height, hair type, to fit local geographies (11). Along with these more obvious physical variations came variations in both brain size and structure. As we note today, even within closely inbred families or social groups, variations in personality and qualitative intelligence are extremely wide. This should testify to the minute and myriad genetic elements that enter into each person's individuality. Thus any inbred social group would have a "family" resemblance in intelligence, potentially a culture. Since most of the variability took place at a level of brain expansion beyond the very adequate 600 cm³ of *Homo habilis* about three million years ago, our brain variability could diversify in an almost infinite number of human directions without external selective interdiction except by the surfacing of extremely sensitive mutants, or contact with competing human groups.

*Homo* retains that ancient mammalian characteristic of large wandering creatures, a great tolerance for genetic interfertility, even while the surface appearance of the individuals may seem to vary in the extreme (12). Today, many anthropologists would concede that those peoples that we call *Homo sapiens sapiens,* Cro-Magnon man (30,000 B.P.), could have interbred with typical *Homo erectus* types of 500,000 of B.P. (13).

In fact, this is probably what happened when Cro-Magnon, in his first migrations outward from his frigid northern incubation about 150,000 years ago, pushed the ancient erectine laggards of the southern hemisphere (see Chapter XVIII) over the border into sapiency. One or two hundred thousand years in the history of a species or genus is not too long.

What we see around us today is the incomplete resolution of that ancient process, now lifted onto a new international level. We are still variable in intelligence. The ancient racial differences decline in geographical, cultural, or biological meaning. The result is the gradual settling in of an international intelligence level that seems to be in a free fall decline in most parts of the world. It is the result of an almost totally myopic disregard for the underlying biological dynamics of civilization change.

# Cortex, Symbol, Destiny

A number of years ago, Mary Leakey found in Kenya fossilized footprints of a human being. She rated these prints at about four million years old. They were completely modern in form, indicating that this ancestor of ours was already as fully bipedal as we were going to get.

The great difference, as is true of all the subsequent fossils that have been discovered of *Homo habilis,* the probable owner of the footprints, and thus between this creature and ourselves, lay in endocranial capacity, and the internal structure of the brain. From that early stage of human evolution, the skull continued to expand at an increasing rate, in turn to be restructured toward the more gracile paedomorphic form exemplified in Cro-Magnon, of about 30,000 years ago. Cro-Magnon's was the acme of brain size (14). The expansion also coincided with the explosive advance of cultural artifacts both in their practical utility (for hunt and war) as well as their esthetic impact. Enormous amounts of what we now can call brain power went into the creation of this material civilization of the last years of the Pleistocene Ice Ages.

We cannot know when protoman made the decisive shift away from at least a partially instinctually controlled repertoire of behaviors to a symbolic or cultural determination of behavior. At some point, the growth of the cortex, its relationship to our ancient linguistic abilities shifted human action into a new learned, conventional pattern. This has been our evolutionary destiny ever since. Our future is irrevocably entangled in the working out of this new meaning structure of intelligence.

Other intelligent animals exhibit clear linkages of intelligence to instinctually controlled adaptive behavior. For twenty million years, the predator mammals and their prey have gradually become more intelligent, more capable specialists, than were their more generalist Miocene ancestors (15). We, too, have been honed in specialization, becoming ever more corticalized, symbol-using creatures. The past is littered with the bones of maladapted failures, competitor mammals, primates, even humans.

The human cortex constitutes the source of our bedevilment concerning the biological nature of all that we attribute to culture and civilization. It is that immense overlayering of a mass of billions of brain cells that has transformed our behavior from the mildly adaptive jungle flitterings of the proto-anthropoids to the symbolic cultural expressions of all human groups, no matter the intellectual level of their symbolic musings. However, even though humans can participate in the seemingly nonpractical involvements of cultural communication does not mean that we can ignore biology. Rather, we are challenged to find within culture the biological principles that mark our progressive encephalization.

What has happened to *Homo's* traditional mammalian biological urgings is that they have now been transformed by the interdiction of thought, itself a spontaneous neurological product of the brain's transformation. At certain minimal levels of intelligence, humans do not "climb out of themselves," so to speak, to analyze their actions and situation. The traditional forms of culture suffice to absorb their interests and behavior. As long as the circumstances of life remain stable, primitive peoples survive.

On a higher level, the cortex demands considered, abstract objectified analysis, thinking. Here, the entire span of human culture remains at hand to be "thought through," evaluated. Thus art, religion, technology, politics, sexuality all are suffused with a qualitative "dimension" as we soar in cortical power. In a sense, we can say that as *Homo* discovers and can utilize the forms of objective thought, he has capacitated himself to go beyond the environmental restraints that were imposed upon transitional man. It must be reiterated that highly abstract symbolic thought, though it still issues in the basics of what we call culture, has a special biological/neurological reality. Perhaps it even can be given a quantitative measure as compared with more concrete, immediate levels of cultural behavior.

The power of biological intelligence at its most highly

developed articulations in culture—the literate civilizations of the post-Pleistocene north—now constitutes the challenge. It raises crucial questions for the future of *Homo*. It is clear that not all cultures, nor all individuals within these cultures, have the same abilities to engage in what seems to be a paradigm of human intelligence in action.

Today, *Homo* thus lives in two worlds, reflecting his as yet uncompleted revolution. For many, the symbols of cultural life point backward to man's hominid and primate heritage. The culture they respond to is as much a vessel for the expression of limbic system motivations and reactions, albeit prototypically human actions. For others, there is the lure of the civilizational, the articulation of human intelligence not only in its adaptive technological or economic power for control and conquest, but also for the transmutation of those deeper biological juices into the symbols of the creative life.

We have experienced in human history tantalizing tastes of such civilizations. However, the contemporary context is now suffused with contradictions and confusions. Do we go forward, and with what consequences? Do we fall back? Then, can we go home again?

# PART 2

---

# *A MODEL OF THE MIND*

# Chapter IX

---

# IN SEARCH OF GENERAL INTELLIGENCE: I.Q.

## Unlocking the Mystery

In this and the chapters to follow, Part 2 of this book, the searchlight will shift to the mind and brain, as viewed by scientists from the various psychological and neurological sciences. The purpose is to create a contrasting set of pictures of the variable structure of human intelligence, in a sense the microscopic heritage of the evolutionary shaping of human beings. However, it is the intention to direct the beacon of evolutionary theory on these findings, to make them meaningful from the evolutionary perspective on intelligence as presented in this series.

Knowledge can be considered to act as a probability ratio that increases, not merely by the addition of new facts and predictions to the existing store of hypotheses, but adds new and related theoretical pictures. Each new domain of experience, theoretically expressed and related conceptually and experimentally to the existing domain of ideas, powerfully buttresses the probability value of the great hypotheses.

We expect that a vision of human intelligence variability will emerge consisting of these interlocking symbolic pictures: (1) evolutionary, (2) psychoneurological, and (3) educational/cultural. Each will be subject to testing, questioning, and confirmation. If each can be supported experimentally and maintain an internal theoretical consistency, we will have some useful knowledge.

Humans are knowledge makers. We begin with our five senses. The web we weave through relationships, both experimental and theoretical, is ultimately based on what information we receive from our human experience. It becomes more objective, less subject to our personal prejudices, by our agreed-upon methods of testing our conjoint experience. It must always go beyond our individual knowing to a structure of relationships that can be used for creating new testing points. We use these tests to bring new information into the web of relational experience.

Thus we are able constantly to revise what we think we know objectively about what exists in the universe. Then we can state that we have some knowledge, knowledge that will organize and clarify our experience, even predict events that lie beyond our awareness.

## Origin of I.Q. Testing

Psychologists point to the commissioning of Alfred Binet and Theodore Simon in 1904 by the French Ministry of Education to devise a simple test that could more easily identify subnormal children as the key moment in the experimental development in the study of intelligence differences. The test was devised so that educational intervention might be more rapidly effected (1). Heretofore, psychologists' experimentation into intelligence function had probed a variety of physical/motor behaviors. Also, there was a heavy reliance on philosophical principles which up to that point had not as yet yielded the kind of predictability long found in the physical sciences.

*from Jensen*

Tests for intelligence had been created in earlier decades, notably by Wilhelm Wundt (1832-1920) and Herman Ebbinghouse (1850-1909) in Germany and Francis Galton (1857-1911) in England (2). In fact, American students of these scholars, James McKeen Cattell (1860-1944) and Clark Wissler (1870-1947), did much experimental work on the relationship of sensory/motor skills, as well as reaction time, perceptual discrimination, and short-term memory skills (3). These concerns dominated in the United States for several decades into the twentieth century.

Much of this research was abandoned by the time Binet's American students, also the students of G. Stanley Hall in the United States, Henry Goddard (1866-1957) and Lewis Terman (1877-1956), began to put Binet's more practical and commonsense testing approach into effect in the United States (4). It should be stated, however, that Cattell's early research with Wundt did yield more important and practically useful results. Developing an instrument that Wundt had utilized, later called the tachistoscope, Cattell in the 1880s had already noted an efficiency factor in the cognitive grouping of separate elements. He found, for example, that random letters exposed for brief moments of time to subjects via the tachistoscope were remembered no better than the same number of unrelated words (5).

Prior to this, reading had been taught to children as one would build a house, brick by brick, letter by letter. What Cattell's work did to revolutionize reading instruction was to suggest to educators that the teaching of whole words as a primary instructional act was more efficient than asking students to memorize strings of unassociated letters. The meaningfulness of the word somehow expanded the capacity of short-term memory, so that a word was equal to a letter in terms of recall. Later, short sentences would be found to be equal to individual words in priming memory over brief exposures of time. Meaningfulness took on a preeminent role in mental activity over such supposedly irreducible units as the letters of our phonetic alphabet.

*NB*

Binet's approach to the testing of intelligence differed from the theoretical approach of the Wundt and Galton experimentalist school. The latter sought the distinctions in intelligence in terms of primary function in the sensory and motor level, feeling that these kinds of discriminations would reveal certain basic intellectual differences (6). Many years later, as we will show further on in this series of chapters, primary processing procedures would be returned to psychological testing but with sophisticated experimental techniques and mathematical analyses unavailable at the end of the nineteenth and beginning of the twentieth centuries (7).

Parenthetically, even in the 1960s, the testing of reading readiness or reading potentiality went through a phase of sensory/motor analysis, even in skill building, with the idea that these fundamental human functions stood as a basis for later developed symbolic skills as reading and writing (8). It is interesting further to note that the predictivity of such analysis was subsequently not borne out. Children who were precocious in discriminating left and right, who had good large and small muscle control, did not necessarily learn to read before the awkward, bumbling types (9).

Binet's approach, in contrast to primary physical analysis and experiment, was to use pictures of such familiar things as blocks, pencils, crayons, papers, to pose simple problems involving information about these items—memory, discrimination, judgment, even reasoning—and to grade the tasks in terms of increasing complexity (10).

*def.?*

The issue of complexity became a central innovation of Binet's approach. Here he utilized Herman Ebbinghouse's insight that such increasing levels of complexity would reveal more clearly the distinguishing variability of intellectual function. It was Ebbinghouse's word completion test that would later become a key testing element in the development of more full-range I.Q. tests (11).

Binet went on to scale these tests, which were quickly successful in making the basic discrimination between children who later would have difficulty learning in a regular school program and those who had a good probability for success. Mental age would be correlated with the number of items correctly answered on a battery of tests, soon encompassing gradatious from three to fifteen years of age.

*school-linked from the outset*

It was Wilhelm Stern (1871-1938) who suggested that by dividing the children's mental age (derived from comparing a particular child's deviation from the average) by their chronological age, we would derive a ratio then multiplied by 100 to get a whole number "mental quotient." Lewis Terman, at Stanford University, later developed the Binet-Simon scale of intelligence for American usage as his Stanford-Binet "intelligence quotient" (12).

# General Intelligence

The question as to what the intelligence was that we were measuring and comparing was first asked by Herbert Spencer (1820-1903). Even before Darwin's influential *Origin of Species* (1859), Spencer had probed the nature of intelligence as a biological and scientific concept. Spencer, essentially, was a philosopher, imbued with the growing sense of the applicability of scientific method to the biological and human disciplines. His text, *Principles of Psychology,* was the first psychology book to examine the nature of intelligence and how it related to individual differences. Human intelligence was a unitary trait that emerged in evolution as an adaptive function (13).

Later, in reaction to Darwin's system, Spencer saw intelligence as part of the selective mechanism out of which the process of evolutionary differentiation took place. Thus intelligence took its place alongside fang and claw as a means of adaptive function. Differences in intelligence became more or less grist for the mill of natural selection. The survival of the fittest applies to differentially intelligent creatures and the true "survival of the fittest," so-called Social Darwinism, in the adjustment of internal to external relations became key to connecting animal and human in the course of evolutionary progress (14).

Spencer has been credited by J. P. Guilford as being the first to put forth the idea of intelligence as a unitary entity (15). However, it was Francis Galton who, in his fascination with the application of mathematical analysis to experimental techniques, advanced the study of the nature of intelligence from broader philosophical considerations to exact scientific inquiry. Galton's basic thrust was identifying sensory acuity as the key to intellectual differences. While his methods of scientific experimentation following Wundt did not bear fruit at that time, they would stand as a research and theoretical paradigm for a later stage in psychology. Galton did postulate, following Spencer, that intelligence is a hereditary element in differentiating itself throughout the human race and that it was a general ability that when found at the highest level of genius could be channeled into a variety of important creative endeavors (16).

Galton saw genius as an extreme on the smooth extrusion or tail of the Gaussian probability curve expressing the varying levels of this common factor of cognitive ability (17). Unlike his contemporaries, Cesare Lombroso and Havelock Ellis, he did not take seriously the nineteenth-century view of creative genius as a form of pathology, a madness that departed from normal intellectual and social functioning (18).

While the ideal of discovering through theory and experimentation a deductive method of analyzing intellectual difference in functioning foundered in the successors to the Galton school, it remained an almost unmentioned ideal. Binet, with a natural Gallic respect for the theoretical elegance and ideals of the British school, still remained primarily a gifted clinician. It is pretty much agreed that he saw intelligence as a composite of a variety of tests of skills and abilities.

As Arthur Jensen puts it: "General intelligence, in Binet's thinking, is not a single function, but the resultant of the combined effects of many more limited functions, such as attention, discrimination, and retention. In his later writings he put greater emphasis on the more complex mental functions . . . of logical processes, comprehension, judgement, and reasoning . . . as the sine qua non of intelligence. He argued that intelligence could be measured efficiently only by using a great variety of items that 'sample' these higher processes" (19). It is important to reiterate that the final result of a Binet test was "intelligence in general, an average."

In this way, the road led away from theory and experiment in the study of intellectual differences to correlational testing for particularly concrete educational and vocational results and predictions. Both Lewis Terman and David Wechsler (1896-1981), who devised the most widely-used batteries of I.Q. tests, were psychometricians, believing that they were dealing with various forms of abstract thinking in examining the heterogeneous results of such testing. Wechsler especially saw intelligence as an aggregate of abilities that extended even beyond the cognitive sphere into the realm of affect, motivation, and personality (20).

The Englishman Charles Spearman (1863-1945) received his doctorate in 1897 in Leipzig for work done under the supervision of Wilhelm Wundt. He returned to England in time to witness the great expansion of psychometrics and the concomitant decline of the experimental work of the Galton school. Having decided theoretical inclinations, he approached testing with a sure systematic approach. As early as 1904, Spearman introduced the concept of factor analysis. This was a methodology to be used in the analysis of test reliability and the coordination of skills as revealed by various testing instruments (21).

It was clear from the earliest days of educational and aptitude testing that there were many kinds of skill tests, all seeming to measure different abilities. The multitude of faculties proposed, especially with the lack of any overriding conceptual unification, seemed to disintegrate the concept of intelligence. Spearman's solution was the use of "correlation." "If two or more nominal faculties were claimed to be distinct, it should be possible to devise tests of each one, to administer the tests to a group of persons who show individual differences in the power of the faculties in question, and show that the measurement of the different faculties are uncorrelated" (22).

Spearman's conclusions, after much practical application of his ideas in the English schools, were that the differences in the supposed separate faculties indeed were only nominal. The intercorrelations of these tests, worked out through a variety of novel statistical techniques, suggested "that all of the measurements reflect a common factor, that is a common or unitary source of the covariance among the variables. Individuals who scored exceptionally high on any one variable tended to score above average in all others as well" (23).

In addition, a hierarchical picture began to emerge among these correlations, the matrix of intercorrelations revealing a common factor that Spearman termed $g$. This common factor appeared in those tests more heavily conceptual in character, i.e., where inductive or deductive reasoning was required. He called *g* a unitary form of "mental energy," of which certain kinds of tests required more than others.

Whether or not his hunch about the nature of the unitary type of intellection that seemed to underlie all higher types of mental activities was accurate, the concept of *g* became a powerful heuristic tool for uncovering the structure of a great variety of testing materials. It seemed to be the focus of a complex theoretical program for examining mental functioning, and became a powerful tool of prediction.

What might lie beyond the unitary psychometric concept of *g* was unknown, and not required of the theory. It was enough that tests of high *g* loadings had important predictive outcomes that were confirmable in schooling as well as in life. Spearman did set out additional group factors that certain tests seemed to invoke: verbal, mechanical or spatial, mathematical, and memory factors. However, he was cautious enough to see in his work a basically theoretical description as to how the testing process worked. What *g* stood for besides the metaphor of mental energy could not be decided by the available evidence (24).

Others such as Edward Thorndike (1874-1949) would argue for the concept of "neural connections," wherein individuals were distinguished in terms of the "breadth and altitude" of the intellect. To Thorndike, no unitary *g* factor existed, no underlying mental energy. To him, tests represented an average number of differing neural bonds which they sample. The *g* factor resulted from the fact that certain tests sample common bonds. Spearman called this view anarchic (25).

The subsequent work of Louis Thurstone (1887-1955), J. P. Guilford (born in 1897), and Raymond B. Cattell (born in 1905) contributed to the position that there were distinct and separate factors, and that, basically, *g* was a test artifice. Their contributions—Thurstone, primary mental abilities; Cattell, intelligence-fluid, intelligence-crystallized; and Guilford, structures of the intellect (150 of them)—pushed the discipline of psychometrics into a state of conceptual confusion. The question in the post-World War II period remained: is intelligence, that which lies behind the academic tests, that which is tested in life and praxis, is it one or many (26)?

Arthur Jensen, Spearman's leading disciple, argued, utilizing highly sophisticated mathematical and statistical techniques, in a steady stream of influential papers, that yes, there is something holistic behind the tests that we can call intelligence *g*. The predictive psychometric power of *g* and at the same time its theoretical limit are reflected in the following statement by Jensen about the current dilemma now faced by the tradition of correlational testing initiated by Binet:

> . . . certainly *g* exists as a product of factor analysis of any sizeable collection of diverse mental tests. The fact that a very substantial *g,* in the sense of proportion of total variance accounted for, is found in virtually any sizeable collection of diverse tests, and that the *g* is largely similar for different collections of tests, provided that each collection is reasonably diverse in form and content, is a fundamental and important discovery . . . . To argue, as do some psychologists, that because *g* is a mathematical abstraction, it cannot be thought of as having a cause, is fallacious, in that it fails to take account of the fact that a *g* factor *need not* be found at all. If all mental tasks involved only specific activities, no *g* factor could emerge by any method of factor analysis, and persons' scores on tests would vary solely as a function of the particular collection of tasks (or items) included in the test, plus errors of measurement. All the correlational evidence, however, completely contradicts this possibility. But this fact alone cannot prove that the *g* factor has a single or a unitary cause. The *g* factor could be explained, as did Thorndike, by hypothesizing a multitude of independent components (S-R bonds, neural elements, or whatever) of ability, a number of which are necessarily sampled by any task, and a large number being sampled by the more complex tasks (27).

# Discovery and Prediction of Talent

Let us go back to life, for this is where ideas are tested for their ability to clarify or predict. For seventy-five years, I.Q. tests have been used in various formats—ETS-SAT, various Wechslers, Stanford-Binet, Raven's Progressive Matrices, Armed Services Vocational Aptitude Battery. Over this period, during which the debate over the unitary or disparate character of these test factors continued, certain observable outcomes should have appeared concerning the relationship of the life results of individuals having taken the tests, reading back into the record of their test predictions.

The use of tests is constantly expanding. That testing is done now on a massive scale—precollege, armed service aptitude tests, vocational screening—argues for a measure of predictability here. What is it though? Certainly, persons can be distinguished in the three major intellectual categories that fall within those standard deviations that can be roughly described as below average, average, and above average. What with the inevitable variability of one's score in successive testing situations, which often may vary significantly around one's norm, prediction becomes essential, and, if borne out, often pays for itself.

From that point on, tests can be given that are more subject-matter oriented and may allow for a finer breakdown in ability assessing. Essentially then, the mandate given to Alfred Binet has been fulfilled. Even a short test, such as one of the various Wechsler instruments, can make a fairly accurate set of distinctions between individuals (28). We can spot potentially slow-learning students and the seemingly average, distinguishing them from the student with really exciting potentiality.

Most important, these tests have more often uncovered talent, as well as, more rarely, disabilities, that would have gone unnoticed without the exposure given by these apparently objective instruments. Through the medium of these tests, whole groups of underpriviledged people—socially, culturally—many with psychological handicaps, have shone through the environmental clouds that masked their intellectual potentialities. Whereas when fixed in an environment that trumpeted certain assumptions about them, neglected by family and school, such individuals, through these brief testing instruments, exhibited intelligence that "should not have been there." Most unbiased observers would agree that from this broader educational and social perspective, I.Q. tests have revealed something of importance, something that argues for *g* as a unitary dimension—educability (29).

Robert Sternberg has written recently (1983) to argue for the reality of the general factor in intelligence testing and in a sense to bring down the curtain on almost three quarters of a century debate.

> One of the most well-established findings in the literature in human intelligence is the existence of a "positive manifold" among the correlations of the varied tests of intelligence: these tests all tend to be positively interrelated . . . .
>
> Curiously, there is not even one respectable psychometric (correlational) psychologist who denies the existence of this manifold. Such consensus is curious only because there is so little else on which psychometricians agree! Thurstone (1938), who originally argued against the existence of a general factor, eventually was forced to admit that a higher order general factor could be extracted from his "primary mental abilities." Guilford (1967) originally eschewed higher order factors (which result from correlations among factors), but more recently has started extracting such factors (Guilford, 1982). The point is that even the psychometricians most resistant to the idea of a positive manifold have eventually been forced to deal with it. (30)

That the concept of general intelligence was not merely a research artifact, but revealed itself in the life cycle of human beings, was shown in the now-classic longitudinal study begun by Lewis Terman in the 1920s. Terman chose 1500 junior high school age children on the basis of parental and school recommendations as well as I.Q. tests. The cut-off minimum for these children was 140 I.Q. on the Stanford (Terman)-Binet version of the usual Binet-Simon series developed earlier in France. The mean I.Q. was 153. The purpose of this longitudinal study was to trace the destiny of these youngsters throughout their lives and thus to test the predictability of these instruments. A further purpose was to inquire into the long-term social and personal character of such giftedness. Terman, in hyperbole, called them geniuses (31).

Sixty years later, this group has largely retired. At the very least, we know what they have accomplished in their maturity and are now beginning to glean from their life summaries the personal meaning of their being designated as "special" in early youth. It is clear that this group's high intelligence was in some way instrumental in their rising to positions of authority, civic distinction, personal wealth in virtually every area of life that we judge to be important socially. The sense that the tests were echoing some general ability, which with further education, as Galton early intuited, would take them into a variety of careers of distinction, was borne out (32).

The tests themselves were a complex of $g$ loadings. From this standpoint of looking back, we are unable to see which skills dominated at that period in their educational development. All that we know is that for such highly talented youngsters (over three standard deviations beyond the norm), distinguished life careers were far more probable than chance, and that by all indices of health, personal and social happiness, and longevity, they likewise revealed a clear superiority. High intelligence seems to have been part of a complex of biosocial characteristics of superior social nature. Mind and body were here part of another unity.

Let us move forward in time to the late 1960s and early 1970s and a new longitudinal experiment in intelligence. At

Johns Hopkins University, in Baltimore, Maryland, under the guidance of Julian Stanley, a program in the study of mathematically precocious youths had been undertaken. The impetus had been only in part one of psychological analysis. An educational and economic crisis of national development was also a stimulus. The United States needed more mathematical and scientific talent (33).

Here we must introduce a puzzling, as yet unexplained, fact. It is known that talent in mathematics as well as in the classic game of chess manifests itself early in life. Mathematicians tend to reach their creative peak in their twenties and early thirties (34). Thus there was a practical reason to attempt to throw a net widely throughout the state of Maryland to find the most precocious mathematical talent.

The SAT of the Educational Testing Service of Princeton, New Jersey, was used, the same test that is given to high school seniors, the scores of which accompany their college applications. These tests are in effect I. Q. tests. Those students who were recommended for the Johns Hopkins study took both the verbal and the math sections. While it was their math scores that were crucial in qualifying (a score of 600 was necessary), these junior high school students exhibited a fairly good correlation with their verbal scores (35).

Many who would receive between 700 and 800 (the latter a perfect score) would often be in the 600s on the verbal. Nevertheless, it was clear that we were seeing a special ability chosen from the rich unity of *g*, and that though math intelligence was accompanied by high verbal scores, something else accompanied it, something special or unique, so high was this mathematical talent among the best candidates.

The longitudinal/time perspective in this study of uniqueness of talent in the special mathematical program (now extended to science students) has not been long. Yet already it is clear that the most talented of these mathematical whizzes are rising rapidly to the top both of their graduate school classes and in the world as successful performers (36). We will not know for some time how creative or powerful their achievements will turn out to be.

There are hints that the one dimension of predictability in which the I.Q. test fails at this point, and for good probabilistic reasons, is in the area of creative achievement (37). First it should be pointed out that while the verbal fall-off on the SATs as compared with the math achievement of these precocities is not great, the pattern for those with high verbal achievement is *not* likewise symmetrical. There seems to be a greater fall-off in the math SATs by the high verbal.

SAT verbal and math scores both seem to invoke important aspects of *g*. It is also clear that great and powerful achievements in one area do not evoke a symmetrical score in the other. The average combined scores do give a strong predictive picture of the future. However, a person with powerful achievements in one aspect combined with weak achievements in the other, for example, an 800 and a 400, should not be viewed by educators in the same way as a person who scores 1200, with 600 in the verbal and math components respectively.

The mathematical "genius" seems to be able to mine her/his innate *g* more efficiently and deeply through mathematical than through verbal means. Yet the verbal skills of mathematically precocious youth are by no means uncorrelated with their mathematical skills. The assumption seems to be that these mathematical and verbal scores are second-order manifestations of something deeper, even enigmatic. Here the existence of general intelligence is indicated, its nature still garbled.

# Chapter X

---

# THE ENIGMA OF GENERAL INTELLIGENCE: THE NEW EXPERIMENTALISM

## Nature/Nurture

We are at a stage today in the debate over *g* of general intelligence and I.Q. in which certain probabilities loom large. After eighty years of research and study, it is clear that I.Q. tests are predictive in areas where limited verification is required. It is also clear that a general factor in intelligence does exist, yet at the same time it also seems probable that the so-called "factors" reveal a mind that is not homogeneous.

Most people of seemingly similar intelligence drift into certain vocations and not others. Also, those individuals whose high intelligence reveals clearly articulated skills do seem to excel in certain fields. While high intelligence *g* is a necessary condition for achievement in any particular area, considering the longitudinal studies we have examined, it is not a sufficient condition for greatness.

*def. ?*

There is another issue that has gone through the controversy mill for at least two generations. This is the extent to which this intelligence of ours, call it *g* or a summation of factors, in its variance from one individual to another, is derived from hereditary or environmental factors. Indeed, there is so much social policy planning that hinges on the resolution to this conundrum that the violent fire fights concerning it are easily understandable.

How much of our differences can be attributable to genetics, how much to family and community? Interestingly, within the professional community at least, a quiet consensus seems to have developed that a major proportion of the variance has to be attributed to individual differences that derive from our "nature" rather than "nurture" (1). Of course, differences between individuals in terms of their (a) academic or scholastic performance or (b) life achievement are not completely subject to psychometric prediction. The instruments or tools for use in analyzing human differences have not yet been perfected.

*?*

At the very least, one half the variance between individuals on the basis of testing can be attributed to heredity. Interestingly, since the extension of these sciences to Europe and much of the modern world has by now dredged up an extensive international literature on the analysis of intelligence, in academic performance and in life, the North American and European profiles have been confirmed. A consensus is that the overall variance lies between seventy and eighty percent, depending on the social and educational homogeneity of the population examined. Even in the Soviet Union, I.Q. tests have revealed hereditarian results and have been accepted in practice (2).

*ok*

Differences show up in testing that lead us to believe that human biological intelligence, as expressed in such academic situations, reveals slightly different statistical ranges in differing populations. For example, among females, the standard deviation of test scores from the norm is somewhat smaller than among males (3). Also, fewer individuals are to be found at the extreme ranges of intellectual performance. This is also hypothesized to be true for other populations, such as among black North Americans or the Japanese as an ethnic group (4). This characteristic of a differing distribution of intelligence around the norm is naturally neutral to the claims about the differing norms (higher or lower) relative to Caucasoid North Americans or Europeans and other identifiable groups.

The most powerful beacons for revealing the hereditarian character of intelligence have been the innumerable studies of monozygotic and dizygotic twins. For example, identical twins reared apart in differing life circumstances are much more similar intellectually than fraternal twins reared under the same roof. Arthur Jensen's statistical analyses of the phenomenon of inbreeding depression in I.Q., where such examples can be found and tested, have proved important (5). It can be shown that a mathematical pattern of declining intellectual function in children who are a product of incest can be established on the basis of the genetic closeness of the parents, for example, children of brothers and sisters, or fathers and daughters, of first cousins, of second cousins (6).

These theoretically rooted studies of intelligence interacting with the environment as well as the massive evidence from factor analysis elicited from a variety of tests of cognition, have punctured the hopes of those who dreamed that an egalitarian world of uniformly intelligent and cultured persons could be created by waving a magic wand of philanthropic social, economic, and educational policies.

Even the evidence within families reveals a puzzling,

often dismaying fact. Parents having equally "high" and equally "low probability" I.Q.s will in the main give birth to children with only average I.Q.s. "Regression toward the mean" is the term used for this phenomenon, i.e., these children, while usually superior, will tend to be less so than their *rara avis* parents (7). This alone ought to be some consolation to the sociological egalitarian. Hereditary aristocracies created even on the basis of intelligence will be ever unstable. The dynamics of human intelligence reflected in populations will militate against such phenomena. There will always be room for that mysterious gift to be passed around the family of man.

## Experimentation

In recent years, psychometricians have shifted from the scene of past controversies presumably of indefinite resolution, i.e., whether intelligence is one or many, the pros and cons of factor analysis, to new areas. One of the most interesting is what is being called information processing. Now involving actual experimental procedures in the analysis of simple human behavior, information processing presents new possibilities for bridging the gap in psychology between the statistical and the experimental which Lee Cronbach as long ago as 1957 decried as a scandal and challenge for the profession (8).

Many terms and levels of concepts have been put forth to explain what is occurring. Distinctions abound between elementary information processes and metaprocesses (executive functions that deploy and integrate these elementary processes). The central term that behaviorally describes the experiments from which these abstractions are derived is *RT* or reaction time (9). Because what we call informational or metaprocesses are themselves hypothetical constructs seeking to describe the actual events and terms, it is probably wiser first to describe these experiments and some of their unusual correlations with ordinary I.Q. tests—the WAIS (Wechsler Adult Intelligence Scale), Raven Advanced Matrices, ASVAB (Armed Services Vocational Aptitude Battery).

One such experiment tests the speed of processing digits. This test was developed in 1966 by S. Sternberg. The subject, seated at a console, observes, in sequence, a series of from one to seven digits each for two seconds. After a one second interval, a simple probe digit appears. The subject's task is to indicate whether or not the probe digit was a member of the series of from one to seven digits that had previously appeared on the screen. The subject does this by raising his finger from the home button as soon as the probe digit appears and quickly pressing either a "yes" or "no" button close at hand. The RT, reaction time, that is recorded is the time it takes between the appearance of the probe digit and the release of the home button (10).

The interval between the release of the home button and the pressing of the correct response button ("yes" or "no") is called "movement time" (MT). Naturally when more digits (one to seven) are presented, a slower RT and MT are recorded because of the greater complexity involved in making the choice.

Speed of retrieval of information from the long-term memory, LTM, was recorded by Goldberg, Schwartz, and Stewart (1977) (11). The subject is shown twenty-six pairs of common words to be identified as either the same or different. Two tests are used here. In the first test the words are literally the same or not ("dog"-"dog" or "log"-"dog"). In the second test, the twenty-six pairs are either synonyms or antonyms ("big"-"large" or "big"-"little"). In each test, the word pairs are selected so that half are the same, half different. Here, too, both RT and MT are recorded. The subjects here also have to press a "yes" or "no" button.

In a test developed by Arthur Jensen in 1979, a subject is seated at a response panel with a home button and a template over the console which allows either one, two, four, or eight lights to appear with buttons below each light (placed six inches from the home button). The subject presses the home button, hears a warning beep, then waits for a random interval of one to four seconds for one of the lights to come on. The subject immediately releases the home button and presses the button adjacent to the light. RT is the time it takes to release the home button after the light comes on. The more lights to which the subject has to prepare himself mentally to respond (choice RT), the larger the expected RT. If only one bulb is shown from the template, no decision has to be made. If eight, a moment of indecision exists before one light goes on (12).

*[handwritten margin note: ie willingness to play the game]*

The correlation with I.Q. scores is high. Measures of individual difference in choice RT have shown substantial correlations with scholastic achievement, particularly reading comprehension (with a correlation over 0.60 in a junior high school sample), even though the RT tasks do not involve reading or any other verbal symbols or scholastic content (13). "Evidently, certain basic cognitive processes are common to both the RT tasks and scholastic achievement" (14). It should be further pointed out that, in all these information-processing experiments, the goal is never to present tasks that require more than a third grade level of education. This is to minimize errors and to measure only the speed of a patently correct response.

*[handwritten margin note: could just as easily mean schools reward RT but what abt familiarity with lights + buttons]*

To find the meaning of this research insofar as it may impact on broader generalizations concerning intellectual function, the intercorrelation of these results with traditional I.Q. has become standard. The results uncannily reflect the same kind of differentiation of variable intelligence as I.Q., except that there is a lessening correlation with I.Q. test scores the simpler or more basic the RT experiments.

The more choice that is involved, or the more complicated the memory recall required is, even the use of more numbers and words, the closer we get to approximate I.Q. correlations. For example, Jensen's and Vernon's research on black-white vocational school students shows only small differences in simple RT. As the tests became increasingly complex, however, perhaps involving the use of scholastic skills, words, or numbers, they take on the distinctions typical of black-white variability as well as the scoring patterns found in the ASVAB testing procedure.

We are thus at an early stage in understanding what goes on in the relatively simple (third grade) level RT experiment. Sternberg and Gardner, in 1982, developed a distinction between elementary processing of information tasks: stimulus encoding, discriminative working memory capacity, speed of access and retrieval from LTM (here using synonym-antonym combinations), and short-term memory (STM) capacity. They distinguish a metaprocessing or executive level of function that controls, guides, and employs these elementary functions, chunking or grouping stimuli, verbal memory, etc. (15). Jensen wonders whether such metaprocesses of executive control involving problem solving, predicting outcomes, and monitoring one's own performance are trainable through education (16).

What seems to have occurred is that the very simplicity of the RT experiments has allowed the researchers to study the elements involved in the human response to the task at hand. A simple challenge elicits a complexity of behaviors. That the executive processing element here postulated involves more than drive or pure will power to succeed at the task is shown by the invoking of the by-now ancient Yerkes-Dodson principle (1908). This asserts that the motivation to perform well on those tests is inversely related to the outcomes of the superior g. Thus, will power, drive to succeed, improvement, and ambition are not necessarily linked to the abilities that execute and sharpen the actual intellectual efficiency of the brain.

*[handwritten margin note: the processes are defined in terms of the socio-economic needs of this society Oh?]*

As a matter of fact, accepters of the concept of *g* as a unitary reality in the description of intelligent behavior, such as Hans Eysenck and his associates, have bravely taken on the tasks of probing into the strategies that are employed by an individual in the "name" of *g* when taking a traditional I.Q. test (17). They have "split the I.Q." into these elements: (1) speed, (2) accuracy, (3) rechecking. Certainly the latter two elements involve a measure of executive processing of the purely intellectual factor. This itself constitutes a kind of methodological meta-analysis of I.Q.

Here the question is not the actual intellectual subject matter or skills. Rather, the focus is on the mental machinery involved in doing the task. Interestingly, the Sternberg-Jensen view is that speed seems to encompass those primary processes of mental functioning here described as being "more closely linked to the neural substrate of mental activity" (18).

Elsewhere, Cohn, Carlson, and Jensen describe the considerable differences between academically above-average suburban high school students and exceptionally gifted mathematically precocious students in the Johns Hopkins study discussed in Chapter IX as being "attributed to differences in elementary cognitive processes, rather than to higher-level problem-solving strategies, planning, executive control, or other types of metaprocesses, the latter very likely playing an important role in long-term real life intellectual achievement" (19). It should be stated here, too, that the difference in the I.Q. scores of the two groups was somewhat greater than their difference in a variety of RT experiments.

*NB*

At this point, let us admit another and even more mysterious set of experiments being conducted in England under the general guidance of Hans Eysenck, expecially those by A. E. and D. E. Hendrickson (20). Here, electroencephalograph (EEG) studies on the electrical potential of the brain evoked by simple auditory stimuli (clicks), which require absolutely no voluntary behavior on the part of the subject, have been developed and improved to the point of giving some amazing predictions. From the tracings around the zigs and zags made on a graph with a specially designed laser, a profile of "evoked potential" can be made and correlated again with the traditional I.Q. The correlation with the most g-loaded of the eleven subtests of the WAIS gave a $+0.90$ to $+0.95$ scores. As Jensen notes, "It is entirely possible, some would say even likely, that the basis of g at the level of brain physiology would be much simpler than the multifarious mainfestations of g that we can observe at the psychological or behavioral level of analysis" (21).

*[handwritten margin notes: how extensive? age of subjects? NB]*

# Conclusion

The push of intelligence research into the experimental and psychoneurological domain over the last ten or so years has quickly yielded some tantalizing and pregnant insights into the sources and meaning of intelligence variability. In one stroke, it has moved our inquiry into the nature of intelligence onto a wholly new level as compared with the correlational testing tradition begun by Binet in the early part of our present century.

I.Q. and aptitude tests are still useful, but now they are deepened and even disciplined by a whole new factual and theoretical structure of ideas. RT research as well as AEP (Average Evoked Potential) and EEG experimentation not only constitutes a check on our I.Q. results but leads us toward the study of basic perceptual and neurological processes reminiscent of, but now understandably far more sophisticated than, anything that Francis Galton was able to muster. While RT research has raised the question of the meaning of the speed of response in the face of complex decision making with simple sensory/motor tasks, AEP-EEG ex-

perimentation seems to eliminate the need for any overt behavior on the part of the subject as a measure of variable intelligence.

If the Hendrickson's work holds and the correlation with
the traditional I.Q. results is maintained, then truly we will
have entered the inner psychoneurological-processing realm
of the human brain. Who knows where that can lead? A. E.
Hendrickson has proposed that the laser-guided "string
length" of the EEG graphs, which seem to distinguish high
from low intelligence (jagged and irregular = high; rounded
and shallow = low), can be explained neurologically (22). This
argues for a view that the brain structure of highly intelligent
individuals is such as to allow the storage of vast amounts of
experiential materials in an efficient manner, coding these
materials in a way that the brain can renew itself continually,
to accept new knowledge, the old being reutilized efficiently
in practice. The result of high intelligence functioning is
what Hendrickson calls relatively error-free reception, storage, and utilization, all on a microneurological-processing
level (23).

*[margin note: what factors might contribute to /or block error-free reception]*

One wonders if there is already a distant connection established between rapid RT processing and clarity of neurological encoding in AEP graphs of the highly intelligent.
Could the high intelligence efficiency that we see here symbolized in psychological research be related to the millions-
of-years evolution of a primate brain that has attained an internal structural peak of complexity at the same time that it
has tested the limits of the capacity of the female pelvis to
give birth to a large-brained neonate?

Of equal suggestibility is the admission into the theoretical structure by both Hans Eysenck and Arthur Jensen of a
supracognitive element, what they both call executive processing (24). Pure intelligence *g* is here created, conditioned,
and assisted by a mental factor that supervises, coordinates,
organizes, perhaps even subconsciously wills the actual response in the testing situation. Whether it be the quickly co-

ordinated movement of eye and hand in front of a console of buttons and lights in RT or the extended discipline of completing an aptitude or I.Q. test within a required time, the doing seems to require another element beyond speed, understanding, or motivation.

# Chapter XI

---

# THE EXECUTOR: "P" FACTOR

## I.Q. and the Executor

Eighty years after the first intelligence tests had been utilized, an even longer period during which the nature of variable human intelligence had been studied, the inner character of intelligence still remained unclear. The question remained whether intelligence was many abilities clumped into one general competency or a real unity. Yet, I.Q. testing had achieved certain important goals. After years of highly sophisticated mathematical analysis and intercorrelation of such testing procedures and results, it seemed clear that a general factor did in fact exist.

All the tests demanded of their subjects some intellectual manipulation of verbal, numerical, or spatial relationships. The variability revealed between individuals in what was intercorrelated in *g*-loaded tests could be predicted to occur in the academic as well as conceptual arenas. Further, it could be demonstrated that *g* was highly heritable, not a mere facet of social and environmental circumstances.

Research into identical and fraternal twins, of in-breeding depression, consistently precipitated *g* as the unifying conceptual artifact. On the other hand, testers were able to separate verbal and numerical abilities, which although highly intercorrelated seemed to reveal certain fine-tuned differences that were found to be important in predicting special school and professional achievements. At the upper end of the scale, it began to appear highly improbable that ordinary I.Q. testing would reveal anything further than above-average, even moderately-gifted individuals (1). Identification of rare gifts and achievements—verbal, numerical, spatial and diagrammatic, artistic, social—continued to be elusive. We just did not find the clear-cut predictability that a high *g* would pour itself equably (à la Galton) into any field and manifest itself as significant achievement: a Socrates could be a Michelangelo, could be a Mozart, could be a Newton, could be a Yeats.

In the 1980s, a new tool, information processing, began to dominate in the reviving experimental study of intelligence. Starting in the 1970s, experimenters analyzing simple processes—reaction time (RT), short-term memory ability—began to find perplexing, if fascinating, correlations with ordinary I.Q. tests. They were perplexing in that RT experiments presumably involved only rudimentary intellectual processes—speed of observation and recall, movement time after attention to sensory event—all those elements to which I.Q. had been indifferent.

Note that even the Wechsler I.Q. tests in their various versions, some of which can be given in just a few minutes, yield surprisingly close correlations to more elaborate I.Q. tests. The simple RT experiments, although not quite as closely correlated with I.Q. as are the various subtests within their respective batteries, did become increasingly predictive the more intellectual transformations of the basic sensory and physical inputs were required, and the more they approached I.Q. tests in their use of numbers and words (2).

In these kinds of relatively simple experimental sensory/motor tests in terms of the error factor (third grade), we seemed to be tapping into a fundamental structure of brain function that clearly went deeper than the various day-to-day demands traditionally associated with the heterogeneity of learning and culture. This in itself seemed to argue for a physiological and neurological substrate to variable intelligence and the consequent reality for *g*, which could serve as proof for those who saw intelligence as a unitary phenomenon.

Yet there was a methodological caveat. For, in all the RT research, the so-called metaprocesses or executive functions that are apparently mobilized to organize experience—readiness, attention, integration of short-term and long-term memory—loomed as background elements that somehow had to be incorporated. Perhaps, as Jensen suggested, they should be viewed as part of that complex of personality/intellectual factors that account for the long-term social/personal utilization of such skills (3). In an internal analysis of I.Q. tests undertaken by Eysenck and colleagues, it had been shown that in addition to errors of speed and accuracy, checking or rechecking, were elements in the so-called "splitting" of the I.Q. score (4). These argued from another angle for the reality of the so-called executive element.

Clearly then, even if we omit that still tantalizing and puzzling set of experiments being undertaken in England by the Hendricksons in EEG-AEP, this research has precipitated a seemingly noncognitive element in I.Q. The Hendricksons demonstrated that a small set of clicks heard through earphones evokes a graphic map of electrical activity that correlates astoundingly (0.80-0.95) with the higher *g*-loaded subtests on the WAIS (Wechsler) (5). Both the executive element in the organization of intelligent behavior, as well as the diverse manifestations of intelligent functioning (the factors), thus still seemed to constitute unresolved aspects of that yet powerfully appealing and predictive concept of *g*.

As Jensen and others have observed, the way out of this dilemma cannot be found through more of the traditional statistical and mathematical analyses of the various testing instrument results. The new information-processing approach seems to reveal a neurological and physiological reality that scientists have always assumed they would someday need to face (6). After all, human intelligent behavior is rooted in biological functioning; the brain's neurological organization is certainly the source of this functioning.

## Neurophysiology and the Evolution of Intelligence

In this chapter, we will expand our understanding of human intelligence and its various enigmas by going into allied areas of neuropsychological research. The issues of both the executive, organizational aspect of intelligent behavior, and the puzzles of the one *g* and the many ("factors of the mind"), may thus also yield new insight.

In the late 1940s, Ward Halstead was arguing for a four-factor view of intelligence from the standpoint of evolutionary structures (7). This was developed further by his follower David Stenhouse (8). They proposed a set of distinctions: "A," the abstractive/cognitive domain; "S," sensory/motor activity; "C," central integrative, memory; "P," postponement factor. Stenhouse correlated the "P" factor with the frontal areas of brain, arguing that in these areas humans made their greatest move beyond animal intelligence. The "P" factor was the element in human behavior that interdicted purely instinctual drive mechanisms.

It was here, using Freud's metaphor, that man surmounted the libidinal dominance of the "id." To the extent that humans could forestall immediate biological satisfaction, could instead plan and prepare for a world of experience that could only be anticipated by the mind, culture would displace biological instinct. Much of the Freudian argument had an almost literary/historical ring. Yet Stenhouse's argument that the "P" factor concentrated in the frontal areas of the brain had a good neurophysiological pedigree (9). Where he was probably mistaken was in his view that the ultimate human brain expended more in the frontal than in the other areas, notably the temporal-parietal (the area between the ears) (10).

The consensus among anthropologists seems to be that the final expansion of the *sapiens* brain involved both the frontal and the temporal-parietal areas, which reduced somewhat the lateral projection of the occipital areas at the rear, as in the Neanderthals. The tucked-in shape at the rear skull areas of *Homo sapiens sapiens* has reduced the length of the skull, widened it between the eyes and ears, at the same time raised it beyond an already high forehead to a peak above the ears (11).

One wonders whether there is an analogy in the way the "P" factor cooperates in intelligent behavior and the Yerkes-Dodson theorem that describes the outcome of intelligence testing in terms of motivation to succeed (12). The invocation of the latter theorem by Vernon and Jensen has been to argue against interpreting the results of RT experiments as depending upon the "drive-motivated" eagerness that would supposedly stimulate RT speeds (13). There is in fact a negative correlation between motivation to succeed and actual success in various tests of intelligence.

Does this mean that those individuals with powerful "P" factor self-control disciplines can muster more efficiently those skills and reactions necessary for the successful completion of a task? Does it likewise mean that individuals emotionally charged to "win the cup" organize their behavior and intelligence in a less efficient manner? Are we seeing more ancient emotional/intellectual valences interfering with the efficient operation of a wholly integrated cortical set of functions?

## Brain Pathologies and Function

The concern with brain structure and functions involving the frontal lobes has a long tragic history. The Franco-Prussian War (1871) was the first conflict in which modern medicine was able to make a significant contribution in saving the lives of those suffering from head wounds. In its aftermath, much research was stimulated. Earlier, Carl Wernicke had labeled one of the behavioral consequences of such dysfunction as asymbolia (14). Over time, such agnostic (impairments of tactile and visual perception), apractic (impairment of the ability to coordinate body movements), and aphasic language disabilities were seen as singular examples of a regression in human intelligent behavior. Hughlings Jackson in England in his analysis of brain pathologies focused on the peculiar distancing of such behavior from typically human symbolic function that then leads toward the practical, immediate fulfillment of needs (15). Despite a patient's physical survival after a serious head wound or a stroke, cortical function would still, in one way or another, have been violated. This violation invariably affected a general mental attitude first, then specific dimensions—language, perceptual/motor, etc.

After World War I, Henry Head in England and Kurt Goldstein in Germany simultaneously brought under careful clinical scrutiny the affliction known as aphasia, the language disability associated with such cortical impairments (16). Goldstein, working in Frankfurt, stimulated by the philosophical input of his brother-in-law, the philosopher Ernst Cassirer, focused on this loss of the abstract attitude and the reversion in both behavior and language toward the concrete (17).

The 1920s saw the nature of intelligence assiduously researched. It became clear in these studies too, that the unique quality of high human intelligence—relational thinking—was the first evidence of such brain impairment. It was Goldstein's conclusion, especially after he came to the United States following the Nazi occupation in Germany, that the symbolic dimensions of thought, uniquely relational and abstract in humans, were located in the frontal areas of the brain (18). This conclusion was drawn from his clinical research in Germany, and it was developed by the more philosophical and scientific perspective provided by the neo-Kantian scientific tradition espoused by Cassirer.

What was interesting about the research was that it was the voluntary dimensions of language and behavior loss that had impressed both Head and Goldstein. Aphasiacs seemed to have been robbed of their will, their enactive energies. Along with the loss of the ability to step back from experience, to relate different aspects of a situation objectively and dispassionately, these aphasiacs seemed to have been reduced to an almost animal-like specificity of behavior (they could not remember common names or general categories for colors and animals). They were left even without the instinctual automatic mechanisms of animals.

The use of prefrontal lobotomies, beginning in the 1930s, throws more light on this aspect of brain function. Antonio Moniz and Almeida Lima used this surgical technique (which grew to approximately 70,000 worldwide between 1935 and 1955) to diminish neurotic, obsessed, violent behavior (19). The disconnection of the frontal areas from the other parts of the brain did reduce the uncontrollable mental behavior of such persons whose mental illness seemed beyond repair. However, the consequences of the prefrontal lobotomies were instructive. Such patients often became apathetic, irresponsible, lacking in creative energies, occasionally even diminished intellectually.

Perhaps the most interesting research into brain specialization came out of World War II in the work of A. R. Luria in the Soviet Union and Roman Jakobson in the United States (20). The subjects of their research were, again, for the most part, victims of war. In this case the focus was language dysfunction (aphasia). The results of their work, a step forward in sophistication and analysis from its predecessors, were again, to show a clear distinction at least in language function between the parts of the brain.

Simply, the frontal areas seemed to be the source of these enactive, dynamic, voluntary aspects of intelligent behavior. At this point, the temporal-parietal areas came more fully into their own. Language itself seemed to be divided up into a cooperative venture contributed to in separate ways by the temporal-parietal and the frontal areas. Indeed, we have by now learned that at least three areas of the brain are responsible for language function—Broca's area: anterior frontal; Wernicke's area: generally temporal-parietal; and the midbrain areas: connecting the left and right hemispheres.

What Jakobson and Luria discovered was that the semantic function seemed to be mostly concentrated in the temporal-parietal areas and that the grammatical-connectivity aspects of language seemed to be contributed to by the frontal areas. For example, loss of frontal function would still allow the individual to create one-word sentences, to see analogies or synonyms in words and ideas, yet not be able to put whole sentences together (21).

On the other hand, individuals with afflicted temporal-parietal function (frontal areas working) could call into use elements of prepositions, subject, and predicate relationships. Yet their language skills seemed flat. They were able to muster little in the way of metaphor. Their understanding and use of language seemed almost one-dimensional, as if the inner content were gone, leaving only the surface structure of syntax (22).

In cases of progressive language loss, the disappearance of temporal-parietal function (Wernicke's area) still allowed the individual to mouth words and sentences, but understanding rapidly declined, eventually to affect the voluntary expression of the remaining sentence elements. When the frontal areas disappeared (temporal-parietal working), the individual would frequently lose sentence structure, eventually even lexicality and one-word sentences, yet comprehension, passive as it might be, remained intact (23).

The conclusion from this research was fairly clear. The frontal areas of the brain would no longer be seen as the paradigm of human thought as Goldstein had surmised. The temporal-parietal areas seemed to hold the key to the purely intellectual, semantic capacities of humans, while the frontal areas seemed to articulate the particular linguistic grammatical elements, apart from the logic of thought in general (24). Obviously, in a whole human being, these elements were drawn together into a unity of function.

## The Message of the Frontal Lobes

Genetic psychologists in analyzing human behavior from the standpoint of the genetic correlation between brain structure and behavior argue for a polygenic view of human intelligence. They argue that intelligence in the individual is the reflection of a wide variety of different genetic vectors, developmentally articulated and rooted structurally both cortically and subcortically. Hans Eysenck has estimated that at least fifty genes go into the creation of that unique individual intelligence that psychometricians seek to measure (25). There may be in addition many more genetic elements at work in creating that larger intellectually relevant aspect of intelligence, personality.

When we add the complex of language functions as they interact with other aspects of thought and behavior, as well as the complicated and unpredictable interactions between the genes, both within and between chromosomes, we can intuit the enormous complexity and variability that go into the shaping of each individual intelligence. Yet, as regards that supreme human element of individuality that we call personality, a consensus does seem to exist among those scientists who study the matter without ideological lenses, that a general factor continues to be observed in behavior that orders individuals as to their overall capacity for abstract thought and creative potentiality.

There exists today a neurological structural hint of what is appearing in the closer analysis of I.Q. tests or in the various types of RT experiments. The temporal-parietal areas seem to be the home of that abstractive function, intelligence "A," of which Halstead and Stenhouse speak, and which may be the structural correlate of that pure function of mental power or $g$. At the very least, we can say that the enormous cortical expansion that took place in *Homo sapiens sapiens* in those brain areas must as a consequence have given rise to certain discrete behavioral qualities of mind.

On the other hand, the myriad tamperings that have occurred in the area of frontal lobe functioning reveal a powerful voluntary element, quite close to those attentional, interpretive, executive elements, seemingly the dynamic force that brings intelligence into play. In an earlier volume in this series, *The Form of Man,* a medieval philosophical debate over the nature of God was used to reflect metaphorically an early recognition that the human mind is two-fold in its exemplification (a rational versus a voluntaristic God) (26). We do not have to stop with the Freudian metaphor: libido versus ego versus superego. In the voluntarism of Duns Scotus and the rationalism of Thomas Aquinas—God as reasoner of truth; God as the willer of truth—we have an as yet opaque recognition of the two sides of intelligence.

Let us conclude this section with a consideration of our almost anecdotal evaluations (albeit by professional psychologists) as to the personality and intellectual characteristics that describe individuals who have made important contributions, whether in business, scholarship, politics, or the arts. Obviously, intelligence is a key, the ability to handle complex ideas of an abstract symbolic or linguistic character, to deal with large quantities of information, memory, but also the ability to transfer these materials into a nexus of relationships, into a map of experience relating to the world about us. This is not always enough. Any activity worth doing takes great cultivation, attention to detail, long-term training, to develop one's skills.

Here we begin to speak about the "P" factor, the ability to concentrate, focus, plan, persevere, above all to postpone the momentary gratifications with which life tempts us, all for the sake of the long-term goal. Sometimes it is called monomania, yet it is something created from will power and enormous energies of concentration. Great achievement, in short, requires of its exemplars a combination of high cognitive intelligence, the capacity to deal with complex and abstract concepts. It also requires the frontal area "P" factor which contributes energy, commitment, the discipline over an unruly mind/body concatenation of elements.

Totted up, it is what we all would call high achievement. In analysis, we can separate elements. In practice, the parts either work together or there is no functional intelligence. Then, there are those with potential, yet with little will or focus, classic underachievers. The other extreme can be even worse. These are individuals of enormous drive, ambition, ego, who lack the cognitive, evaluative skills that would provide those ethical and qualitative censors that add to great effort the leaven of reality and prudence. Pity the highly intelligent underachiever; beware the other.

# Chapter XII

# FACTORS: LANGUAGE AND THE INTEGRATIONAL SYSTEM

## The Message of Language Disabilities

Recent approaches to the measurement of intelligence seem to be able to penetrate apparently simple and primary mental functions. Both RT (reaction time) and EEG-AEP (Average Evoked Potential), experiments have made us realize that the older testing procedures necessarily imply the existence of a fundamental neurological stratum out of which intelligent behavior becomes possible.

In intelligence tests, invariably the verbal factor is central. However, though at the core of I.Q. and aptitude tests, language and verbal performance are really a filter through which the more fundamental intellectual processes are actualized. Thus the language skills, talents, and deficiencies that are uncovered by testing, variable as they are quantitatively and qualitatively from individual to individual, are not a primary reflection of intellectual potential.

The many forms of aphasia that affect language function have displayed often bizarre disabilities. They have led us to wonder if language is a complex of associated abilities akin to what we discussed above about frontal and temporal-parietal aspects of language loss. There is more, of course, in the losses of comprehension, losses in ability to use various parts of speech, grammatical modalities, even specific kinds of words (1).

Often a patient who has lost total language ability still is able to utilize other symbolic modes, to write or read music, to do mathematical problems, to function in the world with intelligence and practical acumen (2). Perhaps that is why psychologists early devised tests that utilized so-called "performance" skills, in mathematics, for instance, or in the areas of sensory/motor or spatial relationships (3). That we were tapping intelligence in the areas of both language and mathematics, as in the ubiquitous SATs, is a recognition that we needed to get as much perspective as possible on this thing called intelligence.

Perhaps the greatest breakthrough in understanding the relationship of language function to larger intellectual issues has come through psycholinguistic research, Especially as regard reading and writing, psycholinguistics has brought language skills into relief. It has enabled us to distinguish the so-called "surface-structure" manifestations of language from the "deep-structural" semantic element (4).

Thus there are purely linguistic or material elements to our language skills that can be distinguished from other purely semantic or intellectual factors. For example, congenital idiots, with I.Q.s in the 30-50 range, often exemplify the full range of human language function. They have absorbed the phonetic elements of the particular language system, can put

*[handwritten margin note: this is an hypothesis]*

words into simple syntax to form crude sentences. Thus there is at least a rudimentary grammatical sensibility. What is especially impoverished is the semantic, the conceptual or ideational character of their language use. Their language is human, but their intelligence is rudimentary. What they say is quite undeveloped and emotional (5).

The work of Noam Chomsky in his search for a universal grammar that will define the peculiar human nature of language function reflects this awareness (6). It has been criticized by such as Thomas Bever for overlooking the powerful semantic shaping of the outer form of language, indeed making grammar a servant of semantics. Yet the universal existence of "shape" to language argues for a dimension, the clothing of language, that tells us that it cannot be completely subsumed to thought, or intelligence. It is not a passing or ephemeral cloak to be easily discarded or transformed (7).

Consider reading, for example. Some children quickly master the sound-to-sight structure of language, from phoneme to grapheme. The maze of inconsistent spellings, the rules meant to be broken, the almost limitless exceptions, do not seem to faze them. They are super oral readers in first and second grade. Then, ask them what they are reading about, ask questions of fact and interpretation, and their faces go blank. Teachers often come up against such problem learners. In the profession, such children are labeled "word callers." They have penetrated the mysteries of language form, but they are not able to penetrate the surface to comprehend what those black marks on white paper mean (8).

The other side of the coin is the affliction we label "dyslexia." The classic manifestation of this problem in learning to read is that the child, more often a male, tangles word order, has difficulty relating graphemes to their sound equivalent, cannot spell the sounds he clearly hears and understands, even words having simple and regular phonetic patterns. Interestingly, here, too, there is no simple one-to-one classic exemplification of the "reading disease" (9).

Neurologists Albert Galaburda and Thomas Kemper have here noted irregular patterns of cell and tissue organization (10). Norman Geschwind has summarized what seems to him to be the paradigm of the dyslexic brain as a "miswiring of the actual basic structure of the brain. It couldn't have been caused by mechanical injury, internal bleeding, or a cut off in the blood supply during or after birth. It *must* have occurred during the formation of the brain tissue in the womb" (11). Other researchers have raised the issue of delayed myelination (the fatty protein substance that insulates the nerve fibers), often associated with reading difficulties in the early school years (12). Some dyslexics outgrow their reading difficulties, others find differing means to overcome theirs, through compensating modalities of learning (13).

That such learning disorders are clumped in families, most often in males, argues for a hereditary link. Many left-handed children suffer from associated learning disabilities, even allergic and other auto-immune difficulties. The puzzle is that an extraordinarily high percentage of such learning-impaired people are extremely bright. Writings on the problem of dyslexia usually list an honor roll of great persons, again usually male, from Leonardo da Vinci to Winston Churchill, who have overcome the burden of their early language disabilities (14).

An even more puzzling set of facts arises from the affliction called "autism." Autism is now considered to be genetic in origin. Individuals afflicted with it are often extremely withdrawn, indifferent to social stimulation, fixated on repetitive routines, and uncommunicative in a normal way with the outside world. There is evidence that the neurological correlate of such impairments reveals itself in abnormal brain-wave activity and lack in brain asymmetry (left and right hemisphere specialization) (15).

Some autistic children give evidence of being "idiots savants." They can make remarkable mathematical or calendric calculations. They can draw, carve, or paint with remarkable skill, often with a kind of "blind" individuality. Some exhibit great musical ability. They may have uncanny memory of absolute pitch, the ability to recall large-scale musical lines, or to learn to play the piano or other instruments in amazingly short time periods. Others can use their verbal skills, memorizing and repeating long poems or prose works (16).

There is a unifying theme to what amounts to a narrow kind of genius. By definition, the idiot savant is unable to generalize, to abstract and extend his skill beyond the rote level. In a real sense, nothing comes forth from such talents that can be called creative or cognitive. In fact, often—but not always—idiots savants are retarded, quite unaware of their unique skills (17). How does one explain such puzzling and paradoxical "gifts"?

Interestingly, many of these almost praeternatural talents and/or defects are attributed to a malorganization of the brain as regards left/right hemispheric division of labor. The anecdotal record of hemisphere specialization in humans indicates that for most right-handed persons (ninety per cent of the population) the left hemisphere is dominant for language and other sequential cognitive skills (18).

By contrast, the right hemisphere is seen as the seat of the spatial/perceptual abilities as well as the more emotional/affective responses. While experimentation has affirmed this general division of labor, it is not clear that those who excel in the visual arts, music, mathematics, architecture, dance, or drafting are virtuosos of the right hemisphere. Certainly not all painters, sculptors, or performing musicians are left-handed by birth, to be retrained to use their right hands in their craft.

Likewise it is clear from experiments by Bever and Chiarello that while the untutored music fan listens with the right hemisphere, those who are educated to appreciate classical music or are professional musicians appear to transfer their range of mental activity to the left hemisphere (19). It seems to indicate that our natural susceptibility to the charms of music derive from one level of brain and nervous system function. At the same time, this affinity and responsiveness to musical affects can be shifted to the cognitive, intellectual domain, seemingly deepened by study and knowledge, yet without losing one's sensitivity to the music's emotional power.

# Reading

Examples abound of how we have misinterpreted the nature and relationship of language to general intelligence. The following is one. It concerns the evolutionary development in our conceptual understanding of the process of reading. If we interpret reading as a skill that is acquired as one matures intellectually, then the general physical and mental developmental sequence of the child will help us predict its future flowering. Thus if the child's sensory/motor development between the ages of two and five is slow, we might very well be right to step in to encourage the development of such areas as left/right awareness, independence in the use of hands and legs, small motor skills, body image, sense of distance, up and down (20).

This was the theory. Retardation in these skills before the age a child was normally expected to read (six to six-and-a-half years) might be predictive in indicating the age the particular child would begin to read. Remediation in these sensory/motor areas might interdict the potential retardation and facilitate a normal pattern of language and reading development.

This hypothesis was not borne out by the facts, however. Many an awkward child, whose physical development defied the norm, learned to read like a "house-afire," often before the age expected for beginning readers. On the other hand are the children with perfectly normal sensory/motor development rates who surprise us by their difficulties in learning to read. Such children often remain problem readers (21).

Another surprise for researchers in reading concerned the so-called "reading-readiness" battery of tests usually administered in kindergarten or beginning first grade. This series of tests, graduated in difficulty, includes picture recognition, picture story interpretation, letter recognition, number relationships, figural design perception. Of all of these tests, the number test was the most predictive of future reading success and excellence. Why? (22)

Apparently, the number test more fully involves cognitive processes than the other tests in the readiness battery. Once the child overcomes the puzzles of the phoneme/grapheme relationships in the spoken and written language, increasingly, intelligent semantic predictions become the key to reading success. Psychologists describe the reading process as predicting one's way across the written material. That is, a fluent reader will not decode written symbols to their sound or spoken equivalent. Rather, the reader will transform the orthographic markings to a structure of conceptual relationships, described as "feature lists," in which in one visual gulp a good reader can often "envelop" the meaning of long sentences and paragraphs (23).

Dyslexic children have difficulty stabilizing this visual material within their spatial/perceptual manifold. Often they are not able to make the jump from the spoken language to its phonetic equivalent. Later they may create their own "semantic feature lists" from the written markings, finding their own personal perceptual/conceptual modality for learning to read (24).

Slow children or those with low intelligence often have operative reading systems, but their semantic power is limited. Thus, their ability for mentally shooting ahead of the actual visual material, confirming what they see, is limited. Their modest predictive powers, which derive from their raw intelligence, experience, or "savvy," limit their reading progress to small increments of increasingly complex written materials.

The picture illuminated by these various departures from the norm confirms our sense that language is a vehicle for intelligence, but that it cannot be absorbed within it. Language is so fundamental a part of our humanness that it is almost inconceivable to think of a whole person without language skills. Yet we know that *written* language, a product of higher culture, is only one of a number of different symbolic structures for the expression of thought; symbolic logic, chess, mathematics, musical notation are others. We like to think of these forms of thought as equally powerful exemplifications of intelligent human behavior.

Language, probably like the other forms, reflects certain valences of the mind. It gives broad but equal scope for this intelligent behavior. There are other equal modalities or dimensions of our mind, however, which clothe and give substance to this deeper intellectual potentiality.

Let us consider another example. We ordinarily believe that in the ontogeny of intelligence one reaches one's full neuronic powers somewhere between the ages of fourteen to sixteen. After the age of sixteen, the individual needs experience, education, and time to develop intellectual and social powers to their fullest (25). There are a few areas of human achievement, however, that rapidly reveal the potential power of this now-matured intelligence.

## The Pace of Intellectual Growth

In the eighteenth and nineteenth centuries, when mathematics was rapidly evolving, it was axiomatic that the queen of the sciences was the domain of young scholars, for great breakthroughs were invariably made by mathematicians in their twenties and early thirties. Even today, as we approach a crisis in the identification and education of the highly gifted, it has become a matter of national importance to find these talents early. At the top of the list is the identification of mathematical precocity. The program at Johns Hopkins University in Baltimore, Maryland, *Study of Mathematically Precocious Youth* (SMPY), has put into affect a search for such talent at the junior-high-school level, i.e., students thirteen or fourteen years old (26).

Such potential giftedness shows up early in mathematics. Students thus gifted can be easily trained not merely to receive further advanced education in pure mathematics but are able to transfer this training to those professional and scholarly areas of study that require higher math skills. The field of mathematics does not require the kind of long, involved experience and study that is necessary for scholars in philosphy, history, the humanities, and social science in general.

What was wont to be said in the old days—the mathematical mind is narrow but deep—has a certain validity (27). The kinds of logical relationships uncovered in the symbolic structure of mathematical ideas seem to require a "purer" intellectual focus, one that does not necessarily involve matured social experience or the bedevilments of meaning that often lie masked in the written language.

The same can be adduced for chess, invariably a game of pure cognitive relationships, that is, for the young. The international grand masters usually achieve their mastery as very young people. The rules, as in math, can be acquired quickly. The next step lies in mobilizing thought to see relationships that involve innumerable permutations and possibilities, to anticipate moves and plan accordingly, for long into the game. In chess, the world champions usually fall by the wayside in their late thirties, a situation summed up by the truism in mathematics that "if you haven't made your great breakthrough contribution by age thiry-five, you never will."

Philosophers, on the other hand, rarely attain their

monumental peak *before* age fifty. In how many other fields of endeavor, even political and business acumen, is this likewise true? In music and the fine arts, a measure of symbolic skill certainly is required. Here, too, we will find a Mozart or a Picasso showing extraordinary gifts practically in their childhood. Certainly we can argue for a distinct and unique "musical" or "visual" talent in these praeternatural geniuses. However, the application of these symbolic "talent" skills so that they touch us creatively requires time. This allows us to make a distinction between the *Wunderkind,* or prodigy, and the mature cognitively rich creative artist of the mature years.

By contrast, great scholars in the verbal areas may develop into their seventies in maturity and genius. The juices of creative endeavors in the narrower logical sense of the mathematician and chess master, or the more enigmatic powers of the creative artist, often seem to diminish with great age.

We should not, however, consider these virtuosi of the nonlanguage symbolic structures narrow idiot savant types. The SMPY study of mathematical talents argues that such virtuosi have generally high intellectual skills. Since they are given the ETS-SAT exams at age thirteen or fourteen, usually geared for the seventeen- to eighteen-year-olds, their verbal scores are of more interest. While the top math prodigies often score above 700 in the math section (out of 800 possible points), their verbal achievements are invariably above average, some being quite high for that age level (28).

## Factors and the Integrational Level

The accumulation of evidence points to the reality of factors in any understanding of human intelligence. While the kind of broad-based study of human achievement does not diminish the reality of *g* as a fundamental power of the mind, it does reveal the existence of a separable level of functioning, one that can be called the *integrational* level. Here are found the various skills of man the culture maker.

The panoply of virtuosic achievements and also those regrettable handicaps that seem to emerge from such an analysis of the integrational domain argues that we are seeing the mind here in its unique qualitatively variable "wiring." The wiring or organizational variability ought not to be seen as a pathological departure from a fixed norm, from which comes that universal Renaissance genius who could do all things in a heroically creative manner, if only he lived in the Florentine culture of Leonardo da Vinci.

There is abundant evidence that argues for a correlation of extremely high intelligence married to a series of integrational level anomalies, (1) in the developmental relationships of the hemispheres to each other—left- and right-handedness—and (2) in the organization of the language areas. The latter extends to hemispheric specialization, each hemisphere with its own internal structure (dyslexia), to myopia and a malfunctioning of the auto-immune system, especially in males, or rheumatoid arthritis in females leading to asthma, allergies, even to psychopathologies. The latter reflects the nineteenth-century view of genius as partaking of madness.

The late Norman Geschwind noted, on the basis of much research, that during embryological development, the human brain was quite capable of meeting a variety of dangerous challenges to normal development through neurological accommodation. In other words, if one part of the brain was in some way deviated from its full developmental potential, other parts compensated. This indicated that the genetic coding for the individual brain could be fulfilled in its major form, but that qualitatively unusual structural compensating over-developments might be noted. Here lay the possibilities of such specialized integrational skills, both of the highly intelligent, the mathematician A. L. Couchy and the composer W. A. Mozart, or the unfathomable abilities of an idiot savant (29).

In sum, the potentiality for high or low intelligence seen as a quantitative dimension in which we humans all share, though in varied amounts, seems to be affirmed at a basic neurological level. Here is the *g* that we are discovering through our intercorrelating I.Q. and aptitude testing instruments, EEG, and RT experiments. However, *g* cannot be separated from the executive "P" factor element disclosed in the frontal lobe function, both linguistic and behavioral.

On the other hand, where we seem to vary qualitatively from person to person, from talent to talent, is in the integrational language areas. The particular organization of our brain and nervous system, even given seeming equal intellectual power, tends to propel us into variable pathways of social and educational development. Here is a real distinction that so-called factor analysis of intelligence testing still reveals.

# Chapter XIII

---

# OUR PSYCHIC INHERITANCE

## Anthropoid Heritage

The anthropoid brain was not an atypical mammalian adaptive machine. It served the essentials. With it, the anthropoid could find the way around the turf, was enabled to remember events and things that might have consequences for future survival. What distinguished the anthropoid brain from other mammalian organs of intelligence were the particular connections with those special adaptive organs. The anthropoids were generalists. True, marmosets, monkeys, and great apes all had their particular assets or characteristics, but in general they were not specialized killers, as were certain canids, or herding escape artists, as were the ungulates.

Their world was the world of the forest. Up and down trees, searching for food only part of each day, prowling through their territories noticing much, but basically evading trouble, they flourished from the Oligocene period some thirty million years ago to the Pliocene, about seven million years ago. At that point, the apes began their precipitous decline (1).

Our ancestors hominids were anthropoids. During the Oligocene when the original template of ape and monkey evolved beyond the prosimians, lemurs, and tarsiers, the range of variation among these primates must have been formidable. Many millions of years later, we observe the survivors, and sometimes those survivors are not the seemingly most adaptable and resourceful of our near kin. This is because successful species usually elbow their closest competitors into extinction (2).

Thus, what we see today among the apes is probably not typical of the most adaptive ape generalists of the Miocene fifteen million years ago, the heyday of ape dominance. While much in our hominid construction reminds researchers of our monkey heritage, it is quite clear that the apes first carved out the center and sent the monkeys into a quite specialized fringe existence (3). With the decline of the apes, the monkeys eventually returned to primate dominance, except for *Homo,* who was the big victor, at least for now (4).

As we pointed out in Chapter IV, the evidence argues for the fact that our ancestors in the Oligocene were exemplars of a conservative primate, having certain specialized characteristics. Our line was able to hang on, while the monkeys were pushed to the environmental backwaters and the mainline representatives of the dryopithecine and ramapithecine apes disappeared entirely. These testify to the existence of the strong positively selective character of a number of hominid preadaptations that at the very least were not critically negative. They worked their consequences for our survival (5).

## Ur-hominid Preadaptations

What were these preadaptations and what was their selective equation? The brief list that follows is not meant to simulate a chronology of development in these characteristics that seems to set us off from the mainline of evolving anthropoids: First, our bodily structure, though the physical characteristics for erect bipedal gait were not yet fully worked out, argues for a creature who was at the least a semi-erect biped. This could have derived from the prosimian trunk-scampering tradition or it could have been an independent variation. Certainly the knuckle-walking of the great apes or the prehensile tail of the monkeys prepared these creatures for a different and specialized direction. Eventually this bipedal potentiality in the protohominids allowed for their adaptive egress onto the plains (6).

Second, the gibbons are monogamous apes, due in part to the loss of oestrus in the female. (She is now often sexually available.) That another ape was blessed with this unique familial characteristic argues also for man that this quality of sexual bonding for the purposes of the protection and nurturing of the young may go far back in hominid history. It is probably part of the original repertoire of anthropoid variation (7).

Third, as in all aspects of physical structure, e.g., size, speed, strength, so, too, brain size and intelligence were subject to the natural Gaussian probability curve. While many of the ape lines burst forth in an adaptive exuberance of expansion, it is quite likely, as with the early therapsid mammals 100 million years before, that the more intelligent forms were pushed to the sidelines. Large relative brain size was here still linked to small physical size, which created a group of small creatures whose intelligence was still not well enough coordinated with their other adaptations to make a competitive difference at that early stage in human evolution (thirty to fifteen million years ago) (8).

Fourth, our peculiar bicameral brain, which seems not to render any special advantage to its possessors as long as it was not linked to an extraordinarily large brain, seems anomalous. We have a language area fixed generally in the left hemisphere and powerful spatial/visual skills rooted in the right. (Many terrible human mental afflictions can be at least pacified by the severing of the links between these two halves (9).) This construction of the hominid brain does not seem especially crucial adaptively as it leads to its eventual full exemplification in man. Other structural possibilities could have led to the final functional result.

Fifth, the language areas in the human brain, (a) Broca's area in the left frontal (anterior), (b) Wernicke's area diffused in the left upper temporal-parietal areas, and (c) upper midbrain areas seemingly connecting the two hemispheres, are peculiar to the hominids (10). The functional uniqueness of language argues that it evolved from a preadaptive potency at the earliest stages of our evolution, along with the bicameral hemisphere division. Language is a cortical phenomenon. The only language functions we have left after the cortical elements are removed are a few primitive ejaculatory vocal responses. We do not even have the glorious variety of anthropoid limbic system instinctive shrieks, whistles, and calls (11).

The original verbal linkage to the cortex may have been a preadaptive fluke. It allowed for vocal responses to be controlled by cortical learning patterns. An interesting example of this, as noted above, is the lack in infant children at all stages in their development of the instinctual "freeze-controls" that quiet the young of other species when in danger. In the beginning, quite possibly the link with cognition of vocal expression was not as tight as it is in modern hominids. However, the fact that language and vocal expression are so clearly under voluntary control in humans, that we whisper, shriek, talk, sing at decibel levels far under the 3,000 cps (cycles per second) of the apes (the human level is closer to 440 cps of the orchestral "A"), gives us a sense of the ancient and special biological nature of human vocal communication (12).

From the evolutionary standpoint, it is probable that

such a "preadaptation" was useful even in the earliest days
of the hominid encapsulation while the great apes expanded.
It argues for an intimacy of communication that is quite defensive in character. This would buttress the evolutionary
fact that the great advances in intelligence usually have been
stimulated in the first stages as defensive adaptations—alert-
ness, evasiveness, protectiveness—in a restricted ecological
domain (13).

*how is this known?*

Perhaps most important in our understanding of the
evolution of functional brain intelligence as regards language
is that it is man's intelligence specialization. As the brain expanded, the role of language became increasingly central to
the expression of this intelligence. The key thing to remember
in all this is that language as it is rooted in human vocal expression is probably of very ancient vintage. Its evolution is
inextricably bound up with that of the brain and intelligence.
Thus, intelligence reveals itself through language expression,
but is not necessarily exhausted or defined by language
abilities.

Sixth, the human pharynx, that specialized organ that
goes hand-in-hand with the language propensities as reflected
in the language areas of the brain, gives additional evidence
and support to the argument presented above. Physiologists
have noted that the various anthropoid vocal structures are
highly specialized to produce particular instinctual calls. The
human pharynx by contrast is quite unspecialized. It is characterized by a large open area in the back of the throat whose
shape is determined in the process of vocalization by a thick,
highly mobile tongue (14).

In sum, this simple, if quite highly developed, set of
structural/vocal relationships must have been a basic Ur-
hominid structure. It seems unlikely that something so simple
and functional should suddenly have evolved from unexcep-
tional ape or monkey vocal tracts. The latter morphologies
seem to have been selectively shaped into highly individual-
ized structures to produce their particular contemporary ar-

ticulations.

Philip Lieberman has argued that the opening into the back of the throat in Neanderthal humans was too small for them to develop the full range of vocal expressions available to modern *sapiens.* Lieberman went on to argue that the Neanderthals could not produce enough distinct and audible phonemes to have had a fully developed language. Lieberman now accepts the fact that only a few distinct phonemes are necessary for language production. (The dot-dash Morse code would have two phonemes.) Most languages today have between twenty and fifty phonemes (clearly distinguishable sounds) out of which to build their language (15).

In humanity's evolutionary journey, it is probable that a few clearly articulated sounds could have constituted enough auditory descriptive material to pass along the necessary adaptive information within the family and then to other members of the primeval hominid band. Naturally with the final explosion of *Homo sapiens sapiens,* the fully articulative power of man's verbosity was released and the mystery of *Homo's* "Tower of Babel" revealed to us all. Even today we note the heritage of articulatory handicaps in some individuals and peoples. Even when they are raised in completely new cultural environments, their pronunciation of the early adoptive language echoes their biosocial heritage (16). Nevertheless the admittedly limited articulatory powers of ancient man's vocal skills must have been enough to allow for a steady increase in size and power of the language areas of the brain, as the brain and intelligence were subject to positive selection.

## The Human Brain and Natural Selection

Evolutionary time and cosmic patience have given us a picture of both ends of the behavioral animal adaptive tradition. Insects and humans, who will prevail? At one time, we would speak of insect intelligence, the dance of the honeybee being the enchanting parallel to humanity's perplexing tango with freedom and the unknown.

The honeybee dance is one of the most stereotyped if complex examples of instinctual specificity of behavior in the realm of life. The guidance system that directs scout bees in their search for nectar is unique in nature. When the scouts return to the hive, they dance a preprogrammed pattern of zigs and zags that varies in intensity depending upon richness of the source, direction, and inclination from the horizon. This grammar and semantics trigger an instinctual response in the workers, who plunge out of the hive in a precise orbit toward the source (17).

We are the obverse. We have relinquished our instinctional preciseness and security for an unknown ambience. Here, it is intelligence in the truer evolutionary sense that releases us from the rigid suzerainty of genetic imprinting. We are free to learn and behave, the genes standing aside, beyond the fray. The genes, however, are the carriers of intelligence, more or less, powerfully or no, carriers of the potentiality to adapt to the new, even to create an environment (sociocultural) that would encourage the cultivation of those inner potentialities for learning and thinking.

Let us outline the three elements of intelligence carried forward by the growing brain. (1) The first is that releaser from instinct, or blockade of affect and drive expression that we have described as the "P," the power and postponement, factor. The postponement factor inhibits the forces in our biology that demand satisfaction—food, sex, fight, or flight. The power factor, on the other hand, spurs the individual to act in the name of thought, reason, to make a map of a situation (18).

Nature seems to have centered these powers in the forebrain. The frontal lobes then have a long evolutionary tradition both of transforming behavior from the instinctual system to the cortical, the evaluative domain of intelligence, at the same time, by interdicting the id, the frontal areas have inherited those peculiar enactive, energizing qualities of the aggressive anthropoid that is *Homo*. The complex of behaviors in symbolic action encompassed in the "P" factor, "planning, practice, perduring, patterning, predicting," were felt by scholars such as Kurt Goldstein and W. A. Halstead to be the essence of human intelligence (19).

Often pathologically aggressive or other disequilibrating mental behaviors are neutralized in a procedure known as the leuctonomy, in which the prefrontal lobes are severed from the rest of the brain (20). While the torrents of misdirected energies are here dissipated and dissolved, often general intelligence is not affected. We do not know what this means. Were frontal lobotomies to be performed on youngsters, would not their ability to learn be limited? It is understandable that the intelligence of an adult might be unaffected by such a surgical procedure. Using the metaphor of Raymond Cattell, it is possible that the fluid learning capacities of a thirty-five-year-old person have already diminished, and what remains are crystallized patterns of intelligent behavior, not as much subject to the debilitating aspect of lobotomization (21).

(2) Here we find the source of intellectual potential *g* that the executor puts into action, the locus of those silent areas of the brain that have grown up in tandem. This concept of growth in tandem is the key to the evolutionary picture of man. It is now clear that inhibitions of libidinal drives and the empowering of symbolically controlled thought in action are centered in the frontal areas. Also clear, there has to be something for which instinct is interdicted and for which power and discipline are exercised.

Here the more relational functions located in the temporal-parietal areas of the brain enter the picture. Intelligence became increasingly selective as the hominids left the forests for the plains fifteen to ten million years ago. The key to an integrative intelligence of adaptive and selective power was the linkage of thought and memory to action, action from which instinct was progressively excluded (22).

By that time (ten million years ago), it is probable that the basic form of what was to be the hominid brain had been achieved. The long-distance receptors, which were now of essential selective import, increasingly were integrated into that basic tandem that existed between the frontal and midbrain areas (23). Language, too, was caught up in this selective packaging of human intelligence. The fact that Jakobson and Luria have found the link in the language use, not merely in the frontal, but also in the parietal areas and have assigned these areas roles that fitted the general morphophysiological structure, behavior patterns that had been established earlier, merely strengthens our model of brain/intelligence (24.)

(3) Language, like our eyes, ears, and fingers, is an organ of human thought and expression. It is the quintessential human specialization. Other animals also have eyes and ears, they touch, smell, and taste. They may communicate vocally. We may hear their cries, their songs; we may know of their fears. Beyond that, the connection is tenuous. Through language, the brain, in the complex interaction of its functions, powers its potential for learning, understanding, and behaving.

The infant born profoundly deaf, cut off from language, that essential flow of human intercourse, is denied one vital entrance into the circle of humanity. Intelligence is at once inhibited in its normal growth, often crippled. Withal, with great effort and perseverance, a profoundly deaf person may be able to acquire the cognitive and behavioral skills that are necessary to survive in our human environment. This is a testimony to language's crucial character in the evolution of human intelligence. It is testimony also that below surface appearance, even beyond natural linguistic reception and expression, as in the profoundly deaf, human intelligence exists and functions.

# Ice Age Reconstruction

The second great revolution in the shaping of anthropoid intelligence came with the creation of *Homo sapiens sapiens,* Cro-Magnon man. The first had been the development of that unique "Ur-hominid" during and after the Oligocene thirty million years ago. The second came in an almost fleeting moment of evolutionary time—the dissolution of a structural biological relationship between brain and body that had existed during those approximately thirty million years. The human brain was freed from its last instinctual encumbrances.

As the honeybee represents instinct articulated into complexity, into art, so, too, with *Homo,* the symmetrical beauty of the Acheulean hand axe, the reverence and philanthropy of the Neanderthal funeral ceremony, are hints that a new behavioral plane has been reached. The heavy Romanesque bony architecture of skull, face, and limbs is suddenly reduced, replaced by a soaring Gothic lightness that transfigures the ancient heritage. The brow ridges that constricted the frontal areas disappear, as does the depression to the rear of the ridges. Instead, a thin high palisade soars beyond the eyes, rounding to a high vault above the ears. Between the ears, the skull is perceptibly widened, then tucked in over the spinal chord, no longer extending bun-like in the rear (25).

In this paedomorphic (scientists call it gracilization) reconstruction, tendencies that are implicit in the hominid tradition become reality. What we see as morphological fact is transformed into intellectual and behavioral reality (26). Enormous abilities derived from the genetic expression and intensification of the neurological richness and connective networking of the brain explode into creative tangibility. We do not see the executive frontal areas nor the contemplative rear as separate functional realities. Functional intelligence impacts as a unitary activity. From this oneness, however, does come the plethora of expressive symbolic cultural possibilities that before were only latent in this physical reality.

Evolutionists have argued whether or not a critical measure of relative intelligence lies in endocranial capacity as it has evolved through geological time or whether there are in addition structural changes that could modify the purely endocranial capacity claims for intelligence of such scholars as Harry Jerison (27). This contrasting view concerning *Homo* is extended by Ralph Holloway of Columbia University (28). A primary example of the difficulty associated with the question is Neanderthal man.

Certainly in terms of endocranial capacity, the Neanderthals were well above the current *Homo sapiens* average. The Neanderthals were *sapiens,* but their cranial structure was more archaic. The skull was long, low and protruding in the rear. In addition, the Neanderthals had massive brow ridges, large chinless jaws, generally a heavy architecture that seemingly limited them intellectually and culturally (29).

The culture of the Neanderthals remained static for over 50,000 years. It is difficult to determine or even to hypothesize how long certain primitive cultures that were discovered in the eighteenth and nineteenth centuries would have remained static had they not been affected by the migrations and the consequent absorption of genes from the north in the last several thousand years as well as the external cultural stimulation of recent historical times.

Unquestionably, the lightening of the frontal brow ridges, the heavy musculature, and the bony jaws were crucial for the freeing and subsequent expansion of the temporal-parietal areas of the brain. Also important was the delay into early adulthood of the closing of the sutures in the skull over the fontanelle of infants.

This was a new brain, thus a new intelligence, vast in its physical size and neurological components. Now there were from 8,000 to 10,000 million nerve cells, any one of which could be connected to as many as twenty-five other nerve cells. Here, again, it was not merely the size of the brain, but the character of the interconnections in an organ controlled by many genes (at least fifty) with their concomitant multitude of components and intercombinations (30).

Bear in mind what was involved in this sudden brain growth. Foremost was the increased capacity of the cortex, that one eighth of an inch of gray mantle, convoluted and folded in on itself in a series of hills (gyri) and vales (sulci). Of equal importance, absolutely no outside selective pressure stimulated this adventitious genetic aberration. The growth was the result merely, as noted in Chapter IV, of the working out of a long tradition of variation, probably selectively accelerated by the internal human social dynamics created by harsh glacial climatic conditions during the Riss glaciation 250,000 to 150,000 years ago (31).

The outcomes of this reconstruction in the physical possibilities for the expression of human intelligence were twofold. The first arose from the parallel dynamics of brain expansion, in reality from the accelerated migration of people, which was facilitated in part by their greater capacity to venture forth from traditional homeland areas. This is the source of the enormous variability in our species. For, in a relatively rapid span of time, perhaps not more than 100,000 years, all the evolving and transitional forms of *Homo* were catapulted over the *sapiens* Rubicon (32).

Now if we consider the enormous number of interconnections in one complex brain—cortical as well as subcortical components, the virtually subatomic kinds of molecular variations that can occur genetically in altering structures from generation to generation, individual to individual, not to mention the significant variability even within one nuclear family—then only can human variability be accounted for from the obvious structural or molecular standpoint (33). To be added to the equation, consider the variability produced by the migrations that occurred at the end of the Pleistocene period.

To think of *Homo* as merely one type of creature is a mistake. Not only were there at least five ancient racial types, but within these races, as for example the Neanderthal and Cro-Magnon Caucasoids, there were innumerable transitional expressions of each of these ancient racial prototypes (34). Some of these were highly retrogressive, others rapidly evolving, all interbred to some extent.

The many Australid forms found even as late as the nineteenth century testify to this variability in intelligence and then in culture and personality. Thus we have the many Negrito types from India, Malaysia, to the Philippines; the various Papuan and Melanesian forms on New Guinea, Andaman Islands paedomorphic forms; the classic Australian aborigine; the now extinct Tasmanian Melanesian type; the Ainu of Japan (possibly a Caucasoid hybrid) and of course the innumerable hybrid forms that mask other possibly extinct Australid varieties from Arabia to the Hawaiian Islands and possibly on to some of the New World Amero-Indians (35).

The final impact of this great evolutionary cataclysm was the Cro-Magnon *Homo sapiens sapiens* brain and its intelligence. Here, in what can only be likened to a stroke of the evolutionary sword shearing through the continuity of traditional animal behavior, the human symbolic behavior system was formed. Before, there had existed, at the very least, a tenuous memory, a thin thread of connectivity with the instinctual past.

Arriving on the primeval Miocene plains so many millions of years before, as did protoman, the distances, the vistas, the sounds echoing through far canyons, all signaled the need to transform a brain dealing with local and immediate jungle messages and dangers, to a world that often would lie beyond our perceptual horizons. Over these subsequent millions of years, the cortical advance in brain size and restructuring now emphasized this substitution of traditional instinctual sureties for the chancy probabilities of intellectual reckoning.

Simply, the result of this evolutionary reconstruction was that the cortical mantle now so dominated traditional physiological and behavioral functioning, not to mention the obvious cultural and intellectual patterns of the hominids, that the ancient instinctive biological controls were enclosed and recentered in those ancient reptilian regulatory life functions. As Jean Jacques Rousseau insightfully observed, this "corticalization" of behavior was basic and unique to humans, still a violation of the laws of living: "L'homme qui médite, est un animal dépravé" (36).

# A Macro-evolutionary Upheaval

It is through this corticalization of thought that humans enter the world of symbolic meaning. What is probably important here is what is revealed in the spontaneous activities of Cro-Magnon and the European-West Asian cultures that stretched from Spain to the Ural Mountains 25,000 years ago. This was a development that fulfilled what had been in the earlier forms of humans an incipient and uncompleted process.

We can make this evaluative assumption on the basis of the rich cultural remains from our Pleistocene past. We can also learn from the remnant primitive peoples that have been studied for the last 150 years. This will be developed more clearly and in detail in the next and final volume of this series. Let it be said here that the dynamic quality of Cro-Magnon culture (25,000 years), which far outspans the stagnant embeddedness of the Neanderthals' 50,000 years, for which we have evidence in their artifacts, reveals the completion of one of the great biological lines (intelligence) equal in importance to the creation of the teleost fish, the birds, even the dinosaurian reptiles.

Looking backward, note the adaptive breakthrough heralded by the appearance of these forms. Without recourse to metaphyscial threnodies, without departing from a strict selectionist analysis of the dynamics that subsequently occurred, we can merely record the occurrence of a classical working out, through mutations, adaptations, and natural selection, of events that allowed the most adaptively competent creatures to contend for and eventually occupy and dominate the particular ecologies which the initial mutational breakthrough made possible.

*Homo's* domination came in the widening arc of power conferred on him by intelligence. We have seen from the Pliocene on, seven million years ago, the increasingly violent outcome of the process of hominid encephalization, in which ever more closely related competitor forms were destroyed. Yet, when all this is understood in the light of traditional fang-and-claw selectivist dynamics, *Homo erectus* and transitional *Homo sapiens* still lived within the biological interstices given to them by nature. Man struggled and survived, but did not obliterate the basic fabric of natural existence (37).

For *Homo sapiens sapiens,* this was impossible. The massive explosion of brain cells, the enormous eruption of predatory psychic energies had revealed man's destructive as well as fulfilling cultural/cognitive potentialities. The question from the standpoint of the evolution of intelligence in *Homo* is whether the consequent uncontrollable ocean of human members and their polluting material techniques can be dammed before they efface what made our advance possible in the first place.

## Culmination

There is a final evolutionary mystery to the expansion in human brain size and content. How far could it have gone? How far has it gone? We know that the size of the female pelvis is not something upon which nature would have made a late and precipitous decision. Like the creation of the language areas of the brain, the structure of the hominid pharynx, there was here a morphological structure whose basic possibilities for expansion were established far back in hominid evolution, probably concomitant with the final turn toward a full bipedal stance (38). This took place perhaps as early as thirteen to ten million years ago, probably when *Homo* departed from the australopithecines, the latter never achieving full bipedal gait.

Obviously the female pelvis that could handle a future two-to-three foot creature had to be different from one that could handle a future five-footer. The modern female *sapiens* had a greatly expanded pelvis and a much more flexible birth canal. However, on the basis of modern experience, even under conditions of advanced medical technology and special eurythmic techniques that neutralize the sedentary modern life of westernized females, birth is still a terribly difficult process. Even as the large-headed baby sometimes succumbs to the difficulties of the delivery process (the male usually being larger in size), those who survive the birth trauma are essentially foetuses, whose heads and brains will expand dramatically in size in the weeks immediately following birth.

Thus the impression is inevitable that the Cro-Magnon females who produced those extremely large-skulled babies were truly heroic. They were the inheritors of that paedomorphic evolutionary fluke that created a superfoetus destined for an enormously powerful cognitive maturity. The selective sieve presumably was never more intensely activated, and from several adaptive perspectives, then it was in those millennia (250,000 B.P.) preceding the final *Homo sapiens sapiens* breakout.

Let us jump ahead many thousands of years. One hundred years ago, at the end of several centuries of truly cataclysmic cultural advances, psychologists began to look back and wonder. What about those unique creative geniuses who had, in effect, mined from the fertile possibilities of human thought such prodigious creative works? How were they different from the average run? To see the toll that had been taken of these eighteenth- and nineteenth-century personages led individuals such as Cesare Lombroso, Havelock Ellis, and others to reject the linking of genius with that smooth Gaussian curve that Francis Galton had proposed for intelligence (39). Was there a causal relationship between these afflicted lives, their frequent mental aberrations, and their creative intellectual insights? The link between genius and madness was thereby proposed.

This hypothesis soon was shot down by the research of Lewis Terman and his associates at Stanford University. They showed in a long and carefully documented longitudinal study that those with I.Q.s above 140 led successful and productive social lives, high in mental health and longevity. Admittedly, the number of creative geniuses in any population was small statistically, here practically impossible to garner, given the population sources that Terman had available to him (40).

Increasingly, however, evidence has gathered from another source. In those individuals who seem to score or achieve at the heights of intellectual achievement, we are witnessing a complex of characteristics that argues that even beyond the size of the female pelvis, nature may have indeed established other limitations, now on the neurological complexity of the hominid brain, given its ancient Oligocene and Miocene prototype.

What is the meaning, for example, of that puzzling high percentage of dyslexic and learning-disabled males of extremely high abilities and achievements, the latter attained despite handicaps in that so-called integrational area of intellectual functioning (Chapter XII)? Also, why are we finding a disproportionate number of left-handed, myopic, auto-immune, asthma/allergy-prone, male youngsters who also have extremely high ability in mathematics? (41) Mathematics, as we have also noted in the previous chapters, may tap the intellectual potential of certain individuals of high intelligence earlier in maturity than in other disciplines and enterprises (42).

Certainly, the most interesting aspect of the variability in human intelligence is the enigma of extremely high intelligence. Here, where we would assume the ultimate consequences of the corticalization of the hominid brain to have taken place, is where we can tally its products. In every area of human involvement, from military charisma and tactical innovations to the moral claims of the religious mystic, from the arts of the painter or the chess player to those of the football quarterback or philosopher, we witness the transformation of ancient, perhaps primeval human activities and sentiments into symbolic expressions of creativity, endless permutations and recreations for our delight and amazement.

Thus it was that the recreative, transformational qualities of the high intellective *sapiens* brain had created in one stroke a whole new realm of biophysical discourse. The symbolic system of culture and its relation to the adaptive destiny of humans in nature became in one moment the essentially cosmic issue, at least for us. Where will it lead us? How should we direct it?

# Chapter XIV

---

# THE ELEMENTS OF VARIABLE INTELLIGENCE

## Judging Intelligence

Intelligence in the abstract is a concept that arises from human experience, from what we see, hear, and feel. Our attempts to understand its nature and workings in the world of living things can go deeply into abstraction, both biochemical and mathematical. Ultimately, these analyses must square, in a predictive manner, with what goes on in society. The need to study this ephemeral set of behaviors that we call intelligence arises from the realities of civilizational life. Eventually, the beacon must be reversed to illuminate the day-to-day dynamics of culture.

True, we define intelligence by our values. Clearly, we cherish literacy, complexity, abstractive power, and dynamic change. These all add up to Western civilization and the values that have been cherished and preserved in its name for the past 5,000 years.

Skeptics point to the incompetence of Westerners faced with the challenges of the natural world, challenges that supposedly primitive peoples can surmount. The stories are often piquant. A car breaks down in the desert outback of Australia. In a matter of a few days, the stranded passengers have perished of heat and thirst. A few yards beyond the car exist sources of water that the Australian aborigine discovers and utilizes as a matter of course. Even the Kung Bushman existing in the desert fastness of Africa's Kalahari can enjoy the leisure of a 4.5-day weekend. In this seemingly barren wasteland, these diminutive people can feed themselves for a week after only 2.5 days of foraging and hunting (1).

Finally, the sturdy adventurous Vikings populated Greenland as early as 986 A.D. Within a few decades, about 250 farms were in operation, over a dozen churches serving these New World invaders. They still retained their ties with the motherland, however. Perhaps it was a sudden climatic change or political or other difficulties that made support and resupply from Norway more difficult; by the 1300s, the Eskimos from the northern part of Greenland were attacking the settlements with some success. The Europeans just could not adapt to the requirements of a subsistence economy requiring such different behavioral skills. By 1500 A.D., the last of the original Norse settlements were overrun (2).

Today, observe the sorry state of these marginally adapted, yet heretofore indigenous successful peoples. The desert has been conquered by well-equipped safari convoys. The invaders of the northern tier bring the appurtenances of civilization to overcome the cold, easily mustering the survival requirements of the extreme northern latitudes. They also bring alcohol and the rest of the civilizational panoply. The Eskimo, the Kung Bushman, the Australian aborigine cannot resist. It is the westerners who ultimately win their Pyrrhic victory over the environment and over the well-adapted primitive specialists.

Here it is again, that ancient test of intelligence, broadly adapted to face the new and the changing, the ability to abstract knowledge from one set of experiences and use it under quite varying conditions. Who is more intelligent, the specialists suited for but a narrow economic and ecological setting or those who bring the environment of our planet earth to its moon and beyond?

*The question*

## The Significance of High Intelligence

Thus, how we judge intelligence must derive from its quintessential fulfillment. Whatever we mean by high intelligence, whether creativity or wisdom, becomes the standard by which we inquire into its specialized nature and components.

*Good God! Who's sorting?*

Let us explore the meaning of the foregoing analysis in the light of reshaping the concept of intelligence as primarily a quantitative evaluator for aptitude, educational and vocational sorting. All judgments in these areas are necessary in a highly complex society. These ways of looking at intelligence are still somewhat crass and insensitive to those obvious qualitative nuances that intelligent people display.

This chapter was described as dealing with the elements of variable intelligence. What follows is an attempt to explain what modern scientific research, including the almost eighty years of psychometric testing, has illuminated in the study of the puzzling thing that is variable human intelligence. The dilemma, of course, is that we do not differ only in that area called abstract relational ability or general intelligence. There is more to our varying intelligence. As the psychometricians have long emphasized, even success in scholastic matters, no less the highly complex requirements of modern civilized life, demands much more of us.

The outcome of this study of the existing research will be a model of varying intelligence that will be somewhat different from other models. Its character has already been hinted at in the three previous chapters. There is more to it, however. A brief suggestion of the additional elements will suffice, in this case the subcortical factors. The final volume in this series of books will contain an analysis of these interactions of the final hominid brain with the product structures of its earlier phases, then progress to the distinction that has to be made in our own day between highly intelligent individuals and populations and less intelligent, perhaps more specialized, forms of human intelligence. In these distinctions lie signposts that might indicate the path to human civilization or barbarism.

This is the crux. While gaining much understanding from pathologies of thought or language, even from such mental aberrations as exist in autistic individuals and idiots savants, as well as from those with the lowest intelligence, morons, microcephalic idiots, and the like, it is intelligence in its highest manifestations that constitutes the evolutionary mark. In observing what is possible, in all its multifarious creative cultural productivity, we can appreciate the truly qualitative variety of social forms that humans must create before intelligence can express itself. Then, our task is to educate, to keep this expression flourishing.

## Potential

Both RT and EEG experiments have heightened our awareness that the *g* of general intelligence, a capacity for thought that often flows into all activities, must exist as a basic component of high intelligence. The work of Luria and Jakobson in language aphasia, which shows a distinction between the frontal and temporal-parietal areas in language expression, as well as the work on prefrontal lobotomies which show that often general intelligence is unaffected, tell us more (3).

This is that there is a power element. Someday perhaps it will be quantified by electrical or neurological symbolism. We have, at least at present, abandoned the idea that brain size alone is the key to evaluating relative intelligence. Carleton Coon, in his final book, still argued, in the tradition of Tilly Edinger and Harry Jerison, that brain weight related to stature was crucial (4). Certainly we cannot rule out a purely neurological equation that may clarify this puzzle.

If indeed the temporal-parietal areas are the center and source of those quiet alpha waves that evoke the electrical potential that indicates high intelligence, then there has to be a molecular substrate that further substantiates those dynamic bits of deductive evidence. Beyond the temporal-parietal regions, the frontal lobes of the cortex are joined in intimate duality of function. They cannot be separated. While it is highly probable that there is a polygenic interaction that apparently can create variability between the frontal and the rear parts of the brain, the evidence still seems to allow for a somewhat independent variability. Still, we must tentatively assert that the basic neurology of power and intellectual potential has to be shared in any analysis of relative intelligence.

The great and powerful creative intelligence manifested by Cro-Magnon, accompanied as it was by a skull of extremely large endocranial capacity, argues here for the significance of a purely quantitative neurological packaging of intelligence when compared to contemporary less developed humans with smaller brains. If perhaps the brain of higher intelligence can be distilled into a smaller size and weight of brain matter, then this will still require internal change such as the kinds of complex and rich dendritic connections, middle meningeal artery blood/oxygen flow (5).

In this sense, we will find that the capacity for highly abstract, complex knowledge and behavior has to have behind it a brain with a great mass of neurological matter, a great V-8 of an engine with power and potential far beyond momentary requirements. RT speeds, information clarity in EEG graphs both seem to argue for quickness and ease in communication of perceptual/intellectual messages. Compare a V-8 Cadillac coasting smoothly along the road at 70 mph with a huffing and puffing four-cylinder Chevette, a car much more likely to suffer from an engine breakdown under tension and exertion.

## Power: The "P" Factor

And the seven years of plenteousness,
that was in the land of Egypt, were ended.
And the seven years of dearth began to come,
according as Joseph had said: and the dearth was in all
lands; but in all the land of Egypt there was bread.

Genesis 41, King James Version

The frontal areas certainly show more personality than the seemingly silent areas of the cognitive brain. Both Kurt Goldstein and Ward Halstead saw those frontal areas as the key to the distinctly human qualitative dimension of intelligence. Goldstein contrasted the possibility for abstract thought with the concrete attitude, a long step back in human thinking, often, tragically, being revealed only after frontal area pathologies or excisions. Halstead saw the ego shining through in the functioning of those frontal areas for the general expression of human intelligence (6).

Certainly the frontal areas of the cortex, working in tandem with the silent temporal-parietal areas, represent the "P" factor, disciplining the self for the future, inhibiting spontaneous, nay, almost animalian instinctual demands. Here the energies to action, not intellectual receptivity alone, but enaction, emerge from the person, to carve out a stake in the outside world. Here intelligence manifests its powerful creative realization.

Is the "P" factor the drive train of intelligence, what the psychometricians call the executive force? Does it give direction and long-term focus to the silent powers represented by g, the total neuronic mass? Certainly in the last stages of human evolution, that quality of mind represented by the frontal lobes, the need for self-discipline, planning for the future was evident. It was a realization that beyond the brief spring and summer of plenitude would come the long fall and winter, great snows that might impede hunting and severely deplete the accumulated stores. Indeed, the frontal areas of the brain inform us that for every seven years of nature's largesse, seven years of want may follow.

Far from the tropical abundance of the south, the northern hominids had to extend their intellectual vistas beyond the mental horizons of today and tomorrow. Inevitably, these drives, the persistent efforts of humans, derived from the activity of certain areas of the brain; these areas also personify our intelligence.

As yet, we can only ponder this distinction between "front" and "rear" dimensions of human intelligence. It is enough now to note that we all know humans who have enormous drives to succeed, to accomplish a task, yet who lack important intellective qualities, whether moral or purely conceptual. By contrast are others, apparently highly able, who do not express that quality of mind and body to exert the effort, the energies that might allow them to explore their own possibly portentous abilities.

In fact, the least successful five per cent of Lewis Terman's 1,500 "geniuses" admitted that their lack of success could be attributed to a lack of personal persistent effort to achieve. Their family histories revealed a tradition of insta-

*the simple fact of the amt of brain growth that takes place in the "paedomorph" postpartum surely argues for the impact of nurture*

*The Elements of Variable Intelligence* **199**

bility, lack of success (7). Why? The reason might thus not lie in the environment. It is quite possible that these deficiencies in what would seem to be personality factors are truly intellectual (genetic) elements, crucial to the total functioning of intelligence. Thus, it is also quite probable that these elements—the elements that comprise the "P" factor—are highly heritable.

In all likelihood, nature has found it useful, selectively, to distinguish in the functioning of intelligence between the potential for absorbing information and meaning, integrating it in terms of understanding causes, then triggering this clarity of information-gathering into overt behavior, always with the idea of attaining adaptive success.

## Memory

Here enters central integrative memory, "C", which David Stenhouse places as an independent evolutionary factor; it stands alongside the "P" factor (power), and "A" factor (abstraction) (8). One could here argue that memory is critical for the understanding of relationships. Relationships arise from the logical contiguity of events, events that involve different categories of things. As we know, the best way to prime memory is, though one may seem to be storing seemingly innumerable unrelated facts, to order these facts and events into a structure of causes and effects. Memory without the power to abstract and relate becomes mental chaos. Abstraction, the power to think without facts, becomes empty [Kant]. The two elements, abstraction and memory, must be inextricably related in that primary neurological mass that distinguishes between the V-8 400-horsepower superspecial and the four-cylinder 100-horsepower economy model brain.

## Putting It All Together

But wait. Remember the idiot savant who often masters towering memory chunks? Dates, facts, names roll forth from a seemingly endless tape recorder of recall. Yet, with this memory, the idiot savant knows and understands nil. Where in the brain does this memory power reside? Why does it not invoke abstract intelligence?

The drive train and gears are to the V-8 and the four-cylinder motor what the "P" factor is to abstraction and memory. It is in the "P" factor that the potential for knowledge and intelligence is given qualitative shape, perhaps even personality, by the unique genetic construction and division of labor contributed by our forebrain. What we know about this area of the brain has developed because of the pathologies that have been traced either through wounds or strokes, or through the tragedies of mental illness. The research lessons learned from such work are invaluable. They can be practically applied in the world of normal to highly intelligent humans living in a complex dynamic society where there are reflections in behavior that allow us to perceive and recognize the same life distinctions pointed to in the more esoteric research.

In conclusion, a hypothesis: the gross quantity of intelligence, the amplitude, plenitude, potential for the highest levels of abstract thought and action are shared by the cortex in general. It seems, though, that the midbrain and rear areas have taken over responsibility for this mass action, or $g$, the capacity for achieving complex forms of thought. The forebrain is the generator of action, seemingly by invoking those anti-instinctual patterns of restraint, discipline, planning, that characterize the evolution of intelligent adapting creatures. Here, in an animal that has lost its instinctual assurance, the power of intelligent behavior is enacted for the use of whatever potential for thought ("A" factor—temporal-parietal areas) is available to the person. The frontal and rear areas obviously are integrated into one intelligence, yet still differentiated in function and probably in genetic individuality.

## Connections

If language were one with intelligence, we would expect to see with every handicap or defect in the language area a concomitant deterioration in functional intelligence. This is certainly not the case. Individuals with language problems, of speech and understanding, of reading and writing, still show a capacity for learning and acting. This is not to say that an aphasiac or dyslexic has an easy job, for language is an integral aspect of practically all learning and social requirements.

In fact, the congenitally and/or profoundly deaf child is the person most deprived of easy access to language skills. The teacher of deaf children must first present to the child either through signed exact English (SEE) or total communication, even the oral method, some sense of language structure. (The close proximity of the auditory and the language areas in the left hemisphere in all likelihood brought both capacities forward in a tandem of evolutionary development.)

Language's unique position in the structure of intelligence is the clue that lends credence to the reality both in structure and day-to-day function of what I have called the integrational system. Observe similarly talented children, the myriad learning styles whether through one or the other perceptual modalities—hearing, seeing, sometimes even touch, and in various combinations. When we consider the odd brain structure relationships between the hemispheres, or of left- and right-handedness, the verbal left as contrasted with the supposedly holistic spatial/visual right hemisphere, we are privy to an insight into the genetic peculiarities of our individual wiring. Here exists a nexus of connections that does not necessarily reflect on the capacity for intellectual achievement in one or another area of human endeavor.

NB

The concept of the integrational system, based as it is on some clear factual behavioral distinctions, has interesting consequences for the traditional debate as to whether intelligence is unitary or multiple, the so-called factors issue. It is clear, for one, that the concept is useful in those testing situations where performance tests are used, such as the Wechsler battery, to contrast with the verbal portion. In addition, the distinctions are sought in aptitude I.Q. tests such as developed by ETS of Princeton, New Jersey, for college-board tests (verbal/math). Intelligence is reflected in our langauge skills. However, language cannot be thought of, empirically, as synonymous with intelligence.

We are brought once again to the factors, those various skills that we perceive as being important aspects of intelligent behavior—numerical, spatial, verbal, musical, perceptual/motor, mechanical. We are unique qualitatively in the organization of our nervous system and the various parts and levels of brain function seemingly regulated by general intelligence. So, here are the human talents, the praeternatural skills of great minds, the mathematical facility of LaGrange or the violinistic skills of Heifetz, the coloristic vision of Renoir. They are not merely high intelligence put to diverse uses. Or are they? (9)

Even in language, philosophers attempting to penetrate the covering garb of words, to express their relational ideas, must have different kinds of intelligence from, say, a Shelley, for whom words themselves were imagistic vehicles for expressing meaning. These meanings mask totally different ranges of verbal imagery, both emotional and intellectual tonalities, as contrasted with those of a John Dewey or an Alfred North Whitehead.

Neurologists such as Wilder Penfield have long probed the brain to find specific losses in function, verbal and others, in discrete parts of the cortex (10). This fits the conception that any particular part of the brain where function has been localized is somewhat differently organized in each individual. We know this to be true, in part from the alterations in brain function that occur in young children when parts of their brain are excised or wounded by actual physical injury or stroke, without permanently affecting their total capacity for intelligent behavior (11).

The integrational function points to the general processing of information among the parts, some, the later accretions of the cortex, others, the more primeval mammalian limbic system areas. More intermediate are those ancient human language areas. Considering the enormous changes in the size and structure of the brain in just the last 500,000 years, the fact of the large number of genes and combinations regulating the growth and organization of the brain, it is likely that much of our biological/intellectual individuality has its origin not merely in cortical potential and power, but in its genetically adventitious connective wiring. The possibilities here for variability are immense, so many factors/elements being involved. We are looking at talents and skills that are unique to our individual intelligence. They parallel a broadening and deepening of that personality variability noted above with reference to the frontal areas of the brain.

When we consider all this, the dimension of "connectivity" becomes as great an element in distinguishing individual intellectual potential as $g$ (temporal-parietal) contrasts with the work of the frontal lobes. "Integrational" individuality is probably a quieter qualitative dimension. It subtly shapes and turns us in the various social, cultural, and vocational directions as we interact with the historically given social conditions of life and the dynamics of the present.

## Our Mammalian Inheritance

More than once, writers have emphasized the role of the so-called limbic areas of the brain in regulating the ancient intellective functions traceable to our 150-million-year-old mammalian heritage (12). All those powerful emotional valences of sexuality, dominance, territoriality, protection of the young, mating behaviors, as well as the finely-honed instinctual repertoires of adaptations, could not have been merely extinguished in the growth and dominance of the human cortex.

The big question lies with this new relationship between the cortex and the complicated wiring of its parts, now including the lower brain. Indeed, it is in these ancient biological connections that we find much of the focus of sociobiological research. Yes, we smile. So do animals. We defend children and mates, as well as kin. We seek dominance in our male-structured social groups. Really though, does this kind of analysis penetrate to the core of human social behavior?

The limbic system (hypothalamus, amygdala, hippocampus, pituitary, testosterone) still sends its enzymes and hormones coursing through our nervous system. As with language and the perceptual receptors, however, everything is now hooked up and modified by the overwhelming mass of brain cells in the cortex. In this sense, we can argue that the limbic system, the older and formerly dominant force in the mammalian brain, is still an element of human intelligence (13). Because all the old categories of mammalian behavior, whether sex, war, or dominance, are modified by cortical processing, we must alternately admit of the coloration of "purely" cognitive behavior by a biological variability that is practically as old as the dinosaurs.

Dogs, cats, chimpanzees have personalities also. Natural selection requires of advanced, mobile, wandering mammals an individuality of response even within an interbreeding population. This allows for variable reactions even given similar stimuli within the given natural ecology. So, too, with humans, the ranges of variability in the flow of testosterone, pituitary function, the character and functions of those crucial subcortical brain elements of the limbic system, all add a baseline of difference to the dynamics and tone of our personalities (14). They delineate the drives, whether we are introspective, extroverted, excitable, or phlegmatic (15).

We cannot as yet discretely analyze those variable contributions of our entire system of biological reactions that have had such an enormous impact on our intellectual interactions with the world about us. So we pile up variable system upon variable system. The result is a truly qualititative differentiation of individuality for which specialized measures of intelligence can never fully account—what truly counts: predicting who will be able to do what. I.Q.s will not resolve such mysteries, nor will RT and EEG experiments. They will tell us many important things. We will get the full picture only when we are able to make predictions that will fully color in that qualititative individual dimension of the highly intelligent—what is actually accomplished as distinct from what is broadly possible.

A few examples may illustrate the ineffable qualitative individuality of high intelligence (to this writer, the only truly interesting mystery about the subject). Florence became a stable ethnic community sometime after 500 A.D. From that point on, few external genetic elements intruded into the small populations that lived in that part of Tuscany.

That the Florentines had a creative genius as well as practical economic and political acumen is well established. The artists were myriad. Dante, Machiavelli, and Galileo testify also to the broad scope of this intelligence. Chalk up a plus for the concept of *g* and general intelligence. The Florentines were second in this respect only to the Athenians of the fifth century B.C.

In the year 1500, two supreme geniuses left Florence for Rome under the protection and sponsorship of one of their own Florentines, Pope Julius II and in 1513, Leo X. Michelangelo Buonarroti, Raphael Sanzio (born in nearby Urbino), and later Leonardo da Vinci all resided for a short period in the Vatican to work for these far-seeing Medici popes.

Leonardo we know to be a man of truly vast interests and capabilities, so much so that he neglected, relatively, his supreme painting skills. He was also learning-disabled in that he wrote in mirror-writing fashion (language/integrational system). Michelangelo, a person of much greater drive and direction, was gifted in almost every area of the visual arts—architecture (he remodeled St. Peter's), sculpture, and painting. He was also a poet. In painting certainly, the scope of his conception often ran ahead of his actual physical skills at realization. At the least, certain art historians see his paintings infused with the design sensibilities of a sculptor. Raphael Sanzio, perhaps the most specialized of the three, perfected his art during his short life, realizing his talents more narrowly, but perhaps more deeply than the other two.

Consider the genius of each of the three. Genetically they derived from a relatively narrow gene pool. Who could say where quantitative I.Q. dominance would fall? Would it be at all meaningful on that level of creative production to argue that one or another of these artists had greater neurological mass and thus a greater "intelligence"?

Leonardo, even with minor writing learning difficulties, had a mind that could penetrate the essence of a number of different intellectual domains, from engineering, architecture, anatomy, and astronomy, to such mundane areas as planning tricky floats for the Sforza family street festivals in Milan or entertainments for the Pope in Rome. He experimented with new painting techniques ("The Last Supper") and in general dabbled insightfully into everything that crossed his inquisitive mind.

Yet, Leonardo admittedly was never the doer, the realizer of aims and goals that was Michelangelo. In viewing the narrow realm of painting skills, we are haunted by a protean conceptual as well as a technical envisionment. It all seemed to come so easily as compared with Michelangelo, but the productivity and realization flagged.

Raphael concentrated and specialized. In his own particular domain of painting he probably went deepest in realizing his potentialities, at the least, considering the premature snuffing out of his life. Each of these three had very different personalities, two of whom, Leonardo, and possibly Michelangelo, were homosexuals, Leonardo flagrantly so. Michelangelo despised Leonardo, the latter disdained Buonarroti.

What explains such vastly diverse creative propensities in individuals who might even have been distantly related genetically? Let us say that each had roughly similar neuronic mass, perhaps even similar "P" factor frontal drives. All three had realized their drives, fulfilled by such clear-cut public acceptance as was reflected in their papal invitation to Rome. Still, the lower levels of brain organization—energy and function—had to contribute important elements of personal and thus intellectual differentiation.

*And nothing from Florence?*

# Reprise

A summary follows of the elements, morphological, evolutionary, and functional, that contribute to the character of variable intelligence in individuals.

1. The new cortex. (A) The temporal-parietal areas of the brain seem to be the locus of the potential for abstract, relational thought, the quantity of $g$ that is the product of I.Q., EEG, and RT experiments. The fact that the comprehension aspects of language function are also located in this area (Wernicke's) seems to confirm this assumption. Also, that the great expansion of the endocranial capacity in *Homo sapiens sapiens* as compared with transitional human forms seems to be in the breadth of the skull between the ears as well as being the high point in the soaring vault of the skull lends additional support (16). The key physiological and neurological confirmation will come from considerations of neuronic mass, richness of dendritic connectivity, and a large arterial

supply of oxygenated blood to bathe this electrical mass, to help maintain the quickness and clarity of communication.

(B) The frontal areas appear to be the locus of the so-called "P" factor, the executor of cortical function. Here we note the inhibition of instinctual responses, the planning, perseverance, the postponement element. Yet, with the repressing of lower mammalian instinct comes the power element, in which are located the syntactic/grammatical elements of language, the energy to act, using the knowledge available from the midbrain areas. That intelligence as I.Q. seems often unimpaired after prefrontal lobotomies gives evidence for the separability of the frontal areas in the equation of intelligence. Yet the two domains, even if under the developmental guidance of identifiable genetic systems, must ultimately work together for there to be functional social intelligence.

2. The integrational system. The source of the mystery lies first in the fact that human verbal communication is overwhelmingly a cortical phenomenon. We do know, however, from innumerable examples, that losses of the various language functions, both auditory and visual (reading) language systems, do not necessarily impede the development of functional intelligence. Thus, the various language defects reveal a quasi-independence in both the genetics and physiology of language and their special morphological areas: Broca's and Wernicke's.

From this and other learning variations in humans, the conclusion is drawn that the organization and transmission of information is participated in by a wide variety of so-called allocortical elements that constitute the interface between the apparently older mammalian structures and behaviors and the new or isocortical realm of the gray mantle (17). The hippocampus in man, for example, is four times the size that we would expect in a creature the size of man, were the ancient primate versions merely blown up to equal the change in stature between then and now (18).

The integrational system begins to illuminate the more qualitative character of personality, intellectual modalities, valences of mind, that are hinted at in the separability of function in the cortex itself, between the frontal and temporal-parietal areas. Language skills become the most obvious, even epochal beacon in this differentiation of individual intelligence.

3. The limbic system. We are mammals and have drives as mammals, heritage of 150 million years of separation from our reptilian ancestors. But our mammalian drives do not trigger automatic behaviors. They are qualitatively modified by the brain accretions accumulated during the hominids' twenty-or-more-million-year separation from the other hominoids.

There is evidence that the affect that the limbic system pours into realms 1 and 2 is channeled upward through the right hemisphere, frontal areas of the cortex (19). This surmise further supports our experience with the frontal lobes as the power element, even the aggressor, the locus of violent behavior, sometimes requiring prefrontal lobotomies. The integration of the variable dynamics, sexual, emotional, phlegmatic, that comprise the human personality, and the language character of each intelligence, by the higher levels of cognitive function finally defines the "kind" of intelligence that each person has.

# PART 3

*HISTORICAL CONSEQUENCES*

# Chapter XV

---

# MALE AND FEMALE INTELLIGENCE: THE EVIDENCE FOR VARIABILITY

## Male Fragility

The purpose in this chapter is not to go into that vast realm of male/female social, psychological, and biological differences per se. Rather it will be a discussion of some of those differences, and of course similarities, that will be used as a base in our analysis of the nature of male/female intellectual differences. For, one of the most important sources of human intellectual variability lies in gender. To the extent that the larger panorama of male/female differences is involved in questions of intelligence, we must discuss this issue. Here, primarily we will present the facts, the evolutionary origins, and speculate as to the meaning of gender difference in the human species.

Let us first note that despite the great increase in medical knowledge that ordinarily would radically reduce such differences, the differences between the genders in basic health and psychic normality still remain. Males are still the more susceptible gender. Nature has endowed males with a fragile constitution. It is even more evident today because the birth process, life-threatening even in the recent past, has been made so much safer by medical science. In this day of medical supervision, in a developed nation such as the United States, females still outlive males by seven years on the average (1).

Males suffer from a variety of sex-linked genetic defects—hyperactivity, susceptibility to schizophrenia, alcoholism, and muscular dystrophy are now acknowledged. (J. Q. Wilson and R. Herrnstein have recently and massively documented the genetic linkage in violent crime committed overwhelmingly by males and throughout the world.) (2) Males also are preeminently victims of mental illness and retardation, and no compensating social conditions can be adduced to reduce the discrepancy between males and females in the domain of overall pathological behavior (3). Later we will discuss male death rates, increased by such common male maladies as heart disease (now traceable to a complex of male-dominating hormonal and blood imbalances), which lie at the core of drives and energies that seem to define the male gender.

It is probably not an accident that these vast differences in health and behavior permeate the entire complex of male and female differences from the moment of conception. As we will note below, the end results are now fascinating if yet puzzling divergences in mental function. These intellectual differences, while interesting as statistics for historical analysis, always, let us hope, examined with a minimum of ideological interpretation, are still barely understood from the standpoint of modern biological and psychological research. Yet they are there, the crowning evolutionary consequences, with all the paradoxical and tragic accretions, of our struggle into biological dominance.

The fragility of the male is underlined in the fact that between 120 and 140 males are conceived to every 100 females. By the time of birth, this numerical advantage has been cut to about 106 to 100, more males having been spontaneously aborted in the interval. Even at birth, the male is at risk. Thirty percent more males die at birth and during the first month of life. Among those who survive, males suffer about thirty-three percent more birth defects than females. The ratio of males to females equalizes by adulthood (4). However, subsequently, males begin to suffer adult debilitations, after which the ratio of mature females over males continues to rise.

*[handwritten marginnote: where do the statistics come from? what period?]*

This male fragility shows up poignantly in the retirement "utopias" in the South. The heavy predominance of widowed women is incontestable. What is contested is the tensional balancing of the functions that we see in the evolutionary consequences for humans in the special role of the male. It is truly only a latter-day expression of this balancing of debits and credits that seems to give the male a domination in the external manifestations of behavior within the human community. Part of the roaming predatory character of the hominid male has emerged in the supersapient brain as an almost feverish proclivity for intellectual and creative symbolic expression.

As we will note in the succeeding chapter, nature did not necessarily intend that the adaptive expression of intelligence in the human species should lodge itself in the male so as to create a Plato, Michelangelo, Immanuel Kant, Abraham Lincoln, Confucius, or Mahatma Gandhi. Here again, one must look at the complex, genetically-rooted adaptations that create a certain kind of high intelligence while still producing a body that falls victim to itself, not to speak of the violence males overwhelmingly inflict upon themselves in addition to females and children.

Outside the realm of foetal debilitation, males have a genetic susceptibility to things like color blindness, a four- or five-to-one ratio over females in cases of autism (subjective withdrawal from reality), aphasia (spoken language impairment), dyslexia (reading disability), and stuttering (5).

## Strength and Intellect

Researchers have focused upon the existence of certain basic male and female hormonal differences that almost from the time of conception determine different ontogenetic journeys. Using the hormonal evidence, sociologist Steven Goldberg concludes that the hormones begin to cause the differentiation of the male into an aggressive dominating individual and the female into a submissive, accommodating, receptive individual: ". . . in embryonic life, gonadal secretion dimorphically regulates the differentiation of structure in the brain, specifically the hypothalamus, that in turn will regulate the sex regulating functioning of the pituitary. In all probability gonadal secretion at this time also dimorphically regulates other structures of the brain that will eventually be involved in the regulation of certain aspects of sexually dimorphic behavior namely those aspects that are phyletically widely distributed (like motherly attentiveness to the newborn or coital posture and movement)" (6).

Goldberg cites the research of John Money that early pointed to the impact of testosterone production in the male in stimulating a wide variety of survival behaviors—some aggressive and combative—and the concomitant production of estrogen in shaping the females to their socially, contextually, and basically submissive behavior (7). *The Inevitability of Patriarchy,* the title of Goldberg's controversial book, argues that just as the social arrangements of most mammal species, within as well as between the genders, are patterned through genetically-controlled instinctual behavior, so too with humans, if not so deterministically biological. Rather, those hormonal differences that give rise to a good measure of di- *we see* morphic body structure—men are much larger, heavier, more *wide* muscular; women are physically weaker, smaller, yet more *variations* resilient—also patterned social roles of males and females (8).

Men will be the patriarchs and leaders, in the hunt, in combat, the women waving handkerchiefs and flags, seeing the males off in heroic drill, prepared to welcome them back to hearth and home in victory. Exemplified here is the traditional German relegation of women to the "three Ks": *Kirche, Kinder, Küchen* (church, children, cooking). As we will point out in the next chapter, as certain basic relationships of life are altered, the past is not necessarily prologue to the future.

Yet is it not true that the basic strength of the male argues for at least a measure of prepatterning in social behavior that will carry with it certain derivative outcomes in various life activities? One cannot help recalling a few years back the challenge by former tennis champion Bobby Riggs, then in his midfifties, to play the then-reigning women's tennis champion, Billie Jean King, she in her late twenties. She later won, but what did it mean?

Is it merely that power and energy derived from male testosterone hormonal flow and its attendant sex-linked physiological and morphological functions and structures that eventually flow into a differently organized brain and nervous system? Traditionally, it has been axiomatic that the males are the scholars, the creative dissidents who rip down the walls of orthodoxy. Women poets and novelists have long been accepted. Women have been noted for their verbal felicity since the beginning of historic time. They have demonstrated this felicity increasingly as they began to gain equal access to educational institutions. Interestingly, the College Board, which supervises the SAT tests given to millions of college-bound high school seniors, reports that for at least twenty years, men have scored higher on the math section (499-452). Surprisingly, men have also scored higher on the verbal section (437-425). SATs are usually seen as equivalent to I.Q. tests (9).

When it comes to hard intellectual work, whether it be mathematical, or—even when involving language—philosophical, females, as notable as they are in quality, are still few in number. Equal access to the chessboard has not turned chess into a coed contest for mastery. Throughout the world, the paucity of ranking women international masters still remains flagrant. Here it is not physical strength, though endurance and speed are factors, but the ability to look ahead for only a few moves, to choose among the thousands of combinations presented to each player in turn.

What is revealing about the mental demands of chess is that the rules can be easily learned, indeed, the basic openings, midgame tactics, and endgame strategies all are possible for children thirteen- or fourteen-years old. Some of our most talented chess masters have been barely postadolescents. Indeed, many researchers view chess as a game purely of the mind.

In 1984, a chess championship took place in Moscow between a thirty-four-year-old champion Karpov against his twenty-one-year-old challenger, Kasparov. In the beginning Karpov seemed destined to clean the slate of the impetuous Kasparov. As draw followed draw, the energies of the relatively young champion waned and he fell into time-induced errors. He was only saved by a bureaucratic intervention that stopped the match but fooled no one. Eventually, Kasparov was to become the undisputed world chess champion.

Here, as in sports or war, where pure relational intelligence is demanded, where the mind requires deep, yet narrow, thinking, the mental energies of youth remain supreme. Mathematics, also a relatively pure test of intelligence, is thought to require the same levels of concentration and narrow but deep mental analysis. It is here, as in chess, that the male-female dimorphic intellectual differences throw into relief the entire issue of intellectual variability.

## Genetic Sex-Linkages

*asserted*

Before we analyze these differences in mathematical ability and their consequences for understanding male and female intellectuality, it is perhaps useful to discuss the general issue of intelligence variability between the genders. Obviously the transition in our evaluation of these differences, from the perspective of modern cultural history, to systematic modes of analysis, came with the tradition of quantification, the I.Q. test, and its various analogues.

It was Lewis Terman, in the early 1920s, in his search for the meaning of "genius," who first brought together American boys and girls in a systematic testing experiment. Of the 1,500 children chosen who scored above 140 I.Q. (who first were recommended by their teachers and others), more boys (813) were chosen than girls (592). Interestingly, in the anecdotal evaluation, teachers for the most part evaluated the girls, on the basis of classroom performance, to be higher than they eventually scored (857 boys, 671 girls) (10).

In general, over the past sixty years of testing—and somewhat confirmed by what has occurred in social life in general—it has been noted that in both extremely high and extremely low I.Q., males predominate. Just as in the health area, or in the areas of physical, emotional, and mental energy, men seem to be the extremists, in the range of mental ability, women hold the center. The statistics have been increasingly accepted that in tested mental abilities for general intelligence—as distinct from purely verbal skill, for example—the variance for women is quite a bit smaller than for men.

Whereas the standard deviation for the genders inclusive is about fifteen points (that is, the population divides itself away from the mean in certain percentages—at every fifteen point separation from the mean, 100 I.Q., i.e., 115, 130, 145, and 85, 70, 55, we find naturally diminishing percentile groupings), the standard deviation difference between male and female is approximately thirteen to sixteen percent. Such a difference in standard deviation away from the mean of fifteen percent is only between one and two points, for example, 14.3 to 15.7 female to male (11).

Robert G. Lehrke, who has done the major research to bring together a large amount of statistical material, points out that this thirteen to sixteen percent increase in variance in male over female intelligence has its consequence at the tails of the I.Q. curve. It makes males overwhelmingly predominant, either geniuses at 160 I.Q. or morons at 40 I.Q. Thus the female I.Q. curve would show a higher midpoint of 100 I.Q., but would fall away rapidly from this point. It would cluster around the average. The male curve would be lower at 100 I.Q. and fall away more gradually toward the extremes (tails) (12).

Lehrke and others now argue that this phenomenon can be explained on one level through sex linkages in the genes. Simply, males have only one X chromosome, females have two. Because the Y chromosome that accompanies the X (XY) is a very small, information-deprived chromosome, carrying all sexual information, the characteristics that reside in the male X show themselves much more openly than the buffered XX of the females (13).

Thus, we find, for example among retardates, families in which all the males are retarded. Compare this phenomenon in the genetics of retardation in the light of the female sex-linkage, where retardation often is hidden as a recessive. In this situation, we will find many families in which there are several normal sisters along with a female retardate. With the males, retardation is fortunately a plague. Their genes are less likely to be transmitted as recessives (14).

The Hendricksons, Allan and Elaine, working in Hans Eysenck's laboratory at the University of London, have developed their EEG experiments into a measure of intelligence graphed into a model called "average evoked potential" (AEP). Elaine Hendrickson, who has specialized in the experimental application of their theoretical model of intelligence, using the auditory/electrical pulse inputs, has found that AEP results mirror I.Q. and aptitude testing but in a theoretical mathematical model, without the masking twenty-to-thirty-percent environmental portion of the I.Q. variance between individuals (15).

Her AEP evidence shows that at 130 I.Q., the proportion of males to females is 2:1, at 145 5.5:1, at 160 18:1. Naturally, as many have noted, as one descends in absolute numbers to the tails of the curve, purely statistical predictions come apart. There seem to be larger numbers at both tails of the graph than there should be. As has been noted, I.Q. distribution may follow a Pearsonian (Karl Pearson) more than the purely geometrical Gaussian curve (16).

What is the meaning of these statistics? Elaine Hendrickson, bringing together her own research with the testing literature on the subject as of 1982, concludes: "If the variance score standard deviations were to be regarded as some indication of the true differences in the distribution of intelligence in the two sexes, it would probably not be necessary to look for further reasons to explain the relative lack of women in higher occupational levels" (17).

The issue of explanation of at least the genetical mechanics of these differences is interesting in that it does phase us into the mathematical domain and thus a relatively secular explanation of such male and female differences. Therefore, on a purely mathematical/genetic analysis, perfectly acceptable scientifically, it is difficult to challenge this model of sex-linkage with the more inchoate political/social arguments of environmentalists.

The predictability of sex-linkage in intellectual differences has been established by a series of wide-ranging interfamilial correlations reported earlier in 1966 by N. Bayley, with regard to retarded children (based on the work of M. C. Outhit in 1933) (18). Using both the mathematical relationships evoked by sex-linkage and checking them against individual I.Q., correlations in I.Q. were: mother-daughter, 0.63, father-daughter, 0.66, mother-son, 0.61, father-son, 0.49, and brother-sister, 0.55. Recall that the son receives only the Y chromosome from the father and a combination of the two X chromosomes from the mother (no X chromosome from the father), whereas in the case of the daughter, the father contributes his X chromosome (19).

What is also partially confirming, retarded mothers are twice as likely to contribute retardation to their children as retarded fathers. Note, here too, the mother will contribute her X chromosome to all her children, whereas the father contributes his X chromosome only to his daughters to be buffered by the X chromosome of the mother (20).

*[handwritten margin notes: retardation is not a unitary "state" it is the symptom usually of other causes; isomorphic; give as the facts, not your conclusions]*

# Mathematical Ability

Shifting to the other end of the variable intelligence spectrum, we note the rarity of distinguished female mathematicians. Not only have few been identified, but all along the spectrum of educational talents, mathematically precocious males have far outstripped females. In 1972, the "Johns Hopkins Study of Mathematically Precocious Youth" began a wide-ranging search for talented junior high school students aged twelve to fourteen (21). During this time, while gifted females seemed to score equally as high as the gifted males in the verbal areas, they lagged behind in their math scores, both before and after specialized tutoring for environmental enhancement of their skills—and these were the best young female mathematicians. The result at the highest range of SATs, those usually given to the seventeen- and eighteen-year-old high school seniors (remember, these were twelve- to fourteen-year-old junior high school students) was a thirteen-to-one ratio of males over females at SATs of 700 and above (22). Such a raw score equated with Elaine Hendrickson's AEP predictions would indicate an I.Q. of about 155 with a 13:1 male:female ratio (23).

Much of the discussion of mathematical talent, perhaps similar to that of chess, has centered around the speculation that there may be one or several genes for visual/spatial skills, (sex-linked in that males have them predominantly). Let us note parenthetically that no one has yet argued that the one high female math talent as compared with the thirteen other males would have a mathematical intelligence in any way inferior to or different from her male confreres. It would only indicate that such talent would occur more rarely among females (24).

The spatial/visual skill is thought to refer, among other things, to an ability to work on map relationships, to visualize mechanical objects so as to be able to replace parts by visualizing their relationships with others in the field of conceptualization. It is thought that such a skill is associated with mathematical ability, and thus explains the genetics of sex-linked transmission.

Interestingly, Ellis Batton Page has argued cogently that the spatial/visual gene, if indeed there is a spatial/visual gene, acts as a recessive in sex-linkage, the daughter gaining an average of her mother's X chromosomes and her father's only X chromosome (25). She would thus correlate more closely genetically with her father even if the I.Q. score seems indifferent to this relationship. However, if the spatial/visual gene is recessive, it will be masked since the daughter has two X chromosomes. Thus the spatial/visual gene would have to be in both X chromosomes to be expressed. Her brother having one X chromosome, the recessive spatial/visual gene will more likely express itself in the male than in the female (26).

Naturally, there is a real question about the relationship between spatial/visual skills as determined by I.Q. and aptitude tests, those abilities in plan reading, mechanical aptitudes, architecture, engineering, topographical and map skills. While it is plausible to argue that math and even chess require a comparable visual-relational quality of the mind, common sense suggests that while we see the equations or the chess board positions, we think about the conceptual relationships. Except in geometry or mechanical work with actual objects, to a certain extent in chess movements, we do not really relate parts to the whole in a spatial sense. We use the visual manifold—our mind/eyes—to seek out intellectual relationships. Perhaps the visual "picture" triggers our conceptions of relations and possibilities in the same way that writing down ideas creates something tangible out of inchoateness, which can then be worked into a set of logical verbal relationships. It is not space—left/right, up/down—that is manipulated, however, but something far more complex.

Thus, to say that math intelligence is related to a single gene or a complex of genes for spatial/visual perception seems to envelop into one category (mathematics) too many dissimilar skills and abilities. Jane Armstrong of the Educational Commission of the States in Denver, Colorado, after testing 1,800 high school seniors, confirmed the superiority of boys in math after neutralizing the number of courses each sex took in math. "The kinds of problems in which boys excelled were those which tested reasoning, not computational or spatial visualization abilities" (27).

Also, how, for example, do we understand the enormous employability of females in fine small motor visual/manipulating skills, from dressmaking and typing to putting together tiny computer elements? That women do these tasks far more satisfactorily than men argues for skills that really must exist in the visual/motor areas. However, these factors must be joined with personality and emotional elements. It may be that women are more placid, patient, and careful, whereas males, often more impatient and irritable, can be corralled less easily into this kind of careful, precise, mostly monotonous labor.

Another enigmatic and fascinating bit of research into mathematical talent is emanating from the Harvard Medical School under the aegis of the late Norman Geschwind. Starting with a concern for the fact that learning disabilities and other associated problems occur predominantly among males, as discussed above, Geschwind found that these defects seemed to be related to abnormal levels of testosterone production from early in the intrauterine environment into the early postnatal period. Following Steven Goldberg's and John Money's work in the same area, yet drawing his own sociopolitical conclusions, Geschwind also postulated testosterone as the focal point for a whole series of hormonal controls that eventually reached up to a restructuring of brain cells. Here, Geschwind saw implicated the bilateral organization of the brain and in certain cases abnormally overly developed right hemisphere regions, the "planum temporale," those regions normally associated with artistic ability and thus with the kinds of holistic perceptions discussed with respect to the supposed spatial/visual gene complex (28).

The trail did not end there. Learning disabilities, left-handedness (right hemisphere dominance), thyroiditis, colitis, migraine, seemed to be implicated as part of a gestalt of factors that flowed out of aberrations in the testosterone complex. The result of the overproduction of testosterone or sensitivity to its production was the creation of a disharmony in the entire auto-immune system out of which seemed to develop those behavioral malfunctions as dyslexia, autism, allergic reactions, asthma.

> Excess testosterone, or increased sensitivity to the hormone, in addition to slowing the development of the left half

of the brain, leads to a higher incidence of auto-immunity in left handers by suppressing the development of the thymus gland in the fetus. Because the thymus gland is the site of maturation of the T-lymphocytes, which have among their functions the distinction of self from non-self, the result might be the inappropriate attack of the immune system on the body . . . . The major histocompatibility complex, MHC, is a large genetic region that controls many of the activities of the immune cells . . . . MHC also affects the weight of the testes, the serum level of testosterone, the sensitivity of organs to testosterone, and other parameters relating to the hormone and its actions. Conceivably, genes that influence the development of auto-immunity may be linked, or identical to, genes specifying high testosterone production or sensitivity which in turn influences the development of the brain, leading to anomalous dominance (29).

We have attempted in this section to trace: (1) the nature of male and female intellectual differences, (2) the mystery of the I.Q. profiles, (3) the nature of the sex-linkage that we find in the genetics of intelligence, and (4) the relationship of the fact of overwhelming math and chess superiority in males and its meaning for sex hormonal linkage. Geschwind took the final step, extending his own research into the male auto-immune deficiencies, to the research of Julian Stanley and Camille Benbow at Johns Hopkins with mathematically precocious youngsters (30).

A survey of the top precocities in math, those scoring above 700 (out of 800), or the top student in 10,000 seventh graders, showed some amazing correlations. Twenty percent of the mathematically precocious were left-handed, twice the general average. Sixty percent had auto-immune disorders, allergies, or asthma, five times the general average. Oddly, seventy percent of the high scorers were near-sighted—a confirmation of the folkloric "brainy" types—another characteristic that Geschwind believes has correlations with intelligence.

As the researchers moved down the list from the high precocities to score the less elevated, they found that the incidence of the above disabilities fell toward the general population average. At the top range of math scores, along with the greatest incidence of defects of the above sort, the males were preeminent, as was discussed above, a 13:1 ratio of superiority at 700 SAT-M (seventh graders) or higher (31). What does this all mean?

# Significance

The theory of intelligence that was outlined in Part 2 of this book is supported by the above research findings. In fact, this theory of intelligence was built partially from the scientific evidence set forth above concerning male and female difference. As will be pointed out in Chapter XVII, we may take with a certain grain of salt the racial divisions about which we speak today, because of the many millennia of mixture that have occurred before and since the close of the Ice Ages. Yet there is still no strong argument to disregard the reality of the sex differences that we have inherited as mainline mammals.

Here is an example from a diverse field of study that throws some light on the meaning of high mathematical ability and high and low intelligence in general. In the field of reading, a test is given to all kindergartners and first graders, either late in the year for the former, or early in the fall for the latter. It is called the *Reading Readiness Test,* usually the Metropolitan, long published by Harcourt Brace. It has a number of parts: object identification, picture meaning, letter identification, shape and figure perception, and numbers knowledge. Interestingly, of all the parts, the number knowledge test is the most predictive of future reading success (32).

The reason is that, as has been discussed previously, the purely language dimension of reading—letter and word identification, sound/sight discrimination, visual acuity—is not critical for the fluent reader. One can read the words of a story without understanding the meaning. This is why I have placed language ability in humans in that middle area called the integrational system.

The integrational system encompasses a complex of skills that translates our primeval humanity in its linguistic and cultural sense, as well as the purely physical skills of our mammalian/anthropoid heritage, into symbolic, cognitively disciplined skills. The key here is to understand that the integrational system seems to filter the lower brain "juices" and proclivities of these varied ancient hominid brain structures, to transmit and organize them for the cerebral cortex. In highly intelligent people, the cortically imposed disciplines extend themselves downward to rule the limbic system. We can become celibate; we can even choose to commit suicide.

Thus the key to understanding the processes of reading and writing and why so many talented and intelligent humans have language difficulties, is related to the manner in which cortex, visual system, language areas are "wired" together and interconnecting. These systems are products of differing phylogenetic periods in the history of the hominids. Thus we find children who read orally easily but do not understand what they are mouthing. They are "word callers." Reading is really the uncovering of meaning in the graphemes on the page. Thus, a child who has good number skills already is revealing high cognitive capacities more purely relational than can be discovered through a test of visual/object discrimination or letter/sound knowledge usually deemed important in these reading readiness tests.

Mathematics is a purer measure of intelligence. In some manner, the meaning/relation between ideas reveals itself more simply and quickly in mathematical manipulation than in language. This is not to say that intelligence does not show itself through other and various symbolic structures of language as in the work of novelists, poets, historians, philoso-

social environment, seem willing to recognize.

We cannot know for sure what this vast span of evolutionary time did to the model and possibilities inherent in our male and female bodies and our minds. The bits of knowledge that we have related in the preceding chapter are symbolic spotlights that illuminate aspects of the evolutionary mystery. Together they form a picture, perhaps a mosaic that organizes itself into something meaningful. Again we have to balance the contemporary image with our ignorance and pro- *absolutely* ceed carefully in what we say, more importantly in what we attempt to put into practice concerning these human differences and similarities.

It is naturally speculation to dip into those inchoate eons in order to sort out the unique evolutionary factors that led to that subsequently unique biosocial relationship, the human family and its larger social forms. Yet we are here today, as a basis for such comparisons, and we do know something about the forces of adaptation and selection that have shaped a variety of living forms into their recent embodiment.

The humans were early bipeds. It was one of those accidents of evolutionary history that endowed us with the pre-adaptive structures that could subsequently be acted upon by natural selection. If we were on the scene along with most of the Miocene ape generalists (fifteen to ten million years ago), we must have been a bit more erect in our posture—with the hip girdle structure that made such a stance possible—and thus a bit more variable in our living habits both on the ground and in the trees (1). That we had a bit more intelligence per body size is probable; some creatures had to have more intelligence than others in a variable, hotly competitive environment. As it happened, we did, and we have suffered the consequences.

Other facts enter our equation. Our vocal apparatus was more primitive in its unspecialized relationship of a large open area at the rear of the pharynx, a relatively mobile thick tongue to articulate a wider variety of calls than the specialized structures that produced the sounds of the other jungle primates. The several language areas in our cortex argue also for an earlier and adventitious relationship between a vocal system that allowed for murmurs, whispers, quiet conversation, and cortical control of this vocal propensity. Thus language could have been an ancient, even if a primitively simple preadaptation of a peculiar primate at the end of the Oligocene/beginning of the Miocene some twenty-five to twenty million years ago.

We share with some of our monkey and great ape relatives several interesting traits. From the monkeys came the male penis, also the model of the delicate paedomorphic physiognomy that reminds us of a tiny homunculus (2). Orangutans and humans share with the extinct ramapithecine apes thickly-enameled teeth, considered a primitive relic like the human pharynx, but hinting here of an ancient relationship beyond which the other great apes have grown (3).

The gibbon, of all the great apes, is, like us, an extremist. High up, at the very edge of the forest, the gibbon leaps and flies as no monkey can, a virtuoso in its aerial isolation. The gibbon has another interesting social trait, shared with no other of its great ape relatives. It is most likely an ancient peculiarity, one which the gibbon has utilized to no special adaptive advantage that we can see. Perhaps in that specialized environment, it is adaptive to mate for life. The female gibbon has lost her oestrus, and thus she is sexually receptive all the time. Gibbons are monogamous, telling us an ancient truth about our own male/female relationships (4). Anthropologists believe that, as with the gibbon, a causal relationship may exist between the continued sexual receptivity of the female and the male's familial devotion (5). Here, an infant born relatively helpless, whose brain would grow slowly after birth, who needed the continuous nourishment of the female, would in addition require intensive male devotion, commitment, the "P" factor guaranteeing a bonding to the familial future. Surely, here we have a complex of factors coming together that would gradually reenforce the adaptive niche into which our ancient forebears had fallen. It is to this era that Helen Fischer refers when she speaks of the "sex contract" (6). It is in this primary human division of labor that our male/female dichotomy began. The male and female were each shaped in this dyadic relationship by natural selection.

*our M/F dichotomy began in sexual reproduction*

Interestingly, at an early stage in our evolutionary journey, the two hominoids that have lost oestrus and are at least partially monogamous are both inheritors of extreme ecologies: the one whirling among the treetops, the supreme brachiator of the forest, the other increasingly bipedal, trotting on terra firma. What ancient competitors forced these two lines of creature to inherit their particular worlds of survival, then to specialize and succeed in their respective ecologies?

These are the first facts as to why men and women are different, physically and intellectually. Here lies that primeval differentiation between mother/wife and supporter/ protector. Here the male not only needed the persistence and attachment of familial life, but also a measure of defensive energies, a willingness to stand at the "door of his castle" and, without special physical armaments, exert that power of person that would discourage predatory raids.

*why the pair and not the group?*

## Male Plains Aggression

The forested Garden of Eden where the original model of the hominids was shaped was a limiting defensive environment. It was in the evolving plains ecology that the next stage of male/female dimorphism took on its special characteristics. By the mid-Miocene, twelve to ten million years ago, large plains areas had opened up in Africa. The mountains were being pushed up all over the world, the Himalayas in Asia, the Andes in South America, the Rockies in North America (7). A new world of possibilities had developed, and humans stepped out onto the plains and ran.

The vistas were longer, the food sparser, the environment more threatening, but the competition was further away. It was a golden opportunity for a featherless biped with an alert intelligence and few rigidly-defined instinctual patterns. Other anthropoids had made the transition (ramapithecines, australopithecines), but the progenitors of *Homo* were smaller, and thus had to use their evasive intelligence to secure their adaptive flanks while they moved over long distances foraging and scavenging. Gradually, they grew to fit the great vistas of plains life. From this time, we must assume the gradual and modern dimorphic differentiation began between male and female *Homo*. The males had to be bigger, able to travel long distances. As intelligence grew piggy-back-like (allomorphically), strength and intelligence provided psychic powers of ferocious defense and greater abilities to manage a complex environment while *Homo* yet remained physically unspecialized.

For the infant, the die was cast that a large brain accompanied increasing helplessness. This large skull was now accommodated to the female birth tract, her basic pelvic limitations. Thus evolved the specialization of the female to secure the hearth and nurture her young who came along regularly, unlike the chimpanzee female, the latter gradually coming into homeostasis with her environment and producing young every three or four years (8). Male ferocity was gradually expressed outwardly in more aggressive ways as the human family and then the band broke loose from a fixed home in the forested glade and wandered the plains. This ferocity and aggression linked with raw intelligence, with no instinctive censors, created conditions for war and genocide even many millions of years ago. Here, too, began a further element of separation and specialization between male and female.

The war between the anthropoids, hominids, and apes was a war over life space. In the case of *Homo,* higher intelligence was propagated orthoselectively in that the mutations for higher brain-to-body ratios were immediately transformed into positive adaptive patterns and consequently blessed by natural selection to the detriment of both apes and other hominids. This line of evolutionary progress did not stop with the decimation in the Pliocene (seven to two million years ago) of the remnant ape lines, nor the early Pleistocene destruction of the australopithecines (9). It continued into historical times, indeed even into our own era, *Homo sapiens* warring against *Homo sapiens.*

We must realize that our set of genetic structures and their phenotypic exemplifications do not work as independent units. Not only in the linkages between genes, but during fertilization, there are crossover patterns on the chromosomes that create wholly new relationships. In the process of natural selection, when one surface dimension, structure, or behavior, such as the brain and intelligence, becomes highly charged positively, it pulls along with it an entire complex of functions that have worked their way into genetic association. Thus, with high intelligence in the male and female for certain associated behaviors—war, food and shelter procurement in the male; stable child-bearing and -rearing, good health and tensile strength in the female—all the associated hormonal and bodily structures were likewise selected out to strengthen and buffer that facet now strongly under natural selection.

Though the male is characterized in certain obvious ways—he is highly charged sexually or he is viciously aggressive in behavior—we should not be led to believe that these were the aspects of his biological nature that necessarily were being selected. The continued growth of the brain, as seen in the fossil evidence, as well as the logic of contemporary reality, argues that a complex of associated behaviors, reasonably selective in valence, came charging along genetically, then to a large extent phenotypically, with this growth of intelligence.

There is little that can be said against the selectivity of intelligence. Today, as yesterday, it is almost infinitely useful. Of course, our animal aggressivity and genocidal war-like behavior, like our never-ending sexual drives, are often counterproductive. We have to rein them in in order to live with our neighbors. The logic, then, is that the pulsating limbic system energies had to be funneled into the forebrain, giving rise to the power and persistence reflected in the "P" factor; this was the price that males have had to pay in the linkage of thought to practical realization, the rear to the forward parts of our brain. Sexual and aggressive energies originating in the dynamo of the lower mammalian brain, in that they have been channeled into the cortex, became nature's way of saving intelligence from being an ignominious adaptive failure in man.

Who knows whether, in fact, in many varieties of hominids, the existence of high intelligence, without the drives and the passions, could have led to their extinction? The tragedy of the Boskopoids and their failed contemporary Capoid descendants must give us pause (10). The huge crania, i.e., high intelligence, of the Boskopoids did not save them from either the West African Negro migrations nor the earlier North African invasion by the broad-faced Moullian Caucasoids, which moved them into southern Africa. The late coming of the eighteenth-century Dutch to South Africa, along with the Bantu, who already had pushed them out of their old northern homelands to the Kalahari, constituted the final coup de grace to the Bushman (11).

While it is evident that at all stages in humanity's several-million-year residence on the plains, the latter environment acted to develop and even reshape the original forested prototype of the hominids, it is probable that the third and final phase of hominid evolution completed it. In review, these periods were: (1) Oligocence/Miocene forest life, thirty-five to fifteen million years ago, (2) late Miocene/Pliocene plains

NB

existence, fifteen to two million years ago, (3) final, Pleistocene, two million to twenty-five thousand years ago, migrations during the Ice Ages.

# Final Remodeling

The evolution of *Homo sapiens* into *Homo sapiens sapiens,* which presumably took place in the last several hundred thousand years of the Ice Ages, resulted in a new paedomorphic being, as radically different from its erectine heritage as was the original paedomorphic Ur-hominid of the early Miocene forests from its evolving anthropoid cousins. This new human expanded the model of a baby-like intelligence to its ultimate possibilities, delicately-molded skull encasing a vastly ballooning brain. The female bearer of this foetal burden must have been subject to enormous selection beyond the changes discussed above, e.g., structural changes in the pelvic area. The very fact of this remodeling of an already delicately-boned hominid female into the highly sculptured, sexually attractive creature that she is, argues for a powerful element of natural and social selection (12).

Under conditions of enormous climatic stress, an extremely delicate infant had to be nursed through the harsh freezes, often while the group wandered over unknown terrain. The family band had to be welded with powerful affectionate attractions. Indeed, in the art of Cro-Magnons, with its surfeit of sexual symbolism, it is evident that part of the nature of this super*sapiens* was poured forth in an intensification of centripetal feeling toward women, children, including the cultural band (13). Even in the *sapiens* Neanderthals, there is evidence of a measure of evolving sympathy and philanthropy (14). Yet centripetal relatedness and love could not negate the possibilities for outward aggression. The paradox

*[handwritten margin note: Why? Isn't that what we learn from early ritual: that group bonding techniques varied widely?]*

of human existence was even then sharply in evidence.

Clearly, the requirements for successful motherhood during those trying eons were strongly enough in place that the final dimorphic remodeling of the human species did succeed in taking hold. This remodeling did not take place in the course of one or two generations as in our own unbelievably volatile historical moment, but slowly and probably violently in the course of several tens of thousands of generations, enough to put a powerful stamp on the reality of what is a man and what is a woman.

## Our Evolutionary Heritage of Divergence

Let us be clear about what nature is selecting in the evolutionary process. It is not male strength or large size per se. Neither is it *Homo sapiens sapiens'* incessant sexual appetites. Nor is it the males' powerfully aggressive, predatory, and determined attitudes toward humans and nature, their intentions to subjugate and control. These are elements that in a sense ride along on *Homo's* growth in brain size, intelligence. That the above attributes remain core behavioral characteristics merely means that they themselves are not counter-adaptive.

Conceivably, other human attributes that intelligence could have dragged along by their feet might also have been adaptive for that complex thing called human individuality and sociality. As with femaleness, however—the care of the young, the stability and attractiveness that magnetized the male to do her will—it still was intelligence that dominated the adaptive complex.

The female is likewise the bearer and disseminator of high intelligence, equal to the male. Analyses of intelligence tests argue that males and females cooperate in passing down that complex of abilities by which we know high or low intelligence. Even in the area of seemingly sex-linked attributes such as the spatial/visual skills, map reading, mechanical abilities, design capabilities, flying, driving, perhaps even chess or mathematics the female is a powerful transmitter even where the characteristic spatial/visual skills surface as a supposedly male attribute (15).

Ellis Batton Page, as noted earlier, has cited a range of studies in which it is shown that in phenotypic qualities males resemble mothers more than fathers, who, while contributing the small but crucial Y chromosome for gender, possess the mother's X chromosome, fully six percent of the chromosomal material. Since the spatial/visual gene is recessive, the male would have to have his mother's spatial/visual gene in the X chromosome in order to express this spatial/visual talent. Its lack of prominence in females argues that, having the two X chromosomes, one from the father, one from the mother, the female would need both to exhibit it in the phenotype. It is clear then that the female is the carrier of this attribute that seems to appear in such dominance in the male (16).

In general, the enormous energies, creativity, violence, and sexuality that we note in the European-western Asian Caucasoids argue for a line of creatures that was selected for a complex of phenotypic behaviors in which brain size and intelligence were primary. Intelligence brings with it these other behaviors as testimony to the demands and pressures of the variable, challenging climates and ecologies of these northern regions. It is also clear that for Cro-Magnon to have evolved in this context, an enormous expansion of the dimorphism inherent in the traditional hominid model had to take place. This polarization and dependency that occurred were not merely skin deep (primary sexual differentiation); they were and are reflected in the creation of the two forms of human gender intelligence, each supported and stabilized by a wide variety of affiliated hormonal and neurological functions.

Then, how do we interpret the different profiles that men and women show in I.Q.? How do we equate these findings with both history and the evolutionary development of *Homo sapiens sapiens?* Unquestionably, the insatiable and irresistible flow of men into positions of political and intellectual preeminence is a reality. It is reflected in the Gaussian I.Q. profile which shows women occupying the midrange, men dominating at the upper and lower ranges. We now can symbolize this evidence in two ways, elaborating on what was stated in the previous chapter.

In the first, we note that the standard deviation of women from the mean is significantly smaller than that of the men. Both sexes together cluster about fifteen I.Q. point ranges above and below the average. For women, the standard of deviation is less than the male's by from twelve to sixteen percent. In such a calculation, the number of women at the extreme upper and lower ranges of intelligence is relatively small. For the female, the profile of the curve is higher at the center—many more at 100 I.Q.—and drops rather precipitously, as compared with the more rolling curve of the males.

Another way of approaching the difference in purely intellectual, abstract, or relational skills is through the theory of sex-linkage. Here, Robert Lehrke argues that because of the buffering of that second X chromosome, females more often veil these characteristics when they are recessive. They carry the genes, but do not express such characteristics in the phenotype (17).

Males, who are XY, will often exhibit such recessive traits. The males become extremists, manifesting a wider range of characteristics in their phenotypic behavior, whether good or not. Thus, men are the violent criminals, more often susceptible to mental illness, weaker in body function as well. But if high intelligence is lurking in the genotype, it will be phenotypically expressed in males more often than in females.

Nature has thus determined the females to be the center of stability, of longevity, the carrier of evolutionary propensities but not necessarily the exhibitor of them. It is the female who must carry within her body year after year a living entity who will be the fount of hope for the future of the species. Her infant must be protected for nine months. The female body accommodates and provides a vast measure of security even when the female herself may suffer life-threatening starvation or illness. Is it not reasonable to expect that a calm, sober, practical mentality would also be selective for this preeminent role, of conceiving, nourishing, bearing, and nurturing this helpless creature, the bearer of the family immortality?

The price of this new evolutionary breakthrough for females was often death in childbirth, an unusual animal development considering its ancient and ordinary naturalistic roots. The reward for those women who delivered live babies, especially delicate and big-headed males, even at the sacrifice of their lives, was genetic immortality. The price was high for surviving males also. How else can we explain the high incidence of mental disabilities along with giftedness? How else do we explain the extreme delicacy of the male as contrasted with the female?

Males suffer an enormous number of stress-related diseases, hypertension, heart disease, drug/alcohol addiction, high blood pressure, stroke, hardening of the arteries, and ulcers, which take many men at the height of their productive lives. Indications are that the same hormone that is at the root of maleness—testosterone—can cause, in the blood, the high density lipoproteins and cholesterol that lead to heart disease. In some, adrenalin is a protective agent, such as against cancer; it allows the males to seek out challenges and stresses (18). In other males, high levels of adrenalin lead to sudden death. The vulnerable males, however, may have already made their mark on the future by having families. That is all that nature requires.

Here, the carrier of the penalty, but also of the powerfully selective value, intelligence, is the male. Why? Because

*[handwritten margin note: now, today, in this society]*

natural selection has determined him for that special yet generalist role of provider for and defender of the species' survival and immortality. It is once more testimony to the price that humanity, especially the male, has had to pay for its extremely valuable selective treasure, high human intelligence. It is a Faustian bargain.

# Dyadic Difference

Yes, there is an evolutionary explanation of the historical reality of male/female differences not merely social, but intellectual. What does this signify for our revolutionary present and augur for the long-term future? Can we break with the past?

The evidence is clear to Allan and Elaine Hendrickson that the paucity of females at the upper range of the I.Q. and in the graduate schools and research institutions, which should most purely reflect high intelligence, reveals something important, but explaining the phenomenon is enormously difficult. Allan Hendrickson proposes one of the difficulties: "If there was a genuine superiority of the male brain, it should be manifested as a higher mean level of R [recognition intelligence] which in turn should show up in our conventional I.Q. test norms. As we do not find this to be the case, it leads one to suspect that an additional factor must be posited to explain the shortage of women from even those activities where there seem to be little evidence suggesting social discrimination" (19).

What is the additional factor? Women because of their biological function to bear and nourish children have a greater number of what Hendrickson calls "interrupt conditions" to contend with in their mental life. Those interrupt conditions in their nervous system and brain functions "program the woman to respond to such things as an infant's cry or a possible threat from an external source." Men, too, have to respond to such kinds of stimuli, but ". . . all that we are suggesting is that women have a much larger repertoire of events that they are biologically programmed to respond to . . . ."

> When some of these events occur, we suggest that it may be impossible to effectively "store the context." Chess problems, as an example, quickly get into the combinatorial explosion of having tens of thousands of possible moves, looking ahead only a few turns. If an interruption of sufficient magnitude occurs whilst solving a difficult chess problem, the only way one can return to the problem is to start at the beginning. . . . The task enjoyment is effectively destroyed, and the person is unlikely to persist in the activity. This, we believe, is the reason for the lack of women in the professions which require long periods of concentration. (20)

Thus, the female, being always sensitive and receptive to infant needs, would presumably be attending to the emotional needs at hand. In relation to the psychological model heretofore proposed, she has less ability for sustainable "P" factor persistence and long-range planning. In the modern world, this supposedly prevents her from the long-range concentration, fixations, demonic preoccupations characteristic of males.

This hypothesis is hard to sustain from the standpoint of evolution. The care and sustenance of children demand infinite persistence and patience. Women seem quite able to maintain their mothering for long periods and with large broods. They are not carried away, as men often are, by new enthusiasms, even adventures, that will lure them off and away from the family.

Natural selection seems to have given the female personality and mind less of the emotional and intellectual enthusiasm and waywardness that could deflect them from the task. There is an old and apt Central American axiom: when you want to interdict the revolutionary process, throw open the cinemas and show pornographic films. Somehow this dampens revolutionary ardor, and wild military aggressiveness is transferred to other male preoccupations.

The differences observed in the evolution of the hominids, indirectly it is true, but more persuasively when we add 10,000 years of historical evidence from the postglacial period, can be further understood from the following considerations. Human males are larger and stronger than human females. In every area of physical activity this has proved decisive, even in our unisex experimentations. Part of the difference in physical size and strength is a larger and more rugged cranium.

Inside this cranium, a difference in brain size can be documented of between 150 to 200 cm³ between male and female. Consider, however, the male is larger, and intelligence does relate to the ratio of body-to-brain size (21). Allan Hendrickson may argue that this is not a conclusive bit of evidence, that we have here an adventitious, nonfunctional difference in male/female brain size. Yet it is hard to believe that dimorphisms that have endured for millions of years such as size and strength do not have functional selective significance. So, too, must be meaningful this difference in the brain size between male and female that can be observed in the fossil hominids of three million years ago (and this probably is traceable further back at least an equal span of time). It adds to the overall equation when coupled with gender differences in gross physical size and breeding function.

*[handwritten margin note: but earlier you said brain size was no longer thought imp.]*

Since contemporary evidence argues that both males and females contribute equally to the intelligence of the progeny, it must be argued that the high intelligence of the female is of crucial importance to the selective viability of the family and then to the extended social group. What we have set forth above as probable is that intelligence in the female is expressed differently from the male. First, much of the violent variability is buffered and recessive, explained through sex-linkage. Second, the female hormonal balance is tightly geared to successful child-bearing and to the stability and protectiveness of her body throughout her long and sustained child-bearing years, ages fifteen to forty-five approximately. Those factors shape her intelligence to certain emotional as well as intellectual valences.

Two additional elements in which this difference in average brain size expresses itself in function probably derive in the first place from the mass of brain cells and connections that gives rise to the ultimate powers of abstract thought. This can be seen in the RT (reaction time) experiments as well as EEGs and AEP (average evoked potential) pictures, which seem to reveal purely neurological differences between individuals. The second element to which Allan Hendrickson alludes, sustainability of thought, probably reflects a different kind of "P" factor in males as compared to females. The enormous centrifugal drives and ambitions that nature built into humans in their intraspecific battles for survival—a result of channeled orthoselective mutations—argue for a focusing of vast energies, both emotional and intellectual, on the task at hand.

The sustainability and persistence of the female are thus channeled centripetally, are centered in human relations—the myriad paintings of the Madonna and infant child illustrate this—while the male "P" factor, externally and now abstractly concentrated, makes different use of that extra paedomorphically-endowed brain power. Nature did not gift *Homo sapiens sapiens* with this extra measure of intelligence to do math or philosophy. It produced it accidentally, as it were. Brain growth could be likened to a snowball increasing in size as it speeds down the mountain. So, too, the size of the human brain has grown to the limits of the female body, and the sanity of the male psyche. As long as these bizarre and improbable intellectual/emotional/physical combinations worked for the reproductive success of *Homo sapiens sapiens,* they were carried along.

That Cro-Magnon spontaneously doodled, made chronometric experiments, attempting thus to make some symbolical order of the chaos of ordinary events, shows the naturalness of humanity's mental effusions (22). The aim of natural selection was not to create culture heroes. The success in having a large and complex brain came with the integrative concatenation of mental survival strategies, not with speed or strength, or any specialized morphological endowment, rather, with the undifferentiated skill in predicting events and planning strategies to take advantage of animal, human, and natural ecological and environmental patterns.

That we have been able to produce a Socrates or a Michelangelo is a wondrous but hardly predictable outcome of these purely biological events. Along with the pluses, we have dragged along pathological and violent criminality as well as high blood pressure and learning disabilities. Nature has its way of pricing evolutionary survival.

# Conclusion

What then of the future of male/female intellectual differences? How will social evolution plus ideological commitments modify a heritage of millions of years of biological patterning? The history and evolutionary destiny of the hominids is written in the equation of increasing the average level of intelligence. It does not have to be. Humanity has developed the cultural and philosophical superego by which it can, indeed has, interdicted its biological imperatives.

The great requirement of being male or female still is centered on the procreation of increasingly adaptive progeny. For over ten million years, perhaps twice that time, it has been a positively selective thing to do. It is hard to see how we can violate this overriding message about our evolutionary heritage and still remain adaptive.

Beyond that, nature does not teach us what the potential roles of males and females in all possible social/historical contexts can and ought to be. We live in an era when the birthing process is relatively safe, where the physical requirement for earning one's daily bread does not require the brutal exertions of a Pleistocence cave dweller. Intelligence today *+ technology* can flow into a vastly expanded set of behaviors and social functions. This fact of modern civilized life is as much a reflection of our *sapiens* nature as was life in the icy caves of the late Pleistocene.

Why not let nature continue to teach us? We continue to need to survive; the intelligent men as well as women must participate and enter into the family formation process. Beyond that, it is hard to posit the ultimate potentialities of male and female, even if our knowledge is suggestive, perhaps even predictive.

Let it stand merely as a hypothesis what we have set forth in these two chapters. It may be more fully confirmed in subsequent human experience, or it may not. What we could do at great risk to the future of our progeny is to predetermine the answers and put blockages in the way of the full and free expression of individual talent, whether it be male or female.

# Chapter XVII

---

# THE IRRELEVANCE
# OF RACE

## Prologue

This chapter and the next will deal with the issue of race, an issue that excites gargantuan passions in our human but mammalian souls. Dispassionate discussion of the issue is almost under interdict. To talk about race casts one into the pit with the damned. But we must talk about it. No issue should be beyond rational thoughtful discourse. When we become brave enough to face these troublesome dilemmas, we may find openings for a whole new order of understandings. So, friend reader, let us not fear our own shadows. Let us try to be both rational and moral.

It will not be argued in this chapter that on average some groups identified as this or that race are or are not more or less intelligent than other groups, measured by whatever criteria one wishes to use. What will be shown here is that race in and of itself is an almost accidental element in the evolution of variable intelligence. It is not even of secondary biological importance. It is irrelevant, adventitious, a momentary correlation that could disappear from our consciousness tomorrow, in other words, 500 years, if we could only focus on the real issue. The issue of the "North vs. South" will be the subject of the following chapter. Therein will be presented the real evolutionary circumstances that have led to our contemporary predicament and that, still, today, represent an ongoing dynamic force in the equation of the evolution of high and low intelligence.

# I.Q.

There is no question any more that on the surface and on the average there seems to be some intellectual variability between the races. Psychometricians, those who measure intelligence, have been sustained, despite over a generation of bitter debate, in their views that (1) I.Q. is in some measure predictive of intellectual achievement in school and in life, and (2) I.Q. variance between one person and another is about seventy percent heredity and thirty percent environment. In homogeneous populations and stable social settings, the hereditary factor will rise against environment to almost eighty percent to twenty percent (1).

The so-called black/white differential in the United States has remained remarkably stable since World War I. Only lately has there been some inferential data that the black I.Q. average has begun to drop below 85 I.Q. The white I.Q. has hovered between 100 and 103 during this time. The only explanation that seems to clarify the black decrement is the increase in births among the lowest black social groups relative to the black middle class. Claims for a total increase in United States I.Q. in the past fifty years are likewise hypothetical (2). In this regard, the statistics of the years 1984 to 1986 show an illegitimacy rate (high in all groups) of over fifty percent (fifty-five percent in 1986) in blacks, which has startled social scientists and has moved the black leadership to great concern (3).

What has argued for the reality of I.Q. differences is the fact that the northeast Asiatic Mongoloid I.Q. profiles seem to be both somewhat higher than the white mean and different in strengths and weaknesses. It is now felt that the mean I.Q.s, 104 to 109, achieved by the northeastern Mongoloids (Chinese, Korean, Japanese) could not possibly hold in the upper ranges (4). Thus, there is now postulated to be, as with females, a smaller standard deviation leading to a higher Gaussian curve profile about the mean (5). The educational, economic, and sociopolitical evidence seems to confirm the psychological evidence.

Barely dumped onto our shores, in desperate morale, with nothing to their name economically, the so-called Boat People, ethnic Chinese from Vietnam, have overcome incredible language and cultural handicaps. We have all seen the success stories on the television news—the valedictorians of their respective high schools, large percentage of college entrants, and economically and socially viable in a short while, even in this highly competitive environment that is America. The picture that we get from the home countries—Singapore, Taiwan, China, Hong Kong, South Korea, and Japan—confirms this rising tide of modernization as these peoples throw off the cultural shackles of the past and move into direct competition with the western Caucasoid societies.

The picture of our black compatriots is not quite as optimistic. For large percentages of blacks in the United States, quotas are necessary to guarantee jobs in a competitive environment. This in itself is a tacit admission by the black community of their inability to compete. Of course, the counter argument is that we are still observing the perduring results of enslavement and racial discrimination. Yet, even many liberals—a specific example is former Governor of Virginia Charles Robb in a statement in 1986—would admit that the evidence is not definitive that such enduring racism can explain the lag (6). The social and ecomonic picture is not brighter. Crime and terrifying pathologies of social disorganization are in evidence throughout large portions of the population. It should be reiterated that we speak proportionately, millions of blacks being able to outperform many whites, such is the I.Q. overlap (7).

In the African homeland, the picture does not change, thus challenging the standard explanation of white/black exploitation and discrimination. Africa is either on the verge of mass starvation, or else the colonials are back quietly running and re-exploiting these countries (8). Thus, from the standpoint of confirming evidence from a wide range of human informational inputs—economic, educational, social, psychological—the picture that I.Q. gives us is nowhere disconfirmed.

In addition, the psychometricians through the use of sophisticated mathematical and statistical techniques (standard in the sciences), have shown that the I.Q. profiles of the various social groups are quite similar. The argument here is that from test to tests, skill to skill, factor to factor, black/white, Mongoloid/Caucasian achievement affirms that I.Q. does not measure something that is culturally variable. It is measuring *g*, a universal intellectual potential that is part of the biological heritage of all the so-called racial groups (9).

Despite this seemingly persuasive picture of the reality of intelligence variability between the races, *it is my view that the so-called intelligence differential is not significant historically.* It ought not to be seen as a stigma. Those groups who violently oppose discussions of these matters act as if the black population were branded with the mark of Cain. We ought to discuss these matters. In the short or long run, rational analysis could turn the present dismal picture into something quite different and pleasantly surprising.

## The Myth of the Neanderthal Stage Revisited

Truth must remain inviolate. Distort it, insinuate minute falsifications, stretch it, tear it, and the entire picture is in disarray, out of mental control. Because of political convenience, we have accepted such a distorted truth about the evolution of the races. Those who have demonstrated that the facts are other have been vilified (10). The twentieth century is no better in this respect than the sixteenth, only the accommodation of fact to political myth-making is more sophisticated.

The story of racial differentiation, the facts and its significance, has been shaped into an emotionally satisfying fable. We have believed in the so-called Neanderthal stage of racial differentiation because if fits what we want to believe. This is the myth:

The human species was whole up to the late Pleistocene. Although spread over the great central continents of Asia, Europe, and Africa, and for a long period of time, *Homo* remained a fairly uniform, interbreeding species. What differences existed between even the Asiatic forms, Peking and Java hominids, were relatively tiny, as between adjoining contemporary ethnic groups—long-faced Europeans and beaky Armenoids.

As we completed the *Homo sapiens neanderthalensis* stage of evolution some 35,000 to 50,000 years ago, our progenitors, *Homo sapiens,* separated, spread to the ends of the earth, migrated to the Americas, and were gradually and recently transformed into the various races. Yet, how could the races have separated so recently in the first place? Indeed, the races of man are enthusiastically interbreeding. This is true for all higher mammals. The tolerance for interfertility among these advanced, widely-traveling mammals is great. Look at the phenotypic differences in dogs, in cattle, even cats, and you will understand that surface differences merely mask deeper similarities.

So, too, with humanity. The theory is thus plausible. The differentiation of the races into their geographical homelands was only skin deep. The facts are quite clear on that account. Some mammals that have differentiated into even quite different species can interbreed, though their progeny are sterile. Horses and donkeys, zebras and donkeys, tigers and lions, mammals that separated from each other many millions of years ago are such examples (11). The separation of humans and the maintenance of the interfertility bond poses no problem, especially since *Homo sapiens* is and presumably was a great wanderer and an eager miscegenator. We should note here that intersterility is not the only criteria for species separation. Species that are interfertile, yet that do not voluntarily interbreed unless there are no available males or females of their own species, still can fit the taxonomic standards as separate species.

For the races to have evolved as they have in such a short time, less than 50,000 years, especially considering what complex creatures we are, is baffling. Franz Weidenreich in 1946 wrote an important if neglected book, *Apes, Giants, and Man* (12). During the 1930's, Weidenreich had done the basic analysis of the Peking fossils. His conclusions, so at variance with the post-Neanderthal separation myth, were that the Peking fossils at seventeen points of bone structure showed remarkably similar relationship to contemporary Chinese and to no other races around the world (13). While the characteristics were not crucial morphological features, being mostly secondary uniquenesses, they did establish the historical identity of the Mongoloids as distinct from their other *sapiens* brethren.

In effect, Weidenreich placed the separation of the races at least 500,000 years ago, for this morphological distinction between Peking Man and Java Man was also upheld. These two forms were thought to have diverged long before 500,000 years ago. Carleton Coon, in his *Origin of Races,* 1962, elaborated in enormous documentary detail on this picture of ancient hominid separations (14). The evidence now was pointing to a one-to-1.5-million-year separation of the various groups of *Homo erectus* that seemingly had migrated out of the African Ur-homeland. Simply, the separation of the races had begun to occur at an earlier stage in evolution and, according to Coon, the separation had caused them to evolve into the *sapiens* stage separately and unequally, the northern erectines preceding the southern members of our genus by many thousands of years.

The clinching set of facts and relationships in this study was that a line of morphological continuity could be traced in all the contemporary geographical races to their fossil forebears in situ on the continents in which they had separately evolved. Where Coon has been correctly criticized is in pressing too vehemently his belief that no genetic exchanges could have taken place during those many hundreds of thousands of years (15). Later, he conceded that genetic interfertility was maintained during this period, by genetic exchange between the adjoining populations, the results of which were then transmitted to more internally located groups (16).

How serious then are these racial differences? Practically all scientists are agreed that the original *Homo erectus* template reflects these ancient racial divisions in bone structure, but these are minor aspects of what constitutes a human being. R. Lewontin attempted to prove this through a biochemical analysis of blood and other serological differences. He found that the similarities were in the range of eighty-five percent. The differences, fifteen percent, which could be thought of as a serious percentage of divergences, happily were in minor aspects of bodily diversity and structure, i.e., they posed no serious barrier to blood transfusions, etc. (17).

Coon, for example, found that in all biological respects, the contemporary Negroids and Caucasoids were the most similar. The fashionable use of skin color, for one, was found to be not decisive for Caucasoids—the Bengali Caucasoids (India, Bangladesh) are extremely dark, while the equally Caucasoid Scandinavians have very light skin. Of course, this is a contemporary outcome of the hybridizations that have taken place since the end of the Pleistocene Ice Ages, 10,000 years ago (18).

By the end of the Ice Ages, before the tide of intercontinental migrations occurred, the ancient races of *Homo erectus* were being transformed into *Homo sapiens*. Here is where the post-Neanderthal stage of racial differentiation is completely misinterpreted. It is only at the *close* of the Pleistocene that the significant separation of the races of humanity, and especially their differential grade in the evolution of a larger and more *sapiens*-like cranial (brain) structure, was seriously interdicted and modified toward the more universal *Homo sapiens* form (19).

Even that seemingly most isolated branch of the genus *Homo,* residing along the Yellow River near Peking, was finally joined to the mainline evolutionary dynamics of our form. This occurred with the massive expansion of the Mongoloids throughout Asia and their subsequent hybridization with southern (Australid) and western (Caucasoid) races. Despite the isolation that marks them as the most unique of the subspecies of *Homo,* there has never been any question about the interfertility of these different groups when they encountered each other.

Today, the Mongoloids, even in somewhat hybridized form, retain their basic color equilibrium no matter what their geographical distribution. Along the Amazon River, mostly Mongoloid Indians do not vary appreciably from those Outer Mongolians living in almost subarctic climatic settings (20). Also, although widely-separated geographically, these groups still carry with them the telltale seventeen skeletal uniquenesses of the ancient Mongoloid *Homo erectus* of over one-half million years ago.

At this point, the post-Neanderthal myth of our racial separation falls apart factually, constituting a monumental barrier to appreciating the true meaning of the modern races of humans, in terms of evolutionary causes and future prospects. What caused the transformation of the ancient races of *Homo erectus* into the recent ethnic and racial forms of modern *Homo sapiens?* It is here that Carleton Coon's theories about these evolutionary dynamics of the transformation from then to now understandably have raised a storm. Weidenreich did not propose to answer this question.

## The Meaning of Race

Coon proposed that purely locally selective factors in each of the geographical ranges catapulted the original denizens forward, each at a different evolutionary pace (21). This view has now been modified. Recent evidence suggests that the transformation took place largely within the last 50,000 years, much too short a span for internal selective dynamics to have worked their independent seining of more modern from more retrogressive individuals within the indigenous populations (22).

The clue to understanding the evolving dynamics of change in the races may lie in the close biological relationship of the Caucasoids and the Negroids, closely related geographically as well. The push toward sapiency seems to have originated in mutant Caucasoid strains several hundred thousand years ago, somewhere in the northern Eurasian quadrant. The resultant Upper Paleolithic Cro-Magnon culture that revealed itself about 35,000 years ago is by far the most sophisticated of any of the Ice Age cultures that we have identified. The fossil bones also reveal an extremely advanced creature in terms of encephalization and endocranial capacity. The source of sapiency logically must lie here. We have discussed the matter in Part 1 of this book as well as in *The Form of Man* (1983) and *Triumph of the Intelligent* (1985).

The important hypothesis here is that the genes of those Caucasoids radiated outward, even at a distance, into the homelands of the ancient evolving erectines living on the other continents. It is possible that the ongoing genetic unification of mankind could have been in process as early as 100,000 years ago (23). After all, the Neanderthals do appear on the scene about this time, an odd transitional (erectine- *sapiens)* people of Caucasoid racial origins. So, too, does Wadjak man appear in Indonesia sometime between 40,000 and 80,000 years ago, a large-skulled creature, apparently Australid, who seems to depart from the then-existing and conservative Australid erectines (24).

The result of what was at first a slow absorption of foreign genetic elements was the gradual modernization of the ancient races. The model was that of the most advanced, aggressive, adventurous wanderers, who probably left many hybrid children, even when they may have been single individual stumblers into new lands and places (25).

John Baker, who has done the most careful research into the contemporary races, has generally confirmed Carleton Coon's thesis. To Baker, however, the great differentiator of the races is not a structural one (for, after all, up until fairly recent time, the races have remained within their respective geographic regions). Baker argues that domestication and acculturation have dissolved the natural barriers against miscegenation, protecting the group uniqueness, isolation, broadening and diluting those special ecological adaptations that could selectively protect its evolutionary options (26).

He finds the great differentiating factor in *scent*. While Baker argues that scent could be a disincentive toward the mixing of races, sexually and culturally, he does concede that it is a mostly secondary factor in the differentiation of the races (27). While members of different racial and ethnic stocks would probably breed first with their own, were no other females of one's own group available (Coon also argued this), contemporary experience argues that the scent factor would not ever rank strongly enough to prevent hybridization in humans (28).

It should be noted that there is probably a hidden argument in both Coon's and Baker's discussion on such racial barriers toward interbreeding. No matter if it is scent, the mere postulation of a barrier argues for an incipient species level of taxonomic remove between groups.

The sum total of the racial differences inherited from the past: bone structure, scent, ear wax type, fingerprint patterns, some noncrucial blood group affinities, skin color, hair form, certain facial and skull structures such as prognathism, brow ridges, iris coloration, do not add up to a significant heritage of variability (29). In the crucial areas of behavior and intelligence, there is obviously an on-average difference between the racial groups. There is also a likely variability between identifiable ethnic groups within the recognized racial groups (see Chapter XIX).

As will be noted below, the patterns of I.Q. differences do not point to an easily recognizable purely black, white, or Mongoloid profile of thinking or achievement in any of today's functional areas of intellectual performance. The most that we can discover in the area of behavioral differences are some interesting infant patterns, reactions to irritables, as chronicled by Freedman in his sociobiological research (30). There are also differences in development rates during infancy—Caucasoid children seem retarded in their psychomotor development as compared with Negro and Australid children (31). The latter difference might be pointed so as to show differences within the races also, given existing variable intelligence of the parents regardless of race.

The key difference between the races, disregarding possible personality structures that reflect or are reflected in culture and possibly derive from more ancient separations, biological or cultural, is probably, on the average, intellectual variability. It is here, in a discussion of this issue, even within the races, that tension soars, and it is not merely cultural tension. Intelligence truly defines us, not race. Where differences exist that might distinguish an Englishman from an Irishman, it is not religion or ethnicity that counts. It is how "smart" each group claims to be, relative to the other. Naturally, this is also what burns when the issue of race arises. That is why the problem must be clarified rationally.

## The Sapiens Transformation of the Races - A

Now wait, the reader will want to know, is this not a contradiction? Is there some sense in which the issue could come down to a matter of race and intelligence? No, because as was intimated at the end of the above section, intelligence differences and ethnicity are much more powerfully linked as factors of envy, hostility, and conflict. What we think of today as issues of race are really powerful forces in the identification of ethnicity no matter what the race. As will be pointed out in Chapter XIX, the issue of ethnicity stands at the core of human self-identification.

Here, the intelligence-cultural-economic-ethnicity issue cannot be avoided. The identification of the issue with race blurs the problem. The truly racial separations, which *seem* to argue so ineluctably for differences, for superiorities and inferiorities, cannot be supported as being real and historically momentous elements for conflict, that is, until we transform them into ethnic identities.

This can be explained more clearly if we distinguish between the two stages of racial transformation. The template upon which this transformation was performed was the early-evolving *Homo erectus,* who after migrating from the African homeland about 1.5 million years ago set up shop on the various continents and evolved largely separately and haphazardly.

The random genetic variation that occurred, modestly shaped by the selective power of the environment, certainly resulted in the skin and eye color differences that are to be found between southern and northern humans. As is the case with the seemingly accidental variations in bone structure of the Mongoloids, many of these differences were purely random, they had little adaptive significance. Such other adaptive differences that we do find, e.g., the epicanthic fold over the Mongoloid eye (it buffers the glare and bluster of the northern plains), height (the tall black Nilotids, the short, compact Caucasoid Neanderthals), are all secondary developments. They are the backdrop for the thrust forward of an expanding brain and a bursting human intelligence.

The evidence (solely in the tools) is that the various races of *Homo erectus* had individual rates of evolution with regard to brain size and consequent cultural development (32). For example, fossil evidence found in Torralba, Spain, points to the existence, about 300,000 years ago, of the massive organization of hunting, the technology to make and use fire. It indicates an encampment at the edge of a swamp, into which ancient European elephants had been herded to their deaths (33). The northern erectines seem always to have been in advance of their southern brethren. Sometime after 200,000 B.P. the creation of an incipient *Homo sapiens sapiens,* the ancestor of both Cro-Magnon and Neanderthal must have initiated the first stage of *sapiens* racial homogenization (34).

*Stage one:* Here we see the reshaping of the ancient erectines into the newly-evolving *sapiens* type. Obviously, the ebb and flow of the northern glaciers must have spurred the movement of migrants, and there can be little doubt from the evidence of Omo I and II in Africa as well as other late-Pleistocene African fossils (about 100,000 B.P.) that a genetic domino effect must have been fanning over the east African highlands from the north, perhaps from the Fertile Crescent and Arabia (35).

Even the Choukoutien (Peking) Upper Cave fossils, while indicating well-advanced *sapiens* types, show distinct memories of their erectine past in the brow ridges of the "old man" (36). In the time scale, Choukoutien seems to be at the very end of the Pleistocene, some 30,000 to 20,000 years ago.

The explosive development of, first, the big-brained Neanderthals, then the baby-faced, tall, balloon-brained Cro-Magnon, argues for a center of rate gene reorganization in Europe and/or western Asia radiating outward. That Vértesszöllös, Steinheim, and Swanscombe, all European skulls of from 400,000 to 200,000 B.P., were already so advanced toward *sapiens* status supports these suppositions (37).

The result of the domino-like transmission of sapiency to the transitional erectines of the late-Pleistocene Ice Ages was a human prototype ready for the second stage of racial hybridization. What is important about this first stage is that it probably gave to humanity that basic *sapiens* brain—its structure and its cognitive style—that allows psychometricians to argue that intelligence, as it is analyzed in the so-called living races of humanity, is a homogeneous entity. This means that what differences exist on average between individuals are basically quantitative.

NB

An argument for the reality of intelligence as a quantitative element (I.Q.), an argument, however, derived from evolutionary studies both of lower forms of animals as well as humans, is given by I. Steele Russell:

> If the neuron can be regarded as the "atomic" unit of function in the nervous system, then the "molecular" unit of information processing is the "miniature nervous system"

(MNS) . . . . Considering the MNS as a data processing unit in the brain enables one to speculate on the function of brain size. The increase in the number of such units is perhaps analogous to core storage in a computer. The greater the information storage capacity, the greater the flexibility there is in generating data-processing programmes with optional subroutines. This permits the same data to be handled in different ways in different circumstances; or different data to be analysed as having the same meaning. Thus bigger brains do not need to learn differently; they can simply generate longer data control programmes with option flexibility for changes in context or circumstances. Perhaps this is part of what we mean by intelligence (38).

Specifically, especially at the higher ranges of intelligence, what our common sense suggests to us is confirmed, namely, highly educated people from all the races can think and work together, achieve successfully all the vital tasks of civilized life. If there are differences, as exemplified in those infant irritability experiments of Daniel Freedman, and perhaps more anecdotally in the intriguing style differences of daily behavior and in the verbal expressions of ordinary people of different races, perhaps they reflect those more ancient separations. The older developmental areas of the brain including the allocortex may show certain accretions or patterns that reflect the random mutational directions in the history of each of the races and their subdivisions that were fixed in the population during the eons following the original post-African diaspora (39).

## The Sapiens Transformation of the Races - B

*Stage Two:* The modern evolution of the races is now both more dynamic and more complex. In addition, we see all around us the contemporary consequences of human migrations, which provide a bit more evidence upon which to base our analysis. It begins with some evidence that though substantial is still wrapped in the enigmas of its yet cloudy origins.

The Cro-Magnons, fully *Homo sapiens, sapiens,* the ancestors of the Europeans and west Asians, arrived in Eurasia around 35,000 B.P., probably from the area around the Iranian Plateau, perhaps even north of it. The original group, which eventually gave rise to these migrations, must have been pitifully small (40). However, its success in the northern tundras' big-game-hunting environment allowed for a rapid population increase, which then led, fairly quickly, to the extermination of the resident Neanderthals. Simultaneously, from 30,000 to 20,000 B.P., there were significant migrations in progress. The Australian aborigines arrived on the Australian subcontinent in small groups during this period. Coming from the northern islands, these people are presumed to have been pushed south by oncoming groups of Mongoloids (41).

There is evidence that the Australids were ensconced as far north as southern China, Taiwan, and Japan (the Ainu), even into northeastern Siberia (the Gilyaks, and the other so-called proto-Siberians) by the late Pleistocene (42). Thus, the migration of Mongoloids from their Yellow River homeland must itself have been precipitated by some destabilizing event. Add to this the then-contemporary migration over Beringia into North America of a series of small groups of hybrid peoples now called Amero-Indians (43).

There has been much discussion of the racial background of both the Ainu of Japan and the Amero-Indians. While the latter are indeed Mongoloid in overall cast, Carleton Coon has called attention to the similarity of certain Nepalese peoples to the Amero-Indians, arguing for a Caucasoid-Mongoloid mix (44). Elsewhere it has been hypothesized that the Caucasoid element might have been partially Neanderthal, the large noses of some Amero-Indian groups hinting at the incorporation of various genetic elements at least in some of the Caucasoid groups that had moved east across Siberia (45). Finally, also to be taken into account is the Australid cast of some Indians, such as the California Maidu (46).

Since the Amero-Indian migrations seem to have occurred in the period after 20,000 to 15,000 B.P., they could have represented a remnant hybrid Cro-Magnon Neanderthal population moving away from the aggressive Cro-Magnons who now had taken over the cave networks of the Ural Mountains at the doorstep of Siberia. Quite possibly, small groups of Caucasoid Cro-Magnon or hybrid Caucasoids could have penetrated south into the Yellow River area to be transformed by the ever-absorptive Mongoloids (those represented by the "old man" of Choukoutien), precipitating their advance into sapiency and catapulting other peripheral groups south into the Australid homeland.

We know that languages show their historical affinities for some 15,000 to 25,000 years. Many people of Southeast Asia speak languages related to their partial Australid heritage: Vietnamese (Annamese), Cambodian (Khmer), Burmese (Mon), Malaysian-Indonesian (Austronesian) (47). Thus, we have a massive complex of hybrid Australid peoples extending from the inhabitants of Madagascar to the Maori of New Zealand and the other Polynesians of the Pacific. What is interesting is the probability that, at a later date, in the postglacial Holocene period, horse-mounted tribes swept out of western Asia to reshape the final northeast Asiatic complex and precipitate the expansion of the north Chinese out of the Yellow River (Shang Dynasty, 2000 B.C.) into the present middle kingdom, that is, China (48).

That the Chinese retained their Sinitic language, handing it down in turn to the Burmese, Thais, and Tibetans, is interesting because to the north and the east, the Mongols, the Koreans and the Japanese, horse-riding aristocracies, took with them the Altaic languages of the central Siberian, Turkic peoples. How much of a Caucasoid genetic infusion accompanied the resulting cultural and linguistic impact is hard to say. Even today, among the Koreans, Japanese, and Chinese, one discerns the hint of a Caucasoid profile (49). The cultural traditions of myth and legend themselves are clues that foretell an ancient contact with the west (50).

According to a quasi-historical record such as the *Book of Changes,* predynastic Neolithic China was ruled by an upper caste of red-haired and green- or grey-eyed Hsia nobles, known as the "Hundred Clans," who ruled over "myriad black-haired people" (51). The latter may have been the remnant Australids, or by then, hybrid residents of south central China, who were also described as having dark skin.

C. D. Darlington once noted the importance of the Arabic trading concession in such port cities as Amoy, Foochow, and Canton during the Middle Ages (52). Such traders probably took Chinese wives and had children. It is possible that these children were not ostracized or excluded from family formation, for their trading relationship lasted for many generations. The fact that there are few genetic signs today of this Caucasoid presence argues once more for the enormous assimilative capacity of the indigenous population majority. The critical point is that today's northeast Asiatics, though seemingly pure-blooded "late" Mongoloids, are an amalgam of racial heritages, most certainly with a heavy Caucasoid cast from differing time levels.

Let us return for a moment to the mystery of the Ainu and Amero-Indians. Alice Brues notes the great variation in the Amero-Indian types—some who are very Mongoloid in appearance—the Pueblo peoples (Zuni and Hopi)—and some with Caucasoid qualities—Plains and eastern Iroquois and Seminoles—others, such as the previously-mentioned California Maidu, who appear to have had some Australid racial affinities (53). These observations serve to make the whole Amero-Indian picture a clouded one.

Brues, using the mysterious Ainu and other northeast Asians, Amero-Indians, and perhaps the Australian aborigines as well as the Polynesians (who are at least partially Australid), believes that the Caucasoids and the Australids are the most closely related races (54). Carleton Coon, citing less obvious characteristics than phenotypic appearance, argues for a close Caucasoid-Negroid relationship (55).

We come now to the Japanese. In the period after the Ice Ages (8000 B.C.), Japan was occupied by two quite different aboriginal peoples. In the southern islands was an agricultural Malayan-like people, typical of the then-existing inhabitants of southeast China and the islands and lands to the south (of Mongoloid-Australid racial heritage), the so-called Jomon culture. To the north were the Ainu, who practiced the bear-cult tradition also found among the Cro-Magnon peoples (15,000 B.P.). The Ainu, a hairy folk, seemingly related to the Siberian Gilyaks (who also wear beards but are otherwise Mongoloids and who speak a Uralic-Altaic language), seemingly were not of Mongoloid origin. The Ainu, in addition, had heavy brow ridges. All these elements attest to a complex of Australid-Caucasoid (perhaps both Neanderthal and Cro-Magnon) heritage. Finally, the Ainu were relatively primitive culturally (56).

Add to this the coming from Korea after 500 B.C. of the horse-riding, bronze-smelting, Uralic-Altaic-speaking, Mongoloid-Caucasoid hybrids racially, Japanese aristocracy, and you have a complex racial heritage. The Jomons were quickly absorbed, the Ainu driven north to Hokkaido, the latter probably not without some interbreeding, since the contemporary Japanese, like their Korean confreres across the water, are more heavily bearded than the Chinese (57). What can we say about today's Japanese racial composition?

While it may appear that the northeast Asiatic Mongoloids are more homogeneous racially as compared with their southeast Asian brethren, the above evidence makes such a conclusion doubtful. Certainly, in historic times, it has been the Han Chinese who have expanded southward, politically, economically, and ethnically. There are now enclaves of Chinese throughout this area of southeast Asia. Because of their high intelligence, educability, and capacity to modernize economically, they have risen socially as a minority group in each of these societies. Tragically, they have been thus subject to persecution, even genocide. The Japanese during their scant one hundred years of modernization have made their own political, military, and now economic, aggressive expansionary moves.

This pride and sense of exclusivity in both the Japanese and Chinese mask the fact that the Chinese as recently as 1500 B.C. were controlled by a western group of horse- and chariot-riding aristocracies vaguely similar in their burial traditions to the then-contemporary Scythians beyond the Urals (58). This was the period of Indo-European expansion in Europe and Asia. Thus it is not too extraordinary to raise the possibility that this was the most easterly wave of those migrations. Indo-European-speaking peoples, the so-called Tokharians, controlled parts of the Sinkiang province of China until about 800 A.D. (59).

The powerful Chinese ethnic tradition absorbed that group of conquerers as they absorbed the Altaic-Turkic-speaking of Mongoloids of Kublai Khan, and the Manchu Dynasty of more recent centuries. The events are reminiscent of the Lombards in Italy who came down across the Alps in the seventh and eighth century A.D. as a Germanic group of conquerers, the last of many Gothic invaders. The Lombards were attracted to the remnant Roman towns of the north and settled in among their mixed Roman and Germanic hosts. The power and authority of the ancient tongue and the almost legendary influences of the Roman traditions eventually had their impact in absorbing the northerners.

So, too, with the Chinese. The ancient roots of their lineage along the Yellow River, together with the rich agricultural sustenance that was provided as compared with the desolate standard of living in the postglacial period of the peoples of the northern steppes, help us to understand the resilience, permeability, and infinitely absorbent qualities of the Chinese people and culture. It would be an error to emphasize their Mongoloid racial status. It is, as with the Japanese and the Koreans, heavily endowed with recent Caucasoid elements, possibly in combination with a more ancient Neanderthal, Caucasoid, and Australid heritage going as far back as the late Pleistocene (100,000 B.P.) and continuing even up to the second millennium B.C.

# The Sapiens Transformation of the Races - C

Let us shift to another continent, Africa. The origins of the Negroids is shrouded in even greater enigma. It seems as if only in a blink of time the original residents of Africa—such as the Rhodesian lady, who dates from around 60,000 B.P. and who is a borderline erectine/*sapiens*—have been transformed into *Homo sapiens* (60).

The homeland of the modern Negroids is thought to be western Africa, sometime after the end of the Ice Ages (61). The Capoids, (Boskopoids, Bushmen, and Hottentots) also mysterious in their origin, were concentrated throughout northern and central Africa at the end of the Pleistocene, gradually having been driven south, almost into historical times, into the desert areas of southern Africa. The earliest pressures on the Capoids came from the expansive Cro-Magnon Moullians in northern Africa (c. 20,000 B.P.). The second pressures seem to have been exerted by the expansive Negroids, who emerged from their west African homeland one or two thousand years ago (62).

An early drawing found in the Sahara of post-Pleistocene Africa shows what is obviously a Pygmy or proto-Pygmoid preparing to hurl a spear at an elephant (63). Here the mystery of the Negroids begins. Pygmies show certain sets of characteristics that are ultra-Negroid. The creation of these specialized peoples could have occurred when wandering northern groups entered the homeland of these Ice Age transitionals (64). Carleton Coon and Alice Brues surmised that the small size of the Pygmies must have been a result of subsequent ecological and aggressive human pressures (65). Coon hypothesizes further that some kind of secondary cross between Pygmy and other mixed Caucasoid hybrids probably created a new race of humans (Negroid) that were better adapted to a broader jungle ecology than were the Pygmies (66). Brues hypothesizes that the extreme prognathism (jutting face and jaws) of the Pygmies relates them more directly to the ancient and indigenous African populations (67).

All writers agree that on the basis of blood type, ear wax, fingerprint whorls, and other morphological properties, the African Negro is in all likelihood the subsequent product of a Caucasoid incursion into western Africa during the last years of the glacial era or later. Down the eastern highlands of Africa, from Sudan, Ethiopia, Somalia, Kenya, to Tanzania, the memory of Caucasoid explorers is clearly evident (68).

The sequence of course is unclear. From the meager evidence available, it is quite likely that the ancestors of the ancient Egyptians also sent population spirals, tribal groups southward, as well. It is possible that in the earliest millennia of the post-Pleistocene these were basically Caucasoid populations, which later attracted the expanding west African Negroids.

Today, Somalia and Ethiopia are considered to consist primarily of Caucasoid populations with a strong admixture of Negroid blood. The various Nilotid cattle-raising people of Kenya, southern Sudan, and Tanzania, appear mostly black (Masai, Watusi) as do the tall aristocratic Tutsi of Rwanda and Burundi, but their features retain the stamp of the Caucasoid presence in the east African heritage (69).

In fact, due to the slave-importing practices of Egypt, northern Africa, and the Arab nations of the Middle East, a blended Caucasoid-Negroid population of Mediterranean peoples has been created. The city of Jericho in Palestine was once a way station on the route of the slave trade. This is clearly evident as one walks its streets today. Thus, throughout the Arab world, through concubinage and the normal generation-by-generation processes of miscegenation, a new race of humanity was in the making, if the process was not already so dynamic (70). One sees individuals in the southern Arabian peninsula, in Yemen especially, who have a distinct Australid cast, which argues for the early existence of an aboriginal population of Australids penetrating far into the west (71). So it goes with practically every nation, including the United States. The ancient racial boundaries long have been breached, the flood of peoples gradually effacing our memories of the past.

## Conclusion: The Irrelevance

What defines the five races of humanity—Negroid, Caucasoid, Mongoloid, Australoid, and Capoid—is a series of secondary physical characteristics that with the exception of the Capoids can be traced back to the fossilized *Homo erectus* ancestors of each of these geographical groups. Oddly enough, as Baker points out in his book *Race,* it is the Capoids (he labels them "Sanids"), the most mysterious, possibly the newest racial amalgam, who cannot be traced beyond their borderline *sapiens* ancestors of the late Pleistocene (72). The Capoids, in addition, have the most unique set of physical characteristics separating them from the other races, including their African neighbors, the Negroids (73).

Most important, on the critical issue of skull shape, brain structure, etc., there does not seem to exist any special and irrevocable racial heritage to which we can point. For the most part, in that most selective aspect of *Homo's* evolutionary heritage—brain and intelligence—the modest specializations, both in structure and behavior, that were the likely heritage of the separate races of *Homo erectus,* have been gradually but inevitably overridden by the genetics of advanced forms of intelligent humans emanating from the north.

As we have seen, from about 100,000 B.P., there has been a steady if slow reshaping of the various erectine prototypes probably caused by the spillover of curious refugees from the Pleistocene ice packs searching for their tropical paradise, who shared their genes with whomever and wherever. The explosive paedomorphic creation of this ice-bound super*sapiens* inevitably catapulted it from its homeland in demographic relief to nudge the other races of *Homo* over their respective *sapiens* Rubicons, and to give rise in time to a creature known as *Homo sapiens,* whose intellectual heritage could be shared throughout our world.

What we today identify in a technical sense as any one of the races of humanity is really a group of humans that is in the process of shedding its human "appendix," also a vestigial organ from our vertebrate mammalian past. All the races of man, including the northern Caucasoids who started the late-Pleistocene revolution of sapiency, can look back to a similar erectine racial heritage.

Though we dub *Homo sapiens neanderthalensis* a *sapiens,* he was, only 40,000 to 50,000 years ago, a close cousin of the evolving Cro-Magnon Eurasians who created civilization. Any Caucasoid probably has lurking in his genotype a Neanderthal past. Under certain conditions, this past could return to haunt the haughty Europeans.

Most critical for our understanding of the variability of intelligence in the human species is that while at its quantitative lower levels it reveals our qualitative separations into the racial forms of *Homo erectus,* at its highest levels it points in just the opposite direction. The process of hominization, cortical complexity, and high creative intelligence is not the province of any specific race. It is like a baton in a relay run, it can be handed on from one corner of the world to another.

The key is what we do when it is handed to us. Do we cultivate it, treasure it as we would treasure a garden that will nourish us? Do we ignore the clear message that high intelligence does not belong to just one exclusive group? Indeed, if we are temporarily behind, do we make the extra effort to nurture and protect this gift so that intelligence will multiply among us? Or, do we irrationally destroy it, encouraging the return of our ancient past because of our unthinking disdain, fear, even guilt at being able to contemplate our destiny, our future, our promise?

# Chapter XVIII

---

# "EVERY NATION NEEDS A SOUTHERN NEIGHBOR"
## - Austrian Proverb

## Mankind Separates

The separation of mankind into the "north" and the "south" began as long as one-and-one-half million years ago. It began first with a trickle of stragglers northward out of the African homeland, searching, with their deeply-embedded human *Wanderlust,* for their Eden. During an interstadial (a break in the expansion of the glaciers), the plains teeming with life, opportunity beckoned. It was not only the north that attracted; numerous groups of *Homo erectus* were soon to be found in southern Asia and the east Indies (1).

By about one million years ago, the spontaneous mutations that naturally fix themselves in small endogamous populations began to reflect racial affinities and dissimilarities. As we know, the periods of northern mild climate were inevitably to be followed, in the Pleistocene Ice Ages, by the return of the glaciers, and the onset of cold. It was more difficult for those populations that had set up camp and begun to create an economy for living to move out (2).

The reason was fairly simple: the return of the cold came about in degrees, over the course of a number of generations. People tend to try to adjust to external change where they live. Though the responses of the erectines were probably gradual and modest, given their intelligence, still they could learn and must have stuck it out, and over the course of many thousands of years (3).

Thus, the history of *Homo* took on a two-tiered aspect throughout the middle of the Pleistocene Ice Ages. In the south, the selective pressures were practically nil. *Homo erectus* had by about 1,000,000 to 700,000 years ago disposed of the remaining australopithecines (4). The remnant great apes had retreated to the forests.

An example of the lethargic pace of selective advance in brain size and structure, reflecting quiet social as well as ecological dynamics, is the so-called Olduvai Hominid IX discovered by Louis Leakey. Dating from 1,000,000 to 800,000 B.P., with about 1000 cm³ endocranial capacity, this skull is amazingly similar to the Rhodesian (Zambia) skull found in 1926, which dates from about 60,000 B.P. The latter has an endocranial capacity of about 1280 cm³. This reflects a very slow pace of change over more than 600,000 to 700,000 years (5). We have by contrast the occipital section of Vértesszöllös man found in Hungary, which dates from about 400,000 B.P. It is a thick piece of fossil bone. Yet its estimated endocranial capacity ranges from 1400 to 1600 cm³ (6).

The contrast between Java man and Peking man, both erectines and both reflecting sequences of fossil individuals from 750,000 to 300,000 B.P., is also instructive. Though these fossil erectines show great similarities, already we can

discern those interesting racial variations that had fixed themselves in each of these geographically separated populations.
The endocranial capacities of these forms of *Homo,* reflecting the respective average brain size, continuously seem to
favor the northern erectines by 150 to 200 cm$^3$. The evidence
is that Peking man throughout this period was experiencing a
cyclical climatic set of changes that most likely presented
challenges quite different from those in the ancient tropical
homeland (7).

The contrast in basic cranial morphology as evidenced
by nineteenth-century human populations in the tropical
areas of the world, when these peoples came into closer contact with the West, seems to indicate that these relative differences still existed (8). Since that time, it is probable that the
respective averages in endocranial capacity, which have been
falling worldwide, have come closer together.

Any explanation of these long-term evolutionary differences in the so-called grade of morphological advance in
brain size and structure is naturally hypothetical. We can
only guess. However, an explanation from theory would
argue that the rates of variation north and south, at least in
the early stages of the human diaspora, were similar. Naturally, if there existed or came into being more stringent selective
conditions—cold weather, changes in the migratory patterns
of food animals, even the comings and goings of both old and
new types of animals—these might exert a more rigorous testing of the resourcefulness of the northerners.

NB

Some individuals or groups might not have been capable
of that testing; thus they would not have left their reproductive mark on the future. Others must have survived. If we examine the products of these northern survivors, it is clear that
they did not then muster specially new survival adaptations in
bodily structure or function. The evidence argues that a
larger brain and more of what intelligence traditionally
availed for *Homo* as an adaptive skill were all that was needed.

In the north then, two processes seemed to have worked

in tandem for these human creatures. One was the more intense process of selection between northern groups and also within the groups that favored larger endocranial capacity as well as the adaptive power of the larger brain in a highly challenging environment. Second, since the variation for a larger brain was more positively selective over variations for a smaller brain, or no mutations at all (stasis), a tradition of greater variability in the more intelligent individuals and groups was established. Simply, the others did not reproduce successfully (9).

Still, whether the approximate dates were 500,000 B.P. or 100,000 B.P., the form of man remained stable from what had evolved in Africa over one million years prior. Until the very end of the Pleistocene Ice Ages, *Homo erectus* remained the traditional adaptive model of humanity. He was "Homo stabilis," a universal prototype of a creature, regardless of race, who was destined not to rule the world, but to be the master of the hominoids, including the great apes and all the variants in the model of *Homo*.

For example, the Neanderthals, precursor Caucasoids of Europe and western Asia, began to appear about  100,000 B.P., if not a bit earlier. We have evidence, from his fossil bones and his Mousterian tortoise-core tool technology, of an existence for about 75,000 years. Obviously, he was around for some time before. Then, about 35,000 years ago, he disappeared, probably both absorbed and exterminated by the oncoming Cro-Magnons (10).

What is interesting to note about the Neanderthals is their truly enormous endocranial capacity, over 1500 cm³, larger than the current average. It was an archaic cranium, with massive bony jaws, skull with huge brow ridges, in design, long, low, and protruding in the rear. The result of this external structure, which must have mirrored a likewise less-developed internal neurological makeup, was a rather somnolent cultural evolution, perhaps even more lethargic than the *Homo erectus* Acheulean hand axe culture, which did show a

*[handwritten: 1-1½ million years ago   Homo erectus / 100,000   Neanderthals / 35,000   Cro-Magnon]*

slow but incremental design sophistication. Once the Neanderthals caught onto the method of slicing slivers of flint off a rock core and getting them to work in their few tools, they did not go on to redesign or improve these tools. For 75,000 years, these big, but archaic-brained people, seemingly progressed hardly at all in the cultural/technological sense (11). *[handwritten: yet they survived!]*

We can, therefore, advance the same argument with regard to Neanderthal, who was a true *sapiens,* even if a variant, as we have with the more traditional *Homo erectus* types, including the larger-brained Peking-Mongoloid forms roaming in the area of the Yellow River in China. Had time flowed on uneventfully, both *Homo erectus* and *Homo sapiens neanderthalensis* would have quietly and indefinitely lived within the parameters of their geographies and ecologies.

It is doubtful that the extinction of the mammoth and other great mammalian forms—such as the Irish Elk—which occurred at the end of the Pleistocene, can be laid at the door of either *Homo erectus* or *Homo sapiens neanderthalensis*. It was Cro-Magnon, an entirely new and improbable creature who completed the final decimations and genocide of these creatures. And it was Cro-Magnon, starting about 35,000 years ago, who set humanity and the fate of our planet onto a wholly new course (12).

## An Improbable Human

The fossil bones of Cro-Magnon at about 30,000 B.P. suggest a human that had been radically reshaped. This creature was not *Homo erectus* only more so. Evolutionary revolutions, though we envision them no longer as merely accelerated incremental changes, do not happen overnight. In evolutionary terms, a creature who appears seemingly out of nowhere at about 30,000 B.P. had to have experienced a much longer period of incubation, hidden evolution as Sir Gavin de Beer once termed it (13).

True, there are certain constraints on the rapidity of change. The Vértesszöllös occipital of Hungary at about 400,000 B.P. was huge but rugged and thick-boned. The Steinheim skull sections (Germany), 200,000 to 150,000 B.P., were more delicate yet still capacious. It was probably a female. The Swanscombe skull cap (England) of about the same period could have been either erectine or Neanderthaloid (14). These are cranial fragments that suggest a more accelerated pattern of brain growth than those found in the south, but they do not clearly point to *Homo sapiens sapiens.* As with the Neanderthals, they hint that the dynamics of mutations, adaptations, and natural selection during those alternatively warm and cold millennia were extremely intense.

This tall paedomorph, Cro-Magnon, was probably, as Richard Goldschmidt once labeled such evolutionary sports, "a hopeful monster" (15). We can never know the travail to which our Eurasian ancestors were subject to produce, along with Neanderthal and who knows how many other bigger-brained but unsuccessful sports, the relatively hairless, lanky, baby-faced, delicately-boned, balloon-brained creature who suddenly "took" adaptively and then exploded selectively throughout the continents.

What helps to explain this break with tradition is the memory of that primeval prototype of the hominids far back in the Oligocene, thirty million years ago. Here was a creature (thus far we have not found its fossil bones) who did not "make the cut" with the rest of the anthropoids, a reject who was relegated to a defensive position on the forested sidelines. In consequence, this creature evolved a series of buffering adaptations that ultimately created the hominid form in the first place: gracile in bone, paedomorphic, brainy, bipedal, family-oriented (16).

Success in the Pleistocene from about two million years

ago extruded a more established, well-adapted, stable form of human, *Homo erectus.* His relatively thick bony architecture of skull and limbs testifies to this well-grooved tradition (17). (Such densification also occurred among the australopithecines—*A. boisei.*) Thus, the coming of *Homo sapiens sapiens* in the north must be seen as a desperate throw of the mutational dice, to create, in many ways, a throwback to a primeval form, the "memory of the genes," but now, in addition, a creature whose height could support a brain of enormous energetic overflow.

The consequences of this totally new mental power appeared in several areas, the most obvious being the dispossession from their lands and the probable genocide of the Neanderthals, the Cro-Magnons' Caucasoid first cousins (18). This occurrence was part of a general migration outward, virtually in a 360-degree circle, perhaps from an originating area in the Iranian plateau, else in western Europe or the eastern steppes of Russia. It was at this time, about 30,000 B.P., that the large migrations into Africa probably reshaped the modern Negroids.

Note also that the Amero-Indians, who made their way over Beringia into North America, 20,000 to 15,000 B.P., and who were hybrids of predominant Mongoloid racial stock, came with a repertoire of cultural artifacts that is puzzingly similar to that of the Cro-Magnons. It is not merely the bow and arrow or the flint and stone tools, or the arrowheads, but also the long houses and the tepees of the eastern and plains Indians, the animal skin clothing and decorative beads. The entire economy of the Amero-Indians reminds us of the Cro-Magnon cave culture, except in the area of art.

To the south, a whole series of genetic waves, first from the west, transformed the transitional Mongoloid erectine populations into the precursors of the Chinese. These latter sent waves trickling to the south to create the hybrid Australid-Mongoloid populations of the southeastern Asian islands as well as on the mainland. Language affinities tell us this.

Subsequent genetic migrations created the proto-Koreans and Japanese on the central plains of Asia before their final recent movement into their present homeland (19). The modern Chinese, Tibetans, Burmese, Mongolian peoples cannot help but have been touched by any one of a variety of genetic exchanges. In the extreme south, too many variations on the Australid racial theme exist not to admit the probability of small but significant external genetic infusions over the centuries and millennia (20). This blending, which goes on even today, has and is creating new conditions of cultural life.

# Two Cultures

However, for several thousands of years after the end of the Pleistocene Ice Ages, the heritage of Cro-Magnon inevitably has produced and given rise to the sharp discrepant movement of historical development that we see between north and south. The word "sharp" must be emphasized in discussing the north-south gap that we have experienced since the beginning of the Holocene era, post-Ice Ages, from 8000 B.C. on. If we can judge the consequences in cultural behavior as reflecting difference in brain size and structure, then the differences between north and south during all but the final Pleistocene were differences of degree only. The northern and southern erectines, had they warred with each other, might have ended up like the 1980s Arab Semitic Iraqis versus the Indo-European Persians of Iran—in a no-win situation for both sides.

The coming of *Homo sapiens sapiens* has added something completely new to the cultural equations of our genus *Homo*. It is reflected in the spontaneous cultural creations of Cro-Magnon from the Urals deep into central Spain—a new technology, completely new art forms, even the beginning of a practical chronometric accounting of a world that changes amid stability (21). Can the reader doubt that this new super-*sapiens* brain was the instrument that created this completely unheralded Ice Age civilization? If so, if according to contemporary ideology, societies and cultures create themselves and consequently their human participants, we must be told the mechanisms whereby art creates man and his brain.

*but there is a median position*

It is not always the case that large endocranial capacities correlate positively with the levels of subtlety and imagination necessary for great cultural fabrication. The northeastern Asiatics and the Capoid Boskopoids, the latter with an imaginative and lively artistic sense, had large endocranial capacities. The Boskopoids were eventually overrun by Caucasoid Pleistocene peoples in northern Africa and then, in fairly recent times, the Christian era, driven south by oncoming west African Negroids (22). The onset of the great Chinese art forms came late, after 2000 B.C., when the Shang horsemen from the west, Scythian-like, bronze-making, charioted, overran the existing and quite competent pottery-making, millet-growing Mongoloids (themselves the product of more ancient hybridizations) (23).

We must view primeval culture as a unitary expression of the genetic relatedness of the purveyors of these cultures. That is why we trace the comings and goings of the various Ice Age Cro-Magnon peoples. These peoples took their cultures with them in wandering and war (24). Naturally, as cultures and peoples expand in numbers and assimilate outsiders either as immigrants or conquered peoples, the intimate social and cultural relationships will change, as will the character and institutions of the culture.

*/*

We cannot separate the intellectual power of a people in its social structure—law, literacy, commerce, art, religion, science, technology—and its capacity for war, aggression, expansion. Wherever the northerners migrated in those millennia after the Ice Ages, they took with them their intelligence, aggressivity, and their capability for culture-building on a high civilizational level. They also took their genes and their eagerness to inseminate and miscegenate. In the process, they changed themselves and the surrounding indigenous populations who were drawn into their cultural orbit.

To reflect on the power of intelligence to help individuals and groups adapt to new climates, ecologies, historical circumstances, let us consider the events in those centuries after the ice started to recede. We find almost immediately new economies based on mixed agriculture, herding, and technological fabrication in what are now northern Iraq and Iran, in Jericho, on the Iranian Plateau (from which the Sumerians migrated), along the Danube (and wherever the old European culture is to be found, probably Cro-Magnon-derived), and along the northern Mediterranean littoral, into Egypt. Whole new civilizations sprang up, multiplied, and developed in very different yet civilized and expansive ways. They derived in the main from the Ice Age populations of the north and their long, narrow-faced Mediterranean-type brothers and sisters (25).

The same considerations can be applied to the transformed Mongoloids of the Ice Ages and the post-glacial Holocene. The Mongoloids intermixed first with the indigenous Australid peoples to create the Malayo-Polynesian populations of Southeast Asia, driving the Australian aborigines and their Tasmanian cousins south into the uninhabited Australian subcontinent and its southern island (26). In more recent times, they have established enclaves (especially Chinese) in Singapore, Malaysia, the East Indies, and Formosa.

The comparisons are important. The Australian aborigines were pushed into their continental redoubt some twenty thousand years ago. This was both a more temperate as well as a more rigorous ecology. Yet twenty thousand years has not been enough to produce the genetic combinations that would have subjected these peoples to an internal process of social selection. Such a process might have produced a more adaptive and transferable culture. One million years of mutational quiescence had left their impact. Some anthropologists believe that during these past twenty thousand years there has been some cultural regression among these noble archaic people (27).

The Chinese, by contrast, have utilized their morphogically-derived intelligence, their advanced culture, and have thrived in the tropics as long as they have maintained their ethnic membrane. Also, as noted above, they have recently suffered as a minority presence in the alien south.

## Explaining the Differential

Before Europe's expansion to the ends of the earth, which began in the sixteenth century, the peoples of the southern hemisphere rarely entered European awareness. Of course, slavery out of Africa had begun in a systematic way by the Arabs in the early Middle Ages, and was continued by the Europeans well into the nineteenth century. The Arabs have hardly stopped this practice in the mid-twentieth century.

Slavery is an interesting, if despicable, human institution, that has involved the Caucasoids since perhaps time immemorial. What is odd is how it has touched the Caucasoids and Negroids. The Caucasoids have enslaved each other as well as Negroids. The Negroids have long engaged in forms of slavery themselves. (The other ancient racial groups have remained relatively immune, not being susceptible to Caucasoid institutions of industrial slavery, nor engaging in it themselves in any systematic manner.)

With the technological expansion of contacts with the peoples of the world, one and all have rejected this distasteful human scourge, ending finally with the dissolution of legal-ized slavery. A moral revulsion, arising from the awareness of *Homo's* mysterious alikeness despite differences, has led us to the realization of the seeming necessity of a world order, a family of peoples in a nonexploitative legal setting.

With the mid-nineteenth century decline of slavery came the final onslaught of colonial expansion, not merely in the relative emptiness of the New World, but in Africa, and every other part of the so-called underdeveloped third world. In terms of historical impact, the high colonial period has lasted in Africa about one hundred years, elsewhere, somewhat longer. This is not long from the standpoint of human evolution; thus, the pluses and minuses are still being calculated.

Certainly, the northerners brought with them the modern institutions and knowledge that made their conquest feasible in the first place. The last forty years, during which the newly-emancipated third world has been able to develop at its own rate, in tune with its own cultural institutions, have yielded widely variable results. Surely, today, the so-called "south" and its peoples are in a deteriorating state. On the other hand, the peoples of the temperate climes, meaning the relatively unhybridized Caucasoids and Mongoloids, have moved forward ever more rapidly. The northeast Mongoloids—Koreans, Japanese, Chinese—are seen by some dispassionate observers to be on the verge of dominating the world of the twenty-first century A.D. as they dominated eastern Asia since 20,000 B.P.

During the latter half of the nineteenth century, probably as an outgrowth of this more global awareness, and as an attempt to explain the north/south gap from the northern perspective, Lewis Morgan and Edward B. Tylor advanced theories supporting an evolutionary perspective on historical development (28). Both saw European institutions as those toward which all societies would tend—up from "savagery," so to speak. Even the Marxist perspective, which has given rise to the "exploitative colonialist" model of explanation, was an historical one. Marx argued that a society must reach a certain state of industrial development before it would be ready for permanent relief from exploitation by revolution and the onset of the "dictatorship of the proletariat."

A generation or so later, the anthropological school that emanated from Columbia University's Franz Boas would evaluate the so-called north/south differences from another perspective. Utilizing a cultural relativism model in which societies were judged by their internal institutional coherence, by what personal satisfaction their members gained in social intercourse, already postulated the existence of certain basic and universal cultural patterns in all societies, developed and undeveloped. The supposed superiority of the industrialized nations here seemed to be seriously questioned (29).

In a variant of the Jean Jacques Rousseau/Robinson Crusoe model of the "idyllic" primitive life, the conflicts and chaos of the forward-thrusting industrial nations were seen as decadent. The viability and harmony of the few existing subsistence tribal societies appeared to us as satisfyingly human and whole. Colonialism and social class exploitation were interpreted as being, at least in part, pathological aspects of the behavior of the developed West.

Two or three generations later, most of the assumptions of this cultural relativist school have been punctured. People have a way of voting with their "feet." Most of these heretofore subservient peoples, where they were not implacably limited by island or desert ecologies, have opted for Western modernization. Part of this decision-making has been stimulated by their defense needs and their resultant desire to acquire the technology to wage modern war.

In addition, these peoples are well aware that modern medicine, modern agriculture, and education are crucial if they are to mine their own human potential and not be forever victimized by outside forces both natural and human. Western ways have thus proved to be more instrumental, at the least in providing for the survival of a people. The cultivation of human intelligence to create a quasi-Western society, with its accompanying modern institutions, has become critical for the development of each of these so-called third world nations.

The tragedy is that, unlike the northeast Asiatics and a few other societies, most of these third world countries seem worse off now than at the time of their independence from the ruling colonial elites. We, tenacious in our orthodox ideology of environmental amelioration, insist on political and economic solutions, sometimes supporting our views by placing the blame for this laggard progress on these peoples' ancient and now patently recidivistic cultural traditions. These supposedly can hamper a people from assuming new values and attitudes that will produce the educational instrumentalities that will lead them onto a higher economic plane. Certainly there is a measure of truth here, but is it the major explanation?

If the answer to the north/south gap were an environmental one, the theory would lead its supporters to propose practical solutions. Yet, even the transport of populations long resident in the south to the developed ethnic nations of the north has not issued in a sharp reduction of this gap. The usual explanations for this continuing gap have been slavery, discrimination, racism, and other tragically true episodes in the history of encounters between ancient geographies. Yet, as generations pass and enormous ameliorative attempts result in few tidal changes, we must entertain other explanations. Of course, talented individuals from such handicapped groups, in consonance with all the predictions of genetic psychology, move through and beyond prejudice by dint of their individual abilities. They succeed, and on a par with indigenous northerners.

Peoples coming to new lands of the north from other northern climes, who have experienced prejudice and discrimination in their homelands as well as in their adoptive countries, have found their own ways of overcoming social handicaps. They have utilized the available institutions of self-development to forge ahead, and often in less than a generation. In the south—in Sao Paulo, Brazil, in Costa Rica—Germans act and achieve as Germans do in Europe. In Jakarta, Indonesia, or in Kuala Lumpur, Malaysia, the Chinese prosper and progress despite social and political barriers. Their achievement levels are similar to their confreres in Hong Kong, the United States, or Taiwan.

It has often been noted that in the probability curve of intelligence, highly intelligent and able people will appear in all groups, in the supposed third world and wherever groups of people are to be found. The so-called I.Q. overlap is valid and needs constantly to be borne in mind: no psychometric statistic that may define a group can ever define a single individual. In Africa, ethnic groups such as the Igbo of Nigeria and the Sotho of northern South Africa, in Asia, groups such as the Indonesians and the Thais, all in the southern hemisphere, reveal progressive inclinations and are culturally extremely energetic.

The problem with all of the sociological and political explanations for the continuing loss of ground in the third world despite massive assistance by the developed nations is that ameliorative sociologists are unable to hypothesize how such aid might finally yield the desired results. In effect, the entire environmentalist thesis runs the risk of becoming an academic piety—plenty of moral resonance but pitifully few verifiable predictions. Such hopeful mythologies may redound to feelings of moral rectitude on the part of their purveyors, but will only speed the process of disintegration for the recipients of this new form of condescension and paternalism.

Let it also be stated that the problem of the north/south gap in intelligence and cultural development is not a static given. The accidents of evolutionary history are amenable to conscious human intervention, and reversal. The factual issue is the same today as it was one million years ago. Were southern populations to encourage the more intelligent to reproduce at a higher rate than the less intelligent, change would come to the "south" very quickly. No one questions that there is enough high intelligence in all the ethnic groups of our world for just such an occurrence.

By contrast, northern societies to the extent that they encourage the more intelligent *not* to reproduce inevitably shift their own balances, both cultural and technological. The genetic memory of Neanderthal or Peking man still can erupt into reality. Even if the energy requirement for life in the northern latitudes makes far greater demands on family formation and prosperity than in the south, new technological, social welfare, and economic conditions now allow for the existence in northern societies of a much more intellectually variable population than in the heyday of the Pleistocene glacial ecology.

# Reason's Imperative

With Karl Marx, we can argue that technological and economic conditions of existence have a way of shaping and determining the political and philosophical ideals and attitudes of an historical period. In the late twentieth century, the world, through improved transportation and communication, and an international economy, has become bonded ever more intimately together in space and time. It is to be hoped that the horrors of our era are behind us. Even walled totalitarian segments of our world are touched by the moral resonances of a new climate of opinion.

So, too, the moral dimension conditions our awareness of the north/south gap. To recognize that this gap is probably due to an on-average intellectual variance does not mean that we here intellectually underwrite expoitation, apartheid, or injustice. On the contrary, our recognition of any particular factual cause cannot and has not ever led, either in logic or in reality, to any one automatic response to that reality.

In medicine, we try to heal, even when we know that genetic causes of disease or defect are involved. Thus, were we to learn to base our policy decisions on fact rather than on mythology, were we to have the will and the strength of character, even the confidence in ourselves that only the truth can lead us to do good to others, we may begin to replace those eternally ephermeral hopes with real progress.

To believe in hoary mythological mirages of good, that all people are the same, that human intelligence differences have no causal impact on the character and quality of the lives of people, may satisfy theological or ideological dreams. These utopian murmurings will not achieve what we desire. They will fail to achieve the outcomes of our hearts' desire, inevitably leading to ever more drastic and eventually horrendous actions to achieve the impossible. The resulting frustration will create visions, a demonology that will seem forever to block these utopian mythic ideals. Then, will we not act to extirpate these "evil forces"?

The world is worse for this twentieth-century secular mythology. As we will note in Chapter XX, the genocidal horrors of our time have been unleashed, in the main, because the superego of world opinion has become complicit in viewing those who have moved beyond the mass in cultural/economic achievements as not merely extravagant, even unscrupulous, but as the personification of human evil. After all, have we not been ideologically persuaded of mankind's intellectual uniformity?

In practice, we seem now to recognize that the totalitarian political controls placed on intelligent creative behavior ultimately redound to a society's failure. We intuit that ordinary intelligence is socially adequate, but not for real progress. All over the world, the barriers are being tacitly lifted, and the remaining intelligent asked to show their stuff.

Yet to confront the problem forthrightly, to deal with it

so that we may prepare the ground for a heritage of progress for our descendants, demands more of us. We need systematically and intellectually to confront fact and reality. Further, we need to do this in the spirit of international amity, to address our efforts for the good of all mankind, north and south. Our goal should be the *real* equalization of the peoples of the world, a goal that is within our grasp. We need merely to mobilize the goodwill that all of us have for our neighbors down the street and extend it to our distant fellow sojourners on this very tightly-packed planet.

This will not be possible as long as the intellectual and political community remains fainthearted and reactionary in the presence of reality. It is odd that the practical people of our world often are more efficient in facing facts, by quietly and spontaneously responding in action. Intellectuals seem to require a quasi-religious moral assurance about the character of the facts before they can entertain them even as hypothetical possibilities. That is why in paralysis we nervously stroke our ideological worrybeads. A rigid and dogmatic egalitarianism seems to satisfy and mollify our anxieties about an ever mysterious reality. There comes a time, however, when dissident intellectuals must once more raise the revolutionary cry.

One is reminded of the comment of United States Air Force General Donald J. Kutyna, a member of the Presidential Commission that investigated the tragic Challenger shuttle disaster of early 1986: "No one wanted to be the one who raised a show-stopping problem. No one had the guts to stand up and say 'This thing is falling apart.' "

# Chapter XIX

# THE ETHNIC MEMBRANE

## Culture and Biology

Racial differences excite our curiosity, ethnic differences our passions. Individuals of varying racial heritages, if they are raised within a similar culture and have on-average similar intelligence and education will mingle together in an atmosphere of nonconcern. Where racial differences become transformed into differences of behavior, life-style, and culture, they move to the level of ethnic variance. As such, they become factors in rivalry, alienation, and conflict.

On a superficial level, ethnic variability can be thought of as inhabiting the world of culture. Here, in this world of cultural values created so spontaneously in our societies—or thus the "just-so" story goes—humans are lifted onto a suprabiological level. A new world of cultural relationships, causes, dynamics, comes about to create a truly human environment, *sui generis* (1).

*[handwritten margin note: to see only this + miss the rich- ness is poor vision]*

Here, the modern ideologists would argue, our human heritage of biology and history can be remade in the image of the social reconstructionist. With intensive educational effort, political indoctrination, and progressive social policy, we can realize the Utopia of our dreams (2). Whatever blockades there are to such progress exist only in our minds; they are products of bad education. These too can be eliminated.

Where did our biology go? Is it only in our bodies? Have we in a delusionary moment created a mental entity, freed of a brain, heretofore a billion years in the making? We ask, because according to the contemporary ideology of radical intellectuals there are no biological constraints on the possibilities for social and political policy-making (3).

If fundamentalist religionists deny Darwinian evolution so as to free humans to accept religious "creationism", then certainly this other dogmatic intellectual wing has created its own "creationism" to free mankind from its obligations to our biological past. Now, instead of a supernatural God, we have a supranatural Society with its secular "priest/dictators" free to act upon their political whims.

It cannot be so. Acknowledging the continuity of nature is an ancient and accepted intellectual way of understanding our universe. From time immemorial, we have sought for the laws that would help to explain or regulate the jumbled events of our lives. Without such generalizations, we would have as many sets of laws determining the course of events as there are different phenomena. Yes, of course, we are always finding new and special regularities in biological bits of matter as contrasted with stones, clays, and meteors. The physical laws of the universe, however, apply as much to the physical workings of biological substances as they do to inanimate things. The laws are, additionally, complex. That is why the predictions of biologists are less exact than those of astronomers.

So, too, with culture, and then with ethnicity. We cannot describe the workings of humans in culture with the same exactitude and intellectual control as we can of fish, mollusks, or insects in their natural ecologies. This does not mean, however, that the biological principles that guide us in understanding the structure and behavior of plants and other animals, when applied to humans, in one puff disappear. It merely warns us to tread carefully and go slowly in making the transition from biology to culture especially in the use of laws, regularities, principles, dynamics, that work so well on a nonhuman level.

Culture is complex. The real test of what we write here is, will it bake bread? As in all objective discourse about our world, will we be able to make at least some modest predictions about events and processes? Will we be able to understand the relationship of things and events a bit better through these ideas? Here, the reader will have to decide. For, ethnicity is a most puzzling human phenomenon. In a stroke, *Homo's* precultural biological semi-instinctive behavior is now expressed in his widely-varying material and social creations (4).

The mystery lies in how and why man's biological behavior is expressed to such a great extent through culture. At the center of this biological mystery is ethnicity. One could argue that ethnicity became the central element in that transitional process that enabled humans to view so haughtily the nether biological forces that guided their animal forebears and contemporaries. Here, too, resides the focus for the passions, the enmities, the suicidal sacrifices for the good of the social group. In a moment, biology has become one with culture (5).

# Biological Origins of Ethnicity

The glimmerings of ethnicity go far back in hominid history. The stylistic or technical differences that can be discerned in the fabrication of tools among the various levels of humans indicate different patterns of thought and imagination at each of these levels. *Homo habilis* made an advanced form of Oldowan tools. Barely-shaped stone tools, given an edge for scraping or a point to puncture, they are difficult to distinguish from naturally occurring shapes that could be used as tools. *Homo erectus* was known for his beautifully chiseled Acheulean hand axes. *Homo sapiens neanderthalensis* became monotonously prolific with his Mousterian tortoise-core type of flake tools (6).

Only with *Homo sapiens sapiens,* Cro-Magnon, do we find a dynamic of cultural differentiation both in time and space. Many different cultural traditions can be postulated about the 25,000-year cave residence of these northern Ice Age denizens. They can be postulated from their tools, sculptings, and cave paintings. Sometimes the cultural changes are sudden, as if a new tribe had overrun the residents, evicted or slaughtered them, and then instituted its own world of meanings, both nonmaterial and physical (7).

What is indicated by all of this is that humans have long divided themselves into social groups by their common language, art, technology, and religion. How did these divisions begin? What is the meaning of a cultural or ethnic tradition that is so variable even within an interbreeding species? Do these traditions have biological roots, and if so, what would be their significance?

It is the writer's belief that ethnicity has biological roots. These roots are enclosed in the unique biology of the hominids, particularly in the destiny of *Homo,* over the last ten to five million years (8). Further, ethnicity constitutes the human brain's replacement of instinctual signal behavior by conventional symbolic expression. Ethnicity came into existence as the late mammalian/anthropoid brain was enveloped by the human cortex. We can thus argue against conventional sociobiology that ethnic/cultural symbolic behavior, even as it seems to constitute a replacement for instinctual/signal behavior, retains a close one-to-one relationship with the supposedly adaptive responses that are the consequence of signal behavior in the anthropoids—apes and monkeys (9).

Certain unique qualities in human behavior, as regulated by the particular structure of our brain, do become the leading edge of what we see as ethnic feeling and allegiance. In addition to being the housing for a massive cortex (which has grown as an adaptive means of thinking through decisions rather than relegating decisions to the spontaneous automaticity of the genes), our brain is bicameral. Various functions and behaviors are either processed in one or the other half of the brain or else the hemispheres must cooperate through the corpus callosum to integrate intake and evaluation and their overt responses.

Our language areas in the brain are situated most often in the left hemisphere, adjacent to the auditory domain. As noted in Chapter XII, the simplified pharynx and our subtle vocal apparatus clearly were crucial elements paralleling the growth of the cortex. Language is, of course, one of the most powerful centripetal elements in ethnic identity. That it can be objectified as a means of logical communication of ideas and concepts and express equally effectively the intimacy of ethnic dialect, poetry, and literature, reveals how deeply into the history of our genus this human noninstinctual functioning must go (10).

Language is only one element, as basic and fundamental as it is, in the identity of an ethnic group. Note how ferociously people will fight to maintain the integrity and existence of their language. Often people will fight harder for their linguistic identity than for their religious institutions (11).

The sense of group identity and commitment must have deep roots in *Homo's* mammalian past. It is of a piece with the glue that binds a mammal mother to her young, the passions of the pack and the herd. However, these human emotions are even more powerful, they are irregularly expressed;

*[handwritten margin note: and is the best argument against the bonded pair]*

it is unpredictable when and how they will surface to consciousness and commitment. The only explanation at this point in our knowledge is that the entire panoply of language, religion, art, ritual, and other phenonema that go under the rubric of ethnicity, arises, again, from an interaction between the exploding cortex and the subcortical, allocortical, and limbic system areas of the midbrain, in their quintessential reconstruction into the hominid model (12).

Thus, the symbols that human groups regurgitate spontaneously, the cores of meanings by which humans express the imperatives of life, as given to them by their brain, can be seen as mental effusions now *not* guided and shaped by the adaptive demands of instinct and thus of closely-honed selective processes. Speech expressing bodily feelings and functions, as in barroom conversation, may reflect an ancient memory. The denizens of the corner pub, however, also are able to talk *about* the world. Humans chipped out rocks so that they could scrape down animal hides, but also to carve a pleasing shape. Why did the shape please the human eye and its mind and why did a pleasing shape for one group contrast so sharply with what pleased another group? (13)

As *Homo's* brain expanded, so, too, did the repertoire of behaviors and interests of the particular social groups—bands or tribes—as they explored their ecologies searching for subsistence. With each pulsating expansion of the cortex, the bonding of instinct to behavior was further attentuated. Humans were increasingly alone in the universe (14).

One can argue that the killing off of the competitor open-country apes at the end of the Pliocene (seven to two million years ago) and then the competitor australopithecines in the early-to-middle Pleistocene (two to 0.5 million years ago) was caused by the usual competition for *Lebensraum.* Thus, the probably-existing sense of ethnic uniqueness of each endogamous band was still merged with real and spontaneous biological and behavioral differences aggressively ex-

pressed between *Homo* and his residual evolutionary competitors (15). Gradually, this would have had to change, as the
"others" disappeared, *Homo* prospering and coming into
contact more and more often with his own kind. As the brain
continued to expand, something new began to develop au-
tochthonously, under its own impetus.

Here now was the expression of this free play of the
human brain-thought-behavior along a wide diversity of
lines—constrained then as now by a finite number of biological universals. First, we are animals, mammals, primates.
Then, we are peculiar anthropoids with enormous unfocused
(at least from the standpoint of natural selection) energies
that we use in tool-making, word-smithing, singing and danc-
ing, contests, games, and one-upmanship, and maybe here
and there a good mammalian exercise in "chicken"—going
out and doing a little killing to show how good we and our
group are.

The powerful flood of energies that had been released by
the encephalization of the now-hominid nervous system had
no instinctually-guided focus. Those accidently diverse patterns of behavior—as reflected in personality types, language, art, religion, even history—as man began to look
ahead and remember, all became the symbolic focus of his
centripetal allegiances (16).

What was man's natural focus of survival, the social
group, became the center of his mental life. Once he discovered that the group's mental life was different from that
of other similar human beings, *Homo* passed into the crisis of
cultural and ethnic identity. In the beginning, this recognition
was almost inchoate. Humans sensed the differences, but did
not really objectify them as tangible ideological or religious
entities.

As in the orginal coacervate particles of protolife, the
membrane was thin and flexible. Groups came together and
differences were dissolved, sometimes in slaughter, sometimes in union. Secessionists left, and their linguistic expres-

sion soon bent to the winds. When they returned, they spoke like strangers, even acted and played like "others." They were different—exclude them. One could say that the powerful enticements of ethnic identity are nature's way of returning instinctless *Homo* to a homeland, a nurturing, comfortable niche in the pantheon of living things. Unlike the blind genetic imprintings of adaptation, ethnicity is a free, though often preconscious symbolic creation of social humans. That is why it can be so bizarrely ephemeral.

The source of a group's ethnic uniqueness is neurological. The group does not have to exclude other possible cultural combinations, but it has to be comfortable with the drift and shape of its ethnic destiny.

## Ethnic Consciousness

The paradox is that ethnicity is an extremely variable, spontaneous creation of humans. How many cultures, ethnic groups, have existed in the circle of humanity? How many different cultures are possible? The limit is defined by the internal structure of our brain and our general behavioral system. It is not predictable, because ethnicity is a function of vast numbers of neurons and their internal relationships.

On the other hand this adventitiousness in the differences in language, art, and religion, for instance, both between peoples in geographical space and the spontaneous changes in cultures that take place in time do not negate the fact that ethnicity is *Homo's* substitute for instinct; it provides him his new place in nature. That is why ethnic identity goes so deep.

It is hard to believe today, living as we do in such an inchoate freely-floating world society, that the ethnic qualities of extended national cultures were once produced spontaneously by individuals in face-to-face social settings. The culture that defines a France, Germany, or England, like its counterparts in tribal Africa or Asia, once arose from the tastes, attitudes, biological mind qualities of a small group of people, even a wandering band, that called itself one, the people, unique.

Here is the ethnic membrane that humans wind around themselves first in recognition of the reality that they are alone and different. Gradually, as consciousness broadens and matures, what was a necessity becomes a virtue. If groups have a history of togetherness, a mental and physical place that can be called home, survival over the eons becomes a key to survival in the future. Thus, the sense of exclusivity is born, and with it the symbolic armament to maintain and protect this exclusivity.

Religion is powerful in this respect. Remember how the Marxists once disenthralled us as to the supposed revolutionary character of Protestantism. Sociologists Richard Tawney and Max Weber both revealed the economic underpinnings of this new class that created or at least found refuge in a new religion, one that would rationalize and moralize their economic position (17). Naturally, these people, whether Dutch bankers or Huguenot traders, perceived the newness of their economic involvements, the separateness of their social relatedness and achievements. Protestantism was the means, unconscious at first, by which they would draw the ethnic membrane around them (18).

Soon they would remove themselves from the majority, as their churches became a central focus for culture building, endogamous marriage, and a new vocabulary for coping with reality. Immediately, the awareness of difference—here superiority in dealing with the new, particularly in mastering a new economy—must have become apparent. For many within the ethnic group in a complex society, where the old tribal separations had earlier disappeared, this new ethnicity now became not merely an opportunity for self-identification, but also made for prosperity and, then, immortality.

In the days of tribal myths and roving Indo-European heroes, the word "luck" was used freely to denote success, fortune. Lucky peoples were those endowed with the power of survival as they trekked over the plains of Eurasia (19). That was a colloquial way of expressing the awareness of a separateness/uniqueness that could be revealed tangibly only in language, custom, art, religion. Thus, lucky people were separate and apart, protecting their magical good fortune by "sticking close by."

As yet, in traditional societies, people were not sophisticated in explaining the necessities of inbreeding. The Greeks contrasted their civilizational capacities with the less-cultured foreigners by calling them "barbarians," those who spoke "bar-bar" gutturals, like animals. The Jews wrapped a blanket of religious exclusivity around themselves, the chosen people. The same purposes were served, that is, they maintained that ethnic exclusivity, that membrane of separation that would ostensibly preserve their "luck."

Even when their luck turned into persecution, as with the Huguenots, the Igbos, the Chinese in Indonesia, the Armenians in Turkey, such groups persevered. They persevered because the mere physical power to coerce and persecute could not interdict or dissipate the hundreds or thousands of years of truth/life that substantiated their ethnic commitments. Behind the cultural facade, then, a deeper stratum of awareness and thus psychobiological dynamics was being mined.

# A House Divided

We think of ethnicity as a home place for *Homo*. In the early days, the protohominids had to have been flexible, malleable primates, with only loose instinctual bonds, permitting them to move evolutionary-wise in a number of possible directions. That must have been in the period thirty to twenty million years ago. One would also suspect that as the proto-hominids early carved out a defensive niche in the forest, a certain measure of genetic preprogramming had to have occurred.

Those patterns of behavior, given the type of creature *Homo* was to be, probably comprised the raw family and group social bondedness that over the eons has been transmuted into what psychologists call *affect,* our emotional limbic system mammalian personality. From the beginning, however, there was a cortex. It is clear that in our own evolutionary destiny, which involved the pulling and reshaping of the animal in us, we were blessed by the tremendous selective advantage of a more powerful thinking brain—*Homo's* glory.

The growth of the cortex, occurring almost orthoselectively after *Homo's* transition to the long distances of the plains, carried all else in the structure of the brain with it, allometrically (in tandem). Thus began a duality in the evolution of *Homo's* noninstinctual social behavior between the old bonding emotional forces of ethnic affinities (our defensive survival machinery) and the more calculating, external, cool considerations of cortical thought.

This was not merely an academic relationship; it was and is extremely intense, one that we can observe today but still rarely understand. Human beings' more universal aspirations in the world of material, military, economic activities, are attitudes of mind that take us away from home base. Observe sophisticated intellectuals reject their fellow religionists, their own people of origins, and tear off on crusades whether in the name of abstract intellectual ideas, or merely for the sake of world economic plunder (20).

The ethnic emotions and bondings can be transferred to a broader domain. The apartheid of South Africa is an extreme example, a situation effected through intellectually unjust political behavior. Our feelings of sympathy for the re-pressed and exploited take on all the colorations of the home defense emotions of the cultural or ethnic group, only now the mind leads us to make political and social decisions on the basis of a more universal ideal, the brotherhood of mankind.

As I write this on the 100th anniversary of the Statue of Liberty July 4th celebrations, the other side of the ethnic coin is obvious. Here, peoples from the four corners of the world have been blended into a vast and heterogeneous tribe that extends across a continent. The deeply-rooted blood ties of endogamy, language, and religious communion do not exist to bind this people together. So a clever leadership (vide the Romans in their own internationalist/imperialist phase) pulls out all the stops—patriotism, defense of the flag. All the im-ages and symbols that traditionally celebrate ancient ethnic blood-is-thicker-than-water ties blazon forth to recreate that centripetal bond without which national identity cannot be preserved. After all, we have few such instincts programmed into us anymore.

When we note the enormous efforts that great national societies make to stretch that ancient ethnic membrane to en-compass vastly extended boundaries, we bump against a fun-damental social paradox. It is the social tension between the one and the many. In principle, the law of ethnicity involves pluralities of peoples developing the deeply emotional bond-ing glues that set them off from others. The ethnic membrane fundamentally is dependent on the condition of separation.

How far can this membrane be stretched to include transcontinental populations numbering millions of people, sometimes hundreds of millions? It is one thing if they are, for example, Chinese and have inhabited a land for hundreds of thousands of years. It is another when military power or historical accident has created nations such as the Soviet Union or the United States.

Roman law, military protection, commerce and material plenty, a rich Greco-Roman cultural tradition kept an international Latin civilization united for half a millennium. Eventually the glue dried up, and the peoples of the Roman Empire turned to Christianity to restore a historical sense of ethnic unity that had become increasingly vague and meaningless.

The residue was many post-Roman Latin languages, even a Christianity that had to go through a series of centrifugal breakups. It is clear, however, when we examine semi-fragmented Christainity, as well as its splintered offspring, Islam, that the ethnic core of religion can transcend the other symbolic components in a culture, then becoming a universal phenomenon. Both Christianity and Islam still encompass many languages, nationalities, races, a plethora of symbolic heritages.

Thus we see exposed before us the paradox. The actual structure of symbols that human beings express, their meaning, characteristics, and how they focus on man's repertoire of cultural behaviors—language, religion, group social feeling, nationality, the various arts, cuisine, style—can take on the plural or ethnic mode of exclusivity and separation, i.e., cultural pluralism. Else they can jump borders, peoples, and histories, and become part of a universal movement, seemingly joined in cortical exuberance. Sometimes it is expressed in spontaneous cultural communication and acceptance, else economic imperialism, military subjugation.

Yet we cannot be sure that a universal way of life (religious or philosophical) adopted for seemingly positive practical intellectual reasons cannot under certain negative historical circumstances a couple of generations down the line become the focus that will then trigger enormous centripetal ethnic loyalties, as if their very existence depended on maintaining that meaningful symbolic set of identities. Certain kinds of material opportunity have a way of releasing energies in a people, an exit from their ethnic embeddedness. By contrast, a bit of pressure, life becoming once more difficult, a struggle, the ethnic defensiveness is once more invoked, the now-heavy albatross of an international society breaks up as the component parts seek in huddling together to discover once more that mystical luck that will carry them forward.

Millions of years of roaming and struggling to muster the cognitive skills that will ensure the survival of the band have left their mark on all of us. Note that even the persected Jews attribute their perdurance not to their materialistic skills, especially after the Babylonian captivity and the post-Roman diaspora, but to their endogamous commitment to the book, their laws. Unconsciously, the natural outgrowth of centripetal ethnic symbolism, which pluralized *Homo* far more than did his racial separations, became for each tribal, social unit a means of maintaining symbolic integrity. If certain groups were winners over time, then obviously their ethnicity represented a higher cultural (intellectual?) level.

*not necessarily*

The growth of the cortex proceeded to create its own dynamic cultural potentialities. The thinking power that constituted the core element of the victorious ethnics also produced that universal domain of thought that extends to a world of objective laws and social relationships that today transcends ethnicity. The gut feelings of national identity to maintain the integrity of one's group is now buffered by other intellectual valences. The powerful symbolic dynamics of expanding international and objective economic and political institutions war against the conservative defensiveness of the ethnic group, still in the thrall of the ancient forest necessities of surviving the advancing anthropoid host. Now we *are* the anthropoid host joining in a universal economic, political, philosophical crusade that is revolutionizing the symbols of value in our world.

Thus, the Jews and other small ethnic groups tremble. No longer beseiged by the enemy, they burst the boundaries of the ghetto, intermarrying with the majority at an astounding rate, and inevitably, as anthropologist E. A. Hooton of Harvard once predicted, diluting the uniqueness of Jewish intelligence, blending it in with a more neutral majoritarian culture (21).

Everywhere, except in the gridlock of the Soviet bloc, people are alive with interest and commitment to a culture that has renounced ethnicity. Even the Chinese gaze rapturously at advertisements for American gimcrackery on their Japanese color televisions. At the other extreme is the bizarre reaction in the Arab world, especially in Iran, where we see exemplified a last-ditch attempt to rescue an ancient ethnic/religious value system.

The mullahs know well that such a conservative philosophical/religious sociopolitical system could not resist the modernistic technological, commercial political structures that have been loosed upon the world. They know that one crack in the dike would allow a trickle of ethnic dilution to become a river of cultural change. Great as the Islamic culture is, it is yet divided into a number of ethnic subgroups—in Iran's case the Shiite wing of Islam, within a Persian cultural/ linguistic hegemony. Pressed as Iran is by the Iraqis, how long can she survive uncontaminated by land-to-air missiles?

# The Cortical Challenge

The battle here as well as throughout the world has been lifted to a new plane, to that of the cortex itself, the conflict of philosophies, ideologies. The inchoate sense of ethnic exclusivity is being consciously and intellectually undermined in most of the Western world to create interracial, interethnic communities where the old conflicts can be neutralized to prepare citizens for new kinds of ideological wars.

Whereas the old ethnic groups fought to the last—the Igbos, Armenians, Kurds, Afghans, the hill people of Vietnam—to preserve their particular beloved and protective forms of ethnic intelligence, this new world society will have to find more objective philosophical means of protecting the intellectual heritage of mankind. The twentieth century has seen the beginning of the first stage of this epochal evolutionary moment in the history of our genus.

It is ironic that with all the academic studies of our human situation, rarely a word is spoken or written about the state of *Homo,* his condition and prognosis from the evolutionary perspective. Perhaps ignorance is bliss. But the situation is not one of neutrality. The twentieth century has seen the triumph of an ideology that has unleashed a war against this self-same intellectual heritage of mankind and its ethnic carriers that is perhaps unprecedented in the historical record in its concentrated genocidal directionality at one minority. This minority, regardless of its separate cultural heritage, often can be identified within the ethnic membership itself. *It is the intelligent.* It is that group that often has moved the most quickly from tribal encapsulement, to create and exploit the possibilities of this new objective, scientific, international culture.

For millions of years, the steady pace of biological change, perhaps tragically but inevitably, presupposed the triumph of the intelligent. In one stroke, the tables have been reversed. Why, how did it happen, what does it mean? Can it be that we, as a species, so briefly united, exploiting our bioecological possibilities, now hesitate, unwilling or unable to go forward?

In the final chapter of this book, we will consider the meaning of this transition from the world of the preconscious ethnic group struggling for cultural supremacy, and thus genetic immortality, to this new international stage of one ideological culture, one standard of truth, and perhaps one fatal misstep.

# Chapter XX

---

# IDEOLOGY, EGALITARIANISM, AND GENOCIDE

## Reason, Ideology, and Twentieth-Century Genocide

The locus of variable human intelligence is contained within the ethnic community. For several million years, the necessity and then the injunction to breed within the ethnic or tribal community were imperatives. They were also largely preconscious, rarely intellectually expressed, except as "stay with your own."

We humans spontaneously expressed ourselves in the symbolic meanings of cultural existence (1). Our social institutions, our interpersonal behavior expressed our genetic uniqueness both as human beings and as ethnic variations of a model, *Homo.*

A time came when success allowed us the relaxation to

look at ourselves, at what we had achieved over time and space, and even to wonder aloud, "look what we have done, compared to the 'others'—what does it mean?". People began to act out consciously, thoughtfully, a program of development, not necessarily the development of political, economic, or technological possibilities, but a map of human nature and human thought that reflected *Homo sapiens'* spontaneous capacities now objectified into myth, religion, and philosophy.

At the beginning of civilization, as at the beginning of the human odyssey thirty to twenty million years ago, it was a defensive plan, to protect the ethnic group and the good fortune that allowed for life's necessities, even for prosperity. Then, we moved out, we met other groups, different challenges. We fought with these other groups, traded with them, exchanged women, engaged in rape, and discovered that in the act of miscegenation, pleasure won out over pain. At least, this was the case for the passionate moment.

In the prehistorical phases of human progress, the stronger, more intelligent moved the weaker aside, sometimes into oblivion. The stronger had more children who survived into maturity, occupied greater and more productive life space. In a sense, they engaged in a genocidal process that resulted in only one hominoid, *Homo sapiens,* surviving his many competitors of the Oligocene, some thirty million years ago. It will not be too long before the only hominoids (great apes, humans) that remain in the non-*sapiens* category will be those officially protected in zoos and game parks. We see it happening even today (2).

As we have moved into the historical, philosophical phase of our evolution, as we can evaluate and consider our fate, moral questions have intruded. The relations between the weaker and stronger peoples have altered, resulting in sweeping demographic changes that have revived human groups that only one and a half centuries ago were on the verge of dissolution. In fact, the mingling and interbreeding of peoples have resulted in such a rush that the curve of difference symbolized in endocranial capacity as well as cultural civilizational levels continues to flatten out as compared with that of the Pleistocene Ice Ages, a brief ten thousand years ago (3).

Today, we are in the early stages in the universalization of mankind. The technologies created by a highly intelligent segment of our world society have been distributed far and wide. There is no place to hide anymore. What we do not know is what to do with this tidal collision of cultures, ethnic communities, varieties and levels of intellectual and educational capacity.

Events have run beyond our intellectual grasp, certainly beyond the first great intellectual attempts at synthesis: Marxism and Socialism. In terms of turmoil and lightning social and cultural changes, the cautious and dispassionate analysis of ideas, the tentative experiment of hypothesis with truth tends to get ground down into the quick, immediate assumption of surety. Not only do reason and experimental method become trampled in the rush to find quick answers, but a deeper stratum of human motivations is released. Older, limbic system vectors of "they" and "we," which originally protected the protohominids in a web of emotional valences, then to be transformed into a plains aggressiveness, have been re-formed in our modern era—history has gone beyond the control of reason.

The result has been ideology, which *The American College Dictionary* defines as a body of doctrine with reference to political or cultural plans, including the devices, institutions for putting these plans into operation (4). The ideology of environmental egalitarianism is the intellective/emotional device that has been established to explain the *ancien régime,* the heritage of aristocracy, social structure, the domination by the European peoples over the southern peoples of the world.

Even at the time that the philosophical speculations of

Karl Marx had been turned into a pseudoreligious political movement, evidence in the various psychological, biological, and anthropological fields was throwing new light on the biological nature of human variability. As in all new sciences, some of this research was off the mark, some incomplete and tentative (5). However, the wave of political enthusiasm gathered strength with the increasing demographic explosion of peoples, mostly poor, but still the beneficiaries of the new sciences, which resulted in better lives, health, and jobs for the masses.

The ideology of sociological amelioration, socialist political redemption rolled on, and, in a sudden surge, gave birth to its misbegotten progeny, genocide, on a scale never before witnessed, and at a time in human history when expectations for a utopia of rational, educated, middle-class societies were not that far from being sober anticipations. We do not yet have knowledge of the true scope of these many genocidal events of the twentieth century. Nor do we yet understand why they have occurred, how they might be countered so that they can be prevented in the future.

Ideologies, as long as they exert their charm over our minds, are all-pervasive. As did the medieval theologies, they preempt the mind space, refusing to recognize the claims of competing or dissonant philosophies. Modern ideologies may pretend to be secular or scientific. We can recognize the difference, however, because of the emotional commitment of their devotees, the threats that are issued to disbelievers. Eventually, as in our century, punishment for nonmembership can be terrifying.

The reason that we cannot understand our twentieth-century genocidal episodes is that we all still believe in environmental egalitarianism. We cannot accept as possibility that an aspect of differential social status in modern as well as in ancient societies is due to the fact that individuals and groups may differ in intelligence, that the products of this difference may appear in social competencies, in the quality and character of cultures.

Alan Moorehead vividly describes the state of intellectual innocence, where new information is intolerable because it may shatter our well-ordered world, our *Weltanschauung.* Moorehead describes in *The Fatal Impact* Captain Cook's arrival in Botany Bay (near Sydney, Australia) in April of 1770:

At last on April 28—nine days after they had first sighted the coast—they saw an opening in the cliffs and the *Endeavor* put in for shore. There were natives about, some of them spearing fish from canoes, others watching from the rocks and along the cliffs. . . . One can imagine the excitement with which Cook and his men gazed through their glasses as the *Endeavor,* with one of her boats sounding the way ahead, came quietly through the entrance of the bay and soon after midday found an anchorage on the southern side, abreast of a group of huts.

Some odd things were happening on the shore as the *Endeavor* approached. One group of natives, about a dozen in all, went up onto a rise to watch, and when the vessel's boat came near they beckoned the sailors to come ashore. On the other hand, no notice at all seemed to be taken of the *Endeavor* herself. There she was, 106 feet long, with her high masts and her great sails, and when she passed within a quarter of a mile of some fishermen in four canoes they did not even bother to look up. Then when she had anchored close to shore a naked woman carrying wood appeared with three children. "She often looked at the ship," Banks [a member of the expedition] tells us, "but expressed neither surprise or concern. Soon after this she lighted a fire and the four canoes came in from the fishing: the people landed, hauled up their boats and began to dress their dinner, to all appearances totally unmoved by us. . . ." The sight of the *Endeavor* had apparently meant nothing to these primitives because it was too strange, too monstrous, to be comprehended. It had appeared out of nowhere like some menacing phenomenon of nature, a waterspout or a roll of thunder, and by ignoring it or pretending to ignore it no doubt they had hoped it would go away. (6)

## Ideological Egalitarianism

The idea of variable intelligence and the accompanying evolutionary and anthropological evidence that buttressed the existing psychological, educational, and historical knowledge and experience that we had then accumulated came late in the day. The onset of the egalitarian dream had taken hold. The turn of the century saw these sciences beginning to dredge up new facts in our understanding of the historical disequilibrium in the social and cultural development of mankind. However, these were then infant sciences, and, as critics have shown, prone to error, their conceptual reach as yet far beyond their evidential grasp.

At the same time, more mature sciences, physics, chemistry, the applications in engineering, medicine, and technology, had already torn up the traditional social compact. The world was in economic and social turmoil, peoples were on the march throughout the globe, a modernity with unlimited horizons seems to have been created almost overnight. There was no appeal from the warranted assumption that social conditions, in their revolutionary impact on life-styles, beliefs, positions in society made everything infinitely malleable. We were to be whatever the social conditions in this changing world would determine us to be. No limits could be placed on the reeducability of humans.

The existing variability between individuals and peoples could not compare to the power of society to reshape each of us. The molding impact of this all-powerful environment was being tangibly demonstrated around us. Thus, the evident reality of the idea of social determinism transformed itself into an ideology about human nature, about the power of political and economic forces to reshape this nature and about the necessity to wipe the slate of history clean of the recidivistic patterns of the older generations. Echoing Plato, Lenin asked only to be given those first five or ten years in a child's life.

It is fair to note that part of the egalitarian vision of a classless future was built out of revulsion as well as vision. The history of human slavery, serfdom, the ferocity of the criminal justice and pauper system seemingly vindictively directed at the vulnerable poor, place these historical residues at the feet of the old class-structured system. The gulag had not yet been invented, the scope of twentieth-century human horror as yet inconceivable to those then absorbed into a new vision of possibility.

The Marxist philosophy and its various socialistic embodiments promised everything. A utopia of nonexploitation, equality of social and economic condition regardless of race or ethnic background could be achieved, even the withering away of the coercive restraints of state power. First, however, the power ultimately residing in the will of the people, the *volonté générale* of Rousseau, had to be transferred from oppressive, monarchical, liberal, capitalist hands into those of the representatives of all the people (7).

In a time of enormously increased military power, speed of communication, industrial wealth, transport efficiencies, control of the state bureaucratic apparatus gave any leadership group powers that a Louis XIV would have envied. Here, in a nutshell, was the source both for the tragedies of World War I and II and the ensuing genocidal events of our century.

First came the power that a modern technological society gave to any unscrupulous leadership group that could entrench itself through the totalitarian control of a now tightly interlaced modern industrial society (8). Second came an ideology of egalitarianism, in which old social class, ethnic and religious differences were frontally attacked in the name of modern secularism. Most tragically, it was a pseudoscientism, which, in the undeveloped state of our knowledge and the emotional utopian tone of reform lent to all such concepts by ideology, was really beyond critical intellectual reach (9).

Few chroniclers of the twentieth century have noted or

discussed the role of this universalistic mode of thought and behavior that has characterized our century. Along with a blindness to the reality of intellectual variability has come an uncritical assent to those political, social, cultural, even racial unifications that have been spawned as seeming laws of nature (10). The world has come together not necessarily voluntarily, but has been coerced by this ideology, which has striven to dissolve the various cultural and national boundary lines of human history, including the ethnic membrane.

Even against the will of populations, political leadership groups, acting in consort with the liberal vogue for universal solutions, including an egalitarianism of condition, have broken down national ethnic traditions by inviting the world to their respective nations. They have consistently ruled against religious and ethnic privatism, ever in favor of that elusive public by which they lay claim to their legitimacy (11). Ultimately, the final solution had to come. It was a conscious attempt to destroy those religious, ethnic, and social class groups within their respective societies that had acted creatively for civilization, and thus inevitably benefited themselves, attaining a favored social position compared to the mass.

To what can be attributed this ideological enthusiasm that has reduced the soberest of our thinkers, and for almost a century, to the status of passive yeasayers? Much of modern civilization derives from the scientific revolution of the seventeenth century and its largely eighteenth-century political embodiment in the Enlightenment. The core belief of the Enlightenment was in the possibility of rationality in the free citizenry of democratic societies, all acting under the aegis of empirical and hypothetical principles. One can say that the possibility of democracy rested on the capacity of a free citizenry for skepticism (12).

In order to confront an ever-changing world, political leaders, delegated extremely limited powers, would place into effect laws that would, so to speak, test the waters of experience, be ever subject to recall and reconsideration. While there was commitment to equal rights of citizens before the law and an implicit policy in society of equality of opportunity, nevertheless, the variability of skills, talents, inclinations in human beings was acknowledged as a matter of experience, truth, and wisdom. Indeed, Jefferson himself believed that the survival of the United States was dependent on the uncovering and education of an aristocracy of talent to lead the less wise but no less noble and enfranchised citizenry (13).

These views were part of a general Western civilizational thrust that gave us for the first time in two thousand years the hope for a democratic, lawful society that respected the rights both of individuals and their various voluntarily-formed communities. Yet, so abruptly, it all seemed to have ended with the French Revolution and its reign-of-terror aftermath. The European mind shifted toward the incense of historical determinism, idealistic Hegelian philosophy, the first enunciation of the myth of the unlimited nature of the state, and then Karl Marx (14).

# Genocide

It began with the Armenians during World War I. Sultan Abdul Hamid was deposed by the revolutionary Ittihad Party led by Talaat and Enver. The expulsions and killings began in April 1915. Before they ended, over one year later, some 1.5 million Armenians had been slaughtered (15). The revolutionary twentieth-century state had begun its work in ridding itself of privileged minorities, unassimilable to the general will.

The next series of events, the most extensive and horrific in numbers, occurred under Stalin in Marxist Soviet Union. There, a society under the heel of its revolutionary elite for over a decade closed its doors, exercising total control of information, transportation, life itself. Between 1930 and 1940, at least ten to twenty million people died, and perhaps many more, victims of Stalin's crusade against real and imaginary dissident elements (16).

The communist intellectual class, the kulaks—independent peasant landowning remnants of Lenin's New Economic Policy—the Ukrainian peasant classes only recently emerging from feudalism under the czars, all were exterminated. This was accomplished through outright murder, deportation to the gulags in Siberia and elsewhere, and finally by an artificially-induced famine in 1931-32, in which foreign aid was not admitted to the afflicted areas. The world has only recently become aware of this dark episode in socialist revolutionary history (17).

Next was the Holocaust. Under Hitler's National Socialism, some six million Jews, several hundred thousand Gypsies, and an assorted million or so other East Europeans were sucked into the gas chambers and crematoria of the Third Reich (18). Another socialistic final solution to the "cancer" of ethnic indigestibility had been completed.

The post-World War II period saw the end of the colonial order. Throughout the world, socialist revolutionary regimes took over from their once-imperious European "exploiters." New systems of social justice were inaugurated, and on profound Marxist philosophical assumptions. Almost immediately, a torrent of blood poured forth from these third world revolutionary democracies. It is still difficult to disentangle traditional ethnic butchery from the newer, twentieth-century forms of ideological genocide.

Class and ethnic warfare is an ancient phenomenon regularly appearing in early civilizational chronicles. For example, we are well aware of the revolutionary blood baths that occurred both in ancient Greece and Rome in the contests for political and military power. The struggles of oligarchic and democratic groups almost inevitably, with the rare exception of Athens, resulted in tidal bloodletting. Even Athens destroyed the male population of the island of Melos during the drawn-out fratricidal conflict with Sparta. The Melians were innocent noncombatants caught up in events that denied them the right of neutrality (19).

In 1947, Hindus butchered Muslims and vice versa at the birth of India and Pakistan. Later, Muslim and Urdu-speaking West Pakistanis, in a bloody invasion, attempted to put down revolutionary Muslim East Pakistanis. These latter were ethnic Bengalis soon to form a state, Bangladesh (1971-72) (20).

In Indonesia, in 1965, a slaughter of over one-half million communists was undertaken by a right-wing regime (21). There then occurred a genocidal military incursion into East Timor, perhaps to empty it of its ethnically disparate peoples, this in 1975 (22). The Chinese Communists came to power in 1949. We still do not know the extent to which they rid the Middle Kingdom of its "tainted landlord" between 1949 and 1950. One estimate is between one and two million (23). Throughout Southeast Asia, in Malaysia and Indonesia, the Chinese minorities were themselves subject to a series of sporadic genocidal events. This led to the separation of Singapore, largely Chinese in population, from the outlying mainland, different racially, religiously, and ethnically. Certainly the terrible events that have overtaken Chinese populations in the post-World War II period were ideological in nature and contrast sharply with the more basic ethnic and political depredations of the Japanese during the great war (24).

In Africa, unceasing horrors have occurred since freedom was "bestowed" to these long-suffering peoples. How can one describe the reigns of Amin in Uganda or Bokassa in the Central African Republic? In terms of ideologically-rooted genocide, we can point to the extermination of the Arab trading class in Zanzibar (25). Also, the ethnic war between the Hutu and Tutsi (Watusi) in Rwanda and Burundi reflects the attempt to reverse the condition of the underdog Hutu to the ruling Tutsi aristocracy. Both sides can be blamed for almost equal records of bestial slaughter of elites

(26). In Nigeria, the initial tragedy of that former British Colony began with the annihilation of several tens of thousands of Igbo residents in the Moslem north (Christian stranger settlements). The subsequent declaration of independence by the Igbo in Biafra led to a protracted war that probably caused the deaths of two million or so of these industrious and progressive peoples, either killed outright or through premeditated starvation (27).

The final event up to the present in this genocidal wave was the destruction by the Khmer Rouge of its own Cambodian middle class. The Khmer Rouge used the traditional technique of mass expulsion from the cities, systematically slaughtering or starving these peoples under the cover of chaos in the countryside. Here, the estimate runs to about 1.5 million people (28).

There can be no question that this brief chronicle is incomplete. Control of the State under these revolutionary regimes purportedly maintaining themselves through the socialistic functions of the will of the people has been such that much is still hidden about horrors of which the world is yet unaware. The twentieth century is not over and the conditions of jealousy, envy, ethnic hatred, social, economic, and political exploitation and disenfranchisement of every sort remain, constituting a potential tinder box.

To what do these events point? How do they relate to the issue of human intellectual variability and the ideology of social egalitarianism?


# Leadership and Its Rationalization

To answer these questions, we must consider briefly the special adaptive conditions for intelligence as it relates to the human cultural experience. Intelligence has always functioned as nature's solution to the problem of environmental change under conditions far more dynamic than could be adaptively responded to by mutation and the protected genes. Predictive behavior is what allows intelligent animals to survive the process of natural selection.

We humans also draw an experiential map by which we make causal predictions about the natural and social environment. These predictions determine how we will respond to new events. The deeper and more accurate our assessment both of the regularities and the adventitious events in our experience, the more probable will by our success, our luck, and then the favor of lady natural selection.

A protective social net of institutions that would insure our survival has been created by intelligent communities working together to make life a bit safer, and thus more livable. In each community, those with the most useful skills necessary both for the survival and flourishing of the community came to the attention of their fellows. Woe to the community that allowed fools or maniacs to assume positions of responsibility or power. In the natural variability of intelligence both in the quantitative and qualitative sense, the more complex, the richer, inevitably more adaptive communities, leadership was assumed by steady, rational individuals in various aspects of life, from the military to the religious, to the mercantile and agricultural domains. Thus, civilization developed, first in Sumer, on this basis of furthering a plurality of high intelligence (29). The personal scrutiny and the discipline by which the small social group keeps its leaders in line is loosened as societies expand in size and numbers. Surrounded by retinues of sycophants, often enjoying hereditary privilege, the leadership or kingship can fall into the hands of incompetents. The society rolls along through inertia, the steady middle class making things work, that is until critical challenges occur and the leaders are put to the test.

Our explanations of the rise and fall of peoples, societies, even civilizations usually focus on extrinsic events, the amount of lead in the water pipes, the stratification of society, famines, climatic changes, sudden invasions of migrant warrior peoples, the silting up of the irrigation system. Indeed, these are often factors. We ought also look to the knowledge and intelligence factors in the society. What is the character of the leadership? How intelligent, disciplined, uncorrupted is it? What is the knowledge structure of the society? Does its people rely on myth and superstition to guide its behavior or is it a practical, planning people that can separate mythic emotion from the real challenges of concrete experience? Finally, how has the intelligence level of the people fared with prosperity and the settled good life? Often, the decline of corporate intelligence leads to technological indolence, the growth of supernaturalism, and finally a decline in the quality of the leadership group.

The problem of the rationalization of the leadership group does begin with the settlement of peoples, in the post-tribal, wandering, military existence. Before, leaders were wise and charismatic fighters. The criteria were clear as to who would be the good leader. Failure usually meant death at the hands of the enemy or by the many contestants for this supreme position within the group.

There is a point in the development of social existence when humans begin to attempt to reason on the basis of objective written principle. It is not enough spontaneously to create leadership; it must be rationalized, usually first in ritual and myth. Humans love to recount tales. These can have a kernel of fact, but often embroidered from our imagination, desires, even rational conjectures about an outside world of forces and powers that has its impact on us.

What began as conscious chronometric markings on bone or rock in those ancient Ice Age caves, to trace the duration of the moon's phases, women's menstrual periods, the seasons' ebb and flow, eventually grew into a literature regaling a people about a pantheon of gods and forces dealing not merely with nature's regularities but with man himself, his powers and weaknesses, complexities and idiosyncracies (30).

As the leader became more than the warrior, he was endowed with god-like power; he became a focus of holy sacrament, a moral exemplar, sometimes even a figure of tragedy. The real leader of humans is a complex of intelligence, drive, physical vigor, political acumen, and moral respect. We begin to ask questions about these attributes, how they are derived, what are the sources of their charisma. It rises into our consciousness as recognition and question, a mysterious phenomenon.

People see it, feel it, search for meaning, not the least those groups that have the power, seeking to explain and justify this privilege. Thus, we note the close allegiance between priestly and monarchical power. This link has also been duly emphasized by the Marxists, only here linking it as well with economic class controls, for which the royal and religious institutions cloak their privileges in myth, theology, and ritual tradition (31).

This duality of institutional and hierarchical authority existed perhaps universally in the advanced societies. The exceptions in classical Greece and in Republican Rome represent unique, perhaps even ephemeral moments in human history. However, with the Enlightenment outlook on the philosophical and theological claims for divine right, a new element entered, reminding one of that epochal parting of the waters of vested privilege.

The nineteenth century saw the steady erosion of the monarchical position in large part brought about by new economic and social conditions that upended those claims for special privilege. With the revolution in demographics and economics, however, the upthrust of a vast proletarian class, now aspiring to an economic existence heretofore only dreamed of by royalty, the entire system of values that supported the older political and economic structure was thrown into disarray.

Today, we look back in awe to the art and culture, the

science and learning that the aristocracy sponsored and encouraged, even if only to glorify its privilege. We contrast this inundation of genius with the trash that pours out of our automated factories to satisfy the contemporary cultural demands of the masses, the pablum that emanates from the mass media, even the *New York Times Magazine,* the educator of the sophisticates, and we can understand the level of culture that egalitarianism has fostered.

The point here is not to condemn the inevitable cultural effects of a demographic trend that science has loosed upon us. The Marxists are correct here also. An egalitarian philosophy was fostered partially by new economic social trends, not autonomously or deterministically. Rather, ideas that would have had to fight to be heard in earlier days, received a ready hearing in the nineteenth century amid this upthrust of poor people and new technological vistas. Egalitarianism became sanctified. The liberal eighteenth-century European espousal of equality of opportunity that had oiled the engine of material and political progress was transformed into a philosophy of economic and political history that now was viewed as fixed in the stars.

The last vestige of a belief in blood, family, privilege, the inherited mark of the people, has been removed from our consciousness. With this departure also was dissolved any acceptability of the principle of ability or aristocracy. The philosophy of dialectical materialism, now victorious, was transformed into a series of quasi-socialistic ideologies, each with its own peculiar, often national, revolutionary agenda.

It was not enough to topple the kings, the barons, the bishops, but also the capitalists, the wealthy, anyone of status and achievement, all that related in any way to the old privileged order. It was forgotten that Enlightenment liberalism, together with the monarchical system, even in sunset eliminated slavery and serfdom. The civilizational disciplines of restraint, moderate social change, in a time of enormous turmoil, seem to have failed. This failure of human intelligence to maintain its hold eventually resulted in the release of the dark, ferocious side of human nature.

An idea was now about, in a world increasingly in communication and thus subject to the persuasions of this universal grammar of revolutionary egalitarianism. All human beings were to be seen as not merely endowed with certain political rights. Rather, an ideal of "from each according to his ability, to each according to his needs," would be transformed into a new revolutionary paraphrase (32). The very fact of social differentiation, of wealth and status, ethnic or social group identity was taken as *prima facie* evidence for covert immoral behavior. How else, the new leadership argued, could such privilege have been obtained if not at the expense of the less fortunate?

## Conditions of Genocide

The religious crusades of the Middle Ages are the paradigm for what has happened in our century. A war for economic or political ends often can be negotiated, can be made to abide by the rules of gentleman officers. After all, such organized killing is not too different from the contests of skill in a cricket match. However, in an ideological war, whether religious or political, such rational restraints are jettisoned. It aims for the jugular, for in such a war, the enemy is no gentleman. The enemy has no human or moral status.

The fact that twentieth century genocide has been so variable, at one time the result of classic religious or ethnic conflicts, at others directed at one's own people, testifies to the existence of a far more pervasive "world spirit," a climate of opinion that has deeply infected the responses of mankind in general. Indeed, one will find, as in the Indonesian slaughter of communists in the mid-1960s, a reaction and a seeming exception to the ideological thrust that has characterized our time. It only means that bestiality, once its emergence from the underworld of the human brain is sanctioned intellectually, will do its work in a less than neat and consistent manner.

That is why when the Nazis began their final solution to the Jewish problem it was extended rapidly from the remnant German Jews to all the Jews of Europe and almost matter-of-factly to the Gypsies and other East European populations who, for one reason or another, fell into the net. It is clear that one cannot expect to find a rationalization for genocide that will in every case meet the explanatory test (33). It is certainly foolish, and intellectually dangerous, to accept explanations for genocide from the murderers themselves. Genocidal episodes resulting from an ideology based on illusion and lie will be propagandized in the most convenient, not the most rational, manner.

The Stalinists created their own satanical descriptions of the victims who were supposedly acting to block a Socialist Utopia. Here, the link of the residual Russian leadership communities with the older order may have had a patina of truth for those who only heard the lilt of Marxist rhetoric. Even the internal Bolshevik elite could be done in under the pretence of heresy against the true communist teaching. In the case of the Russian general staff, the warrant was that these were secret collaborators with a potential external enemy (Germany) (34).

Much is made of Hitler's racist rantings in *Mein Kampf,* his seeming advocacy of eugenics, the external panoply of pseudoscientism with which he cloaked his clearly-articulated and well-planned vengeance against the Jews. Whatever one might say about his referrals to this "nether race," this "cancerous appendage" to the pure Teutonic *"Herrenvolk,"* which he willed to be freed of this "verminous" race of foreigners that was "poisoning" the fatherland, it cannot be argued that the Nazis or the German people themselves saw the

Jews as pitiful incompetents (35). Every bit of factual evidence points to just the opposite. In a brief two or three generations, the Jews had emerged from their ghettos, flooded into the German cities, whether Vienna or Berlin, and prospered as no Germanic or Slavic inhabitants of these cities had done before them (36).

In so prospering, in dominating, considering their number, every area of cultural and economic importance, save perhaps the military, and even including the political life of these cities and nations, the Jews therefore had not earned themselves the love of the ordinary or even the successful German citizenry that had to compete with them. By the time of the Weimar Republic, Jewish dominance was palpable, now that Vienna—and Austria—had shrunk in opportunity as well as economic and social possibility (37).

It is interesting to note that Austria under the Nazis was even more vengeful against its Jewish compatriots than was Germany proper (38). We would be kidding ourselves, indeed we have stubbornly refused to recognize, that the Germans knew the social status and competence of the people they were exterminating; Stalin knew whom he was slaughtering in the millions. The Turks were well aware of the contributions, the economic, social, and educational level of the Armenians when they drove them out of their communities to rape, starve, and butcher them.

The Hausas saw the Igbo settlements as enclaves of economic and political privilege. Not only were the Igbos ethnically (tribally) different; they were of a different religion. The Chinese Communists under Mao did not need much of an excuse, during the Korean conflict, to round up the remnants of the old order; Mao simply dubbed them "landlords" and brutally destroyed millions of them. The Khmer Rouge, finally, summed it all up, even at the price of their indigenous civilization: they destroyed their educated middle classes and returned their nation to a more pristine form of subsistence agricultural socialism.

These "egalitarians" could not announce through the news media that: "we are destroying the most intelligent, able, educated, productive members of our society, because we are jealous of their achievements in the relatively free give-and-take of the postmonarchical and postcolonial world. If we cannot obtain power democratically, through the free exchange of ideas and achievements, we shall manipulate the people through the myth of socialistic egalitarianism, seize control through every lie that can be foisted on our gullible and mesmerized populace. We will then make them accomplices in these 'final solutions,' so that our power and authority will never be questioned. Our guilt will be theirs; their weakness will be our opportunity."

The concept of intellectual variability was not that developed in the nineteenth century for it to have become a focus for debate for the evolving Marxist ideology. Thus, Marx himself, in "Critique of the Gotha Program," noted the existence of intellectual variability (39). Here, too, just as in the old aristocratic order, was an inchoate awareness of regal achievement, of the importance of family character, of noble blood. Marx could not avoid the facts that have led to the traditional rationalization of hierarchical status, for the ruled as well as the ruler.

In the twentieth century, the concentrated fury of the attack on achieving minorities, whether they be ethnic enclaves within newer populist, socialized societies or traditional successful governing classes within national societies, reminded us once again that this awareness of distance has always existed. However, because the issue of human achievement, intellectual variability, still lay for the most part below the surface of consciousness because it was not articulated intellectually or philosophically, it had no power to resist irrational ideological fury.

Even in the darkest days of the Jews in crusade-ridden medieval Europe, then, facing the pogroms of eighteenth- and nineteenth-century eastern Europe, the venerable reality of a great religious faith somehow secured, even amid the sporadic persecutions and attacks, the existence, the flourishing of these peoples (40). Once religion itself had lost its legitimacy, once human achievement as such became torn from its normal associations with the aspiration for nobility and aristocracy, once a single ideal only, an ideological dogma, seduced the masses, that of the uniformity of talent, intelligence, achievement, then all those who represented anything more than the mediocre became vulnerable to any one of the final solutions. Anything could then be perpetrated, sanctified as it was by the "people's society."

## Contemporary Ideological Liberalism

We are like the Australian aborigines watching Captain Cook's *Endeavor* when it comes to reading the meaning of twentieth-century genocide. It may just as well not have happened. The egalitarian rhetoric in its more sophisticated contemporary Western liberal format is essentially the same in import as that of the savage totalitarian propagandists. The social ills of our time are due to socially-induced inequalities created by political and economic systems that are controlled by immoral people, call them greedy plutocrats, elitists, racists, white male supremacists.

A whole series of social welfare legislation was inaugurated in earlier periods of our century to ameliorate conditions that were deemed to be out of synchronization with what was now possible—the franchise, anti-child labor, public housing, unemployment benefits, labor relations, antidiscrimination laws, etc. The bulk of these programs were put through with the thought that they would provide the needed boost to get people out of their historically-rooted poverty, on their feet, and out into the productive middle class. The idea was social justice, fairness. Take a little more from the haves. Give a little more to the temporary have-nots and allow them to join the haves in a truly middle-class democratic society.

This worked in the United States for the various northern minorities, European and northeast Asiatics. All had made their competitive case in the interaction of social, economic, and thus national development. The problem remained with the peoples of the south, the Negroes, southeastern Asiatics, Latin Americans, in all a very mixed racial and ethnic conglomeration of peoples.

The continued backwardness of these populations, whether in their own homelands or as migrants, willing and unwilling, exacerbated the frustration of the intellectual leaders under the spell of ideological egalitarianism (41). The only obvious reason for this backwardness was the nineteenth-century heritage of slavery and discrimination. Thus, a wide variety of philanthropic and welfare programs was effected to help these deprived peoples.

Variously, rulings were enacted recently that affirmed reverse discrimination, quotas, it was to be hoped equalizing the starting place in the competitive race for position in those democratic societies where free institutions still remained. Immigration from the south was encouraged, presumably to shatter the indigenous monopolies of the native northern peoples and also supposedly to provide refuge from the negative political atmosphere that systematically seemed to infect the southern part of the world (42).

Intransigent to amelioration, this continued backwardness was unanimously agreed upon to be caused by the heritage of discrimination, colonialism, slavery, and oppressive authoritarian governance (43). It would seem that the rhetoric of racial and ethnic hatred that had been dredged up throughout the century by the totalitarian states to rationalize the genocide they had in mind, was still accepted at face value by the liberal community. Thus, a pantheon of social, intellectual devils again was created to represent the ostensible causes for the inequalities of achievement in our world, even in a time when ideological environmental egalitarianism, especially as espoused by the various Socialist/Marxist societies, was losing its forward momentum. There was even a retreat from the egalitarian model in nations such as China, Great Britain, India, and Hungary.

The demons that today are thrust forth to maintain this ideology, especially in the West, are, of course, the slavery and racism that purportedly still taint all our behavior. To prove the validity of this accusation, ideologists only have to point to the patent lack of equal results in our world, even after a century of effort to even out the social scorecard. The next step is to paint the opposition to the reigning ideology with the colors of the K.K.K. Naturally, the existence in any society of the usual small lunatic fringe ostensibly justifies just such accusations.

The ideological egalitarians then launch a vicious attack on a wide variety of scientific approaches to our biological nature, from the eugenics of such leading late-nineteenth-century thinkers as Francis Galton to the I.Q. and aptitude testing movement, which in spite of this persistent opposition still flourishes throughout the world (44). The assumption is that if one believes that humans have a biological nature, or that if intelligence is deemed to be variable between individuals and ascribed to a hereditary genetic origin, these beliefs automatically must give rise to the old and new forms of enslavement and discrimination.

Contrast, for example, Galton's attitude toward eugenics, which today, without controversy, reveals itself in "genetic counseling" and in a wide variety of medical approaches to hereditary defects, and seems to have been absorbed as an integral part of our scientific nonideological treatment of human health. Francis Galton, 1908; "Man is gifted with pity and other kindly feelings: he also has the power of preventing many kinds of suffering. I conceive it to fall well within his province to replace Natural Selection by other processes that are more merciful and not less effective. This is precisely the aim of eugenics.''

Even the noted Jesuit anthropologist Teilhard de Chardin saw the eugenics movement in a similar scientific and moral light: "So far we have certainly allowed our race to develop at random, and we have given too little thought to the question of what medical and moral factors *must replace the crude forces of natural selection* should we suppress them. In the course of the coming centuries it is indispensable that a nobly human form of eugenics, on a standard worthy of our personalities, should be discovered and developed" (45).

Let us contrast these sober, restrained, and rational evaluations of a scientific movement that recognizes that the human genotype has a variability that often expresses itself with tragically negative personal and social results with an example of an alternative view. The *New York Times* literary commentator, Christopher Lehmann-Haupt, is a believer in the ideology of social, environmental amelioration:

> Indeed, the practice of eugenics would seem to have been discredited once and for all by the uses to which it was put in Nazi Germany, which . . . were not just isolated aberrations, but the culmination of elitist, racist tendencies at work from the late nineteenth century onward. Who in these enlightened times would want to re-invoke a theory of racial stereotypes, or return to the practice of sterilizing people judged from a narrowly elitist point of view, to be defective by virtue of their genetic endowment? (46)

Forty years ago, a great anthropologist, Earnest Albert Hooton, of Harvard University, discussed a related and important issue with respect to this Nazi use of racial rhetoric as prelude to genocide:

> In common with all reputable anthropologists, I abhor the vicious nonsense about racial inequality, and particularly "Nordic" and "Aryan" superiority, put out by German

propagandists and by others under the guise of anthropology. Frankly, I do not think that the German anthropologists who emitted this stuff ever believed it themselves. They merely yielded to political pressure and wrote what they were ordered to write. No intelligent person with a scientific training in anthropology has anything but scorn for these unfounded claims, fanatical ravings, and faked facts. Their purpose is simply to arouse the prejudice of ignorant people of their own race against alien races in order to justify aggression, conquest, robbery, and murder. These absurd prevarications and foolish theories require no scientific refutation, because they are intended for consumption and belief by persons of such low intelligence that evidence, proof, reason, and truth itself mean nothing at all to them. Anthropologists only waste their time when they indulge in hysterical polemics against "racism" on the ground that it has no scientific justification. Of course it has not, nor is it intended to have; it is meant to influence minds impermeable to scientific reasoning.

Racial prejudice and racial discrimination are not likely to disappear as a result of the possible findings of scientists that all races are equal or that differences between them are insignificant. They arise from the desire of low grade human beings to dominate and exploit their fellow men, and they serve merely as convenient excuses for such evil behavior. These prejudices and discriminations can readily be transferred from race to nationality, to social class, to religious faith—wherever competition between human beings exists with resulting antagonisms. They will not be cured by preaching nor by the writing of learned treatises on racial anthropology (47),

# Philosophy and Ideology

Philosophies are thought experiments that make certain hypothetical claims about the nature of physical, biological, or cultural reality. They are claims on our intellectual assent.

The next step is to extrapolate the consequences of any philosophy when we seek to apply its teachings in the search for knowledge or human betterment.

A philosophy is a web of interrelated ideas. At the extreme edges of this web wave unconnected strands, which invite our actions. From an established philosophy of human experience, we can venture onto the high seas of practical envisagement. In the end, a philosophy can be transformed into a program of social policy.

Unfortunately, it is difficult to maintain the experimental attitude: (1) how true to experience is this philosophy? (2) Does our practical program amplify and extend the philosophy logically and consistently? (3) Do the people have the self-discipline, the attitude of wait-and-see, to suppress all the momentary emotional seductions that disgorge those primeval limbic system categories of "they and we"?

This is what happens in ideology, whether it be a religious dogma or merely a secular vision of utopia. Those who jump toward rigid and absolute sureties "know" the truth, whether it is given to them directly by deity or by their sainted ideological leaders. This is the tragedy of egalitarianism. As a philosophy, it is innocuous. Its claims on our allegiance ought to be subject to careful experiment and prediction. "Let's try it out and see if it flies," should be the motto. Instead, in the great ideological sweep of the twentieth century, we have been led to assume that, of course, all humans have equal intelligence and that variability, if it may exist between individuals and groups, is a matter of passing cultural traditions and education.

We cannot take seriously the attacks on the morality of the biological point of view, either those against eugenics or I.Q. testing. As Earnest Hooton pointed out, only when abused by the most ignorant and pernicious humans could these have hurt us. For that matter, what idea, innocuous or not, cannot be abused and perverted by the stupid or malevolent?

Our own experience with such views here in the United States has been relatively innocent. Sterilization by force has been rare, I.Q. testing in an open society has condemned few individuals with hidden intelligence and "P"-factored drive from fulfilling their potential. This is because we have been open and questioning as a nation. We see to it that no one idea precludes other possibilities. We have been able to revoke those policies that are clearly in error or have become too rigorous and rigid in their application. This is the character of a truly free, nonideological society. Here, the State stands ready to intervene against fanaticism, against restrictions on competition and enterprise. In the free world, the State never closes the door to new knowledge. It does not seek to create an ideological vehicle out of its own potential for great and coercive powers.

Unfortunately, the reverse has happened in other parts of the world. It does not matter that some nations, such as Germany, were highly sophisticated and educated, others barely beyond the tribal level. The seductions of the ancient mammalian brain structures led them all, under conditions of duress, to throw away ten thousand years of rational, cognitive development of the potentiality for philosophical and scientific thought. That was nature's only gift to *Homo sapiens sapiens.*

When the ice began to melt ten thousand years ago, the possibility of true civilization was born. This possibility was created from that fund of high intelligence that existed as mostly latent potentiality in those northern ice-bound populations. It involved *Homo sapiens sapiens'* ability to objectify human experience in symbols of meaning, then to utilize this symbolic knowledge as a platform of concepts that would lead us toward new horizons of conjecture and envisagement. Here lies the ultimate sociobiological mystery, the relationship of biological intelligence to the creation of those social and cultural institutions and instrumentalities that have brought humans into civilization.

It is the relationship of human variable intelligence to civilization building that underlies the argument of this series of books. However the question is answered, two factors seem preeminent today: (1) Our knowledge of human evolution, of the structure and workings of the body and the brain are now advanced enough so that we can make a few hesitant causal predictions concerning a general theory of mental functioning. (2) We are one world, one people, increasingly intermixed and interbred.

Whatever can be concluded concerning the nature of variable intelligence will probably have to be argued in the universalistic mode. The races and ethnic groups of our planet are too highly melded ever to allow us to return to even the relatively benign European ethnocentrism of the nineteenth century. "Benign" may seem to be an odd word to use here, but it is meant to convey a contrast between the so-called depredations of colonialism and the horrors into which large portions of the independent third world have since fallen.

No matter what our ideas and hypotheses are, they will have to be examined, analyzed, and subjected to dispassionate criticism from the standpoint of one world. Repeat, we are one people. We can no longer tolerate apartheid, just as we must turn away forever, in revulsion, from genocide.

The mandate now is to our educated classes. They will determine the fate of ideology, whether it is to be permanently extirpated from our behavior in favor of secular scientific reasoning, or will continue to haunt us as we search futilely for ever-receding utopias.

This century began with high hopes for science, democracy, social justice. It is concluding with totalitarianism, starvation, and plague. Part of the problem has been our lack of intellectual courage to look reality directly in the face.

# Bibliography and References

## Chapter I
### Introduction: Intellectual Responsibility

1. Rousseau, J. J., 1950 (1762). *The Social Contract.* New York: E. P. Dutton, p. 94.
2. Marx, K., 1932. *The Communist Manifesto* ed. by F. Engels. New York: International, pp. 21-29; Marx, K., 1906 (1859-1870) *Capital.* ed. by F. Engels. New York: Modern Library, p. 837.
3. Gould, S. J., 1981. *The Mismeasure of Man.* New York: W. W. Norton; see also Davis, B. D., 1986. *Storm Over Biology: Essays on Science, Sentiment, and Public Policy.* Buffalo: Prometheus.
4. Lipovechajo, N. G., Kantonistova, N. C., and Chamoganova, T. G., 1978. "The Role of Heredity and Environment in the Determination of Intellectual Functions," *Medicinskie Problemy Formrovanija Livenosti,* pp. 48-59; Eysenck, H. J., 1982. "The Sociology of Psychological Knowledge, the Genetic Interpretation of the I. Q. and Marxist-Leninist Ideology," *Bulletin of the British Psychological Society, 35:*449-451; Jensen, A. R. 1984 "Political Ideologies and Educational Research," *Phi Beta Kappan,* March, 460-462.
5. Scarr, S., and Carter-Saltzman, L., 1982. "Genetics and Intelligence," in Sternberg, R. J., ed. *Handbook of Human Intelligence.* Cambridge: Cambridge University Press, pp. 792-896; Vernon, P. E., 1979. *Intelligence: Heredity and Environment.* San Francisco: W. H. Freeman, p. 262.
6. Lichter, S. R., Rothman, S., Lichter, L. S., 1986. *The Media Elite.* Bethesda, Maryland: Adler and Adler; Ladd, E. C., 1986. "Assessing the Findings," *The World and I,* December, 380-385; Grenier, C., 1986. "Self Appointed Guardians of the Nation's Virtue," *The World and I,* December, 386-394.

## Chapter II
### Humanity's Unfinished Journey

1. Simpson, G. G., 1944. *Tempo and Mode in Evolution.* New York: Columbia University Press; Simpson, G. G., 1949. "Rates of Evolution in Animals," in *Genetics, Paleontology, and Evolution.* Jepsen, G. L., Simpson, G. G., and Mayr, E., eds. Princeton: Princeton University Press, p. 214.

2. Rensch, B., 1959. *Evolution Above the Species Level.* New York: Columbia University Press, pp. 82-96.

3. Tattersall, I., and Delson, E., 1984. *Ancestors.* New York: American Museum of Natural History.

4. Coon, L., 1962. *The Origin of Races.* New York: Knopf, p. 13.

5. Itzkoff, S. W., 1983. *The Form of Man.* Ashfield, Massachusetts: Paideia Publishers, pp. 288-290, Plate 3.

6. Simpson, G. G., 1953. *The Major Features of Evolution.* New York: Columbia University Press, pp. 340-376.

7. Stanley, S. M., 1981. *The New Evolutionary Timetable.* New York: Basic Books, pp. 110-137.

8. Lack, D., 1947. *Darwin's Finches.* Cambridge: Cambridge University Press; Cain, A. J., 1954. *Animal Species and Their Evolution.* London: Hutchinson's University Library, p. 154.

9. Jerison, H., 1973. *Evolution of the Brain and Intelligence.* New York: Academic Press.

10. Portmann, A., and Stingelin, W., 1961. "The Central Nervous System," in *Biology and Comparative Physiology of Birds,* Volume 2, Marshall, A. J., ed. New York: Academic Press, pp. 1-36.

11. Lilly, J. C., 1961. *Man and Dolphin.* Garden City: Doubleday; for a more critical view see Edinger, T., 1955 "Hearing and Smell in Cetacean History." *Monatsschr. Psychiat. Neuro., 129:*37-38.

12. On the paedomorphism reflected in the circumstances of the neonate's birth see de Beer, Sir Gavin, 1958. *Embryos and Ancestors.* Oxford: Oxford University Press; Bolk, L., 1926. *Das Problem der Menschenwerdung.* Jena; Gregory, W. K., 1936. "On the Meaning and Limits of Irreversibility of Evolution," *American Naturalist, 70:*571.

13. Fisher, H. E., 1982. *The Sex Contract.* New York: Morrow.

## Chapter III
### *The Meaning of Biological Intelligence*

1. Itzkoff, S. W., 1983. *The Form of Man.* Ashfield, Massachusetts: Paideia Publishers, pp. 19-43; see also Itzkoff, S. W., 1985. *Triumph of the Intelligent.* Ashfield, Massachusetts: Paideia Publishers, pp. 187-188.

2. On tempo and characteristics of evolutionary processes see the following: Eldridge, N., and Gould, S. J., 1972. "Punctuated Equilibrium: An Alternative to Phyletic Gradualism," in *Models of Paleontology,* Schopf, T. J. M., ed. San Francisco: Freeman and Cooper, pp. 82-115; Mayr, E., 1954. "Change of Genetic Environment and Evolution," in *Evolution As a Process.* Huxley, J. S., Hardy, A. C., and Ford, E. B., eds. London: Allen and Unwin; Mayr, E., 1954. *Animal Species and Evolution.* Cambridge: Belknap-Harvard; Simpson, G. G., 1944. *Tempo and Mode in Evolution.* New York: Columbia University Press; Simpson, G. G., 1953. *The Major Features of Evolution.* New York: Columbia University Press.

3. The following references deal with the development of intelligence and its relationship to basic evolutionary processes: Halstead, W. C., 1947. *Brain and Intelligence.* Chicago: University of Chicago Press; Jepsen G. L., 1949. "Selection, Orthogenesis and the Fossil Record," *Proc. American Phil. Soc., 93:*479-500; Jerison, H., 1973. *Evolution of the Brain and Intelligence.* New York: Academic Press; MacPhail, E. M., 1982. *Brain and Intelligence in Vertebrates.* New York: Oxford University Press; Simpson, G. G., 1950. "Evolutionary Determinism and the Fossil Record," *Scientific Monthly, 71:*262-267; Stenhouse, D., 1973. *The Evolution of Intelligence.* New York: Harper and Row.

4. For the classic arguments for the existence of a unitary factor *g,* see: Spearman, C., 1904. "General Intelligence: Objectively Determined and Measured," *American Journal of Psychology, 15:*201-292; Spearman, C., 1927. *The Abilities of Man: Their Nature and Measurement.* London: Macmillan; Jensen, A. R., 1980. *Bias in Mental Testing.* New York: Free Press. For arguments for a plurality of factors, see: Thurstone, L. L., 1938. "Primary Mental Abilities," *Psychometr. Monogr.,* Volume 1, a; Thurstone, L. L., 1955. *The Differential Growth of Mental Abilities.* Chapel Hill: University of North Carolina Psychometric Lab; Guilford, J. P., 1967. *The Nature of Human Intelligence.* New York: McGraw-Hill.

5. On primates and apes, see: Chance, M., and Jolly, C., eds., 1970. *Social Groups of Monkeys, Apes and Men.* New York: Dutton; Ciochin, R., and Corracini, R. S., eds., 1983. *New Interpretation of Ape and Human Ancestors.* New York: Plenum; DeVore, I., ed., 1965. *Primate Behavior: Field Studies of Monkeys and Apes.* New York: Holt, Rinehart, and Winston; Fossey, D., 1984. *Gorillas in the Mist.* Boston: Houghton Mifflin; Goodall, J., 1986. *The Chimpanzees of Gombe.* Cambridge: Belknap-Harvard University; Szalay, F. S. and Delson, E., 1979. *Evolutionary History of the Primates.* New York: Academic Press.

## Chapter IV
### The Variability of Homo

1. Examples of the implicit and explicit acceptance of such a view can be found in the following otherwise exemplary books, and in practically every standard text on human evolution: Pfeiffer, J. E., 1969. *The Emergence of Man.* Boston: Harper and Row, pp. 309-352; Campbell, B. G., 1982. *Humankind Emerging.* Boston: Little-Brown, pp. 422-429; Brace, C. L., and Ashley Montagu, M. F., 1977. *Human Evolution.* New York: Macmillan, pp. 38-78; Another counter example that at least states the evidence is Sherman, I. W. and U. G., 1975. *Biology.* New York: Oxford University Press, p. 460.

2. Rensch, B., 1967. "The Evolution of Brain Achievements," *Evol. Biol., 1:*26-28.

3. Colbert, E. H., 1973. *Wandering Lands and Animals.* New York: E. P. Dutton.

4. Radinsky, L. B., 1970. "The Fossil Evidence of Prosimian Brain Evolution," in *The Primate Brain.* Noback, C. R., and Montagna, W., eds., New York: Appleton-Century, pp. 209-224.

5. Itzkoff, S. W., 1985. *Triumph of the Intelligent.* Ashfield, Massachusetts: Paideia Publishers, pp. 47-54.

6. Campbell, B. G., 1960. *Human Evolution.* Chicago: Aldine, pp. 55-59.

7. Lovejoy, C. O., 1981. "The Origin of Man," *Science, 211:*341-350.

8. Simons, E., 1972. *Primate Evolution.* New York: Macmillan; Jolly, A., 1972. *The Evolution of Primate Behavior.* New York: Macmillan.

9. Gould, S. J., 1977. *Ontogeny and Phylogeny.* Cambridge: Harvard University Press.

10. Day, M. H., 1982. "*Lucy* Jilted," *Nature, 300:*574; *Nature,* 1983. "Lucy's Lower Limbs: Fully Bipedal?," *Nature, 304:*59-61.

11. Pilbeam, D., 1984. "Reflections on Early Human Ancestors," *Journal of Anthro. Research 40:*14-22.

12. Ashley Montagu, M. F., 1968. "Brains, Genes, Culture, Immaturity, and Gestation," in *Culture, Man's Adaptive Dimension.* Ashley Montagu, M. F., ed. New York: Oxford University Press, pp. 102-113; Sherfey, M. J., 1966. *Nature and Evolution of Female Sexuality.* New York: Vintage.

13. Baker, J., 1974. *Race.* New York: Oxford University Press; Tobias, P. V., 1971. *The Brain in Hominid Evolution.* New York: Columbia University Press. The decline is stated by both authors to be from about 1550 cubic centimeters in Cro-Magnon and his Anglo-Saxon descendants, c. 800 A. D., to about 1350 cubic centimeters today worldwide.

14. de Laubenfels, D., 1983. "The Upper Paleolithic Revolution," *Mankind Quarterly, 22:*324, 329-356.

15. Coon, C., 1966. "The Taxonomy of Human Variation," *Annals of the New York Academy of Sciences, 134:*516-523.

16. Hall, R. R. L., 1965. "Behavior and Ecology of the Wild Patas Monkey, Erthrocebus Patas, in Uganda," *J. Zool., 148:*15; Hall, R. R. L., and DeVore, I., 1965. "Baboon Social Behavior," *Primate Behavior.* DeVore, I., ed. New York: Holt, p. 53; Rowell, T. E., 1966. "Forest Living Baboons in Uganda," *J. Zool., 149:*344.

17. Holloway, R. L., *et. al.,* 1982. "Endocast Asymmetry in Pongids and Hominids," *American Journal of Physical Anthropology, 58:*101-110; Bower, B., Holloway, R. L., and Falk, D., 1985. "Hominid Brain: Advanced or Ape-Like?" *Illus. Science News, 127:157;* Diamond, J. S., and Beaumont, J. G., eds., 1974. *Hemisphere Function in the Human Brain.* New York: Wiley.

18. Wright, S., 1963. "Adaptation and Selection," in *Genetics, Paleontology, and Evolution,* Jepsen, G. L., Simpson, G. G., and Mayr, E., eds. New York: Atheneum, pp. 365-391; Gould, S. J. 1982. "Darwinism and the Expansion of Evolutionary Theory," *Science, 216:*380; Mayr, E., *et al.,* 1982. "Punctuationism and Darwinism Reconciled?" *Nature, 296:*608; Rhodes, E. H. T., 1983. "Gradualism, Punctuated Equilibrium and the Origin of the Species," *Nature, 216,* April 23.

19. Neel, J. V., 1962. "Mutations in the Human Population," in *Methodology in Human Genetics,* Bernadette, W. J., ed. San Francisco: Holden-Day, pp. 203-224; Kolata, G., 1976. "Jumping Genes: A Common Occurrence in Cells," *Science, 193:*392-394.

20. Wallace, A. R., 1864. "The Origin of Human Races and the Antiquity of Man . . . ," *Anthropological Review, 2:*158-187.

21. Holloway, R., 1974. "The Casts of Fossil Hominid Brains," *Scientific American,* July:106:115.

22. The first of the recent acceptance of the almost unrestrained expansion of the hominid cranial capacity, an expansion that defies traditional small incremental mutation interpretations of evolutionary progress, is given in Eiseley, L., 1957. *The Immense Journey*. New York: Random House, pp. 127-141.
23. Oakley, K., 1957. *Man the Tool Maker*. Chicago: University of Chicago Press.
24. Coon, C. S., 1962. *The Origin of Races*. New York: Knopf, pp. 640-642.
25. Shapiro, H. L., 1974. *Peking Man*. New York: Simon and Schuster, pp. 81-83.
26. Howells, W. W., 1974. "Neanderthals: Names, Hypotheses, Scientific Method," *American Anthropologist, 76:*24-38; Dinnell, R., 1983. "A New Chronology for the Mousterian," *Nature, 301:*199; Trinkaus, E., 1983. *The Shanidar Neanderthals*. New York: Academic Press.
27. Itzkoff, S. W., 1983. *The Form of Man*. Ashfield, Massachusetts: Paideia Publishers, pp. 181-209; Marshack, A., 1972. *The Roots of Civilization*. New York: McGraw-Hill; Pfeiffer, J. E., 1983. *The Creative Explosion: An Inquiring into the Origins of Art and Religion*. New York: Harper and Row; Wynn, T., 1985. "Piaget, Stone Tools and the Evolution of Human Intelligence," *World Archeology, 17:*32-43.
28. Coon, C. S., 1982. *Racial Adaptations*. Chicago: Nelson-Hall, pp. 149, 151, 170-171.
29. Van Valen, L., 1976. "Brain Size and Intelligence in Man," *American Anthropologist, 74:*425-427.
30. Howells, W. W., 1977. *Cranial Variations in Man*. Cambridge: Peabody Museum; Brues, A. M., 1977. *People and Races*. New York: Macmillan, p. 131.
31. Jelinek, J., 1982. "The Tabun Cave and Paleolithic Man in the Levant," *Science, 216:*1369; Howell, F. C., 1957. "The Evolutionary Significance of Variation and Varieties of Neanderthal Man," *Quarterly Review of Biology, 32:*330.
32. Day, M. H., and Leakey, M. O., 1980. "A New Hominid Fossil Skull (L. H. 18) from the Ngaloba Beds, Laetoli, Northern Tanzania," *Nature, 284:*55-56.

## Chapter V
### Sociobiology: Selection and Survival

1. Spencer, H., 1855. *Principles of Psychology*. London; Galton, F., 1869. *Hereditary Genius*. London: Macmillan.

2. Watson, J. B. (1913) "Psychology as the Behaviorist Views it," *Psych. Rev., 20:*158-177; Skinner, B. F., 1938. *The Behavior of Organisms.* New York: Appleton-Century-Crofts; Bloomfield, L., 1933. *Language.* New York: Holt, Rinehart, and Winston.

3. Sulloway, F. J., 1979. *Freud, Biologist of the Mind.* New York: Basic Books.

4. Morgan, L. H., 1877. *Ancient Society.* New York; Tylor, E. B., 1871. *Primitive Culture.* London; *Anthropology.* 1881. London.

5. Boas, F., 1940. *Race, Language, and Culture.* New York: The Free Press. Students of Boas included Ruth Benedict, Edward Sapir, and Margaret Mead.

6. Barzun, J., 1958. *Darwin, Marx, Wagner.* Garden City, New York: Doubleday.

7. Washburn, S. L., 1967. "On Holloway's Tools and Teeth," *American Anthropologist, 69:*63-67; Washburn, S. L., and Lancaster, J. B., 1971. "On Evolution and the Origin of Language," *Current Anthropology, 12:*384-386.

8. Childe, V. G., 1936. *Man Makes Himself.* London: Walts. Childe is one of the earliest thinkers in a long line of Marxist environmental determinists in interpreting the evolution of human culture.

9. Hamilton, W. D., 1971 (1964). "The Genetical Evolution of Social Behavior I and II," in *Group Selection,* Williams, G. C., ed. Chicago: Aldine, pp. 23-89; Maynard Smith, J., 1964. "Group Selection and Kin Selection," *Nature, 201:*1145-1147; Trivers, R., 1971. "The Evolution of Reciprocal Altruism," in *Readings in Sociobiology,* Clutton-Brock, and Harvey, eds., 1979. San Francisco: Freeman, pp. 52-97. These are among the earliest writings setting forth the basic arguments of this school.

10. Wilson, E. O., 1971. *The Insect Societies.* Cambridge: Harvard University Press; Wilson, E. O., 1975. *Sociobiology: The New Synthesis.* Cambridge: Harvard University Press.

11. Hull, D., ed., 1974. *Darwin and His Critics.* Cambridge: Harvard University Press (especially Jenkins, F., 1867, pp. 303-344).

12. Hamilton, W. D., 1964, op. cit.; Trivers, R., 1972. "Parental Investment and Sexual Selection," in Clutton-Brock, and Harvey, 1979, op. cit., pp. 52-97.

13. Maynard Smith, J., 1976. "Group Selection," in Clutton-Brock, and Harvey, 1979, op. cit., pp. 20-30.

14. Trivers, R., 1974. "Parent-Offspring Conflict," in Clutton-Brock, and Harvey, 1979, op. cit., pp. 233-257; Kitcher, P., 1985. *Vaulting Ambition.* Cambridge: MIT Press, pp. 213-239.

15. Dawkins, R., 1976. *The Selfish Gene.* New York: Oxford University Press.
16. Wilson, E. O., 1978. *On Human Nature.* Cambridge: Harvard University Press, p. 68.
17. Dawkins, R., 1976, op. cit., pp. 201-202.
18. Kitcher, P., 1985, op. cit., pp. 183-212.
19. Dawkins, R., 1982. *The Extended Phenotype.* San Francisco: Freeman.
20. Hamilton, W., 1964, op. cit.; Maynard Smith, J., 1964, 1976, op. cit.; Williams, G. C., 1966. *Adaptation and Natural Selection.* Princeton: Princeton University Press; Kitcher, P., 1985, op. cit., pp. 77-84.
21. Kitcher, P., 1985, op. cit., p. 83.
22. Melotti, U., 1985. "Competition and Cooperation in Human Evolution." *Mankind Quarterly, 25:*342; Lewontin, R. C., 1970. "The Units of Selection," *Annual Review of Ecology and Systematics, 1:*1-18.
23. Freedman, D. G., 1979. *Human Sociobiology.* New York: The Free Press, p. 16.
24. Freedman, D. G., 1979, op. cit., pp. 141-162.
25. Lumsden, C., and Wilson, E. O., 1981. *Genes, Mind, and Culture.* Cambridge: Harvard University Press.
26. Wilson, E. O., 1978. *On Human Nature.* Cambridge: Harvard University Press, p. 134; van den Berghe, P., 1979. *Human Family Systems.* New York: North Holland, p. 74.
27. Lumsden, C., and Wilson, E. O., 1981, op. cit., p. 21.
28. Lumsden, C., and Wilson, E. O., 1981, op. cit., pp. 85-86, 158-169, 169-176; van den Berghe, P., and Mesher, G. M., 1980. "Royal Incest and Inclusive Fitness," *American Ethnologist, 7:*300-317; Chagnon, N. A., 1977. *Yanomamo: The Fierce People,* Second Edition. New York: Holt, Rinehart, and Winston; Richardson, J., and Kroeber, A. L., 1940. "Three Centuries of Women's Dress Fashions," *University of California Anthropological Records, 5:*1-4, 111-153.
29. Lumsden, C., and Wilson, E. O., 1983. *Promethean Fire.* Cambridge: Harvard University Press; Kitcher, P., 1985, op. cit., p. 371.
30. Alexander, R. D., 1979. *Darwinism and Human Affairs.* Seattle: University of Washington Press, p. 156.
31. Alexander, R. D., 1979, op. cit., p. 131.
32. Alexander, R. D., 1979, op. cit., p. 233.
33. Alexander, R. D., 1979, op. cit., p. 156; Kitcher, P., 1985, op, cit., pp. 292-293; also Melotti, U., 1985, op, cit., 344-345.
34. Kitcher, P., 1985, op. cit., p. 377.

35. See for example the critique of a nonhistorical, noncontextual archeology: Davis, N., 1986. "The 'New' Archeology," *The Intercollegiate Review, 22:*27-32.
36. Kitcher, P., 1985, op. cit., pp. 436-437.

## Chapter VI
### Toward a Sociobiology of Man

1. Alexander, R., 1979. *Darwinism and Human Affairs.* Seattle: University of Washington Press, Chapter V.
2. Simpson, G. G., 1953. *The Major Features of Evolution.* New York: Columbia University Press, pp. 333-376, especially figure 47, p. 373; Goldschmidt, R., 1938. *The Material Basis of Evolution.* New Haven: Yale University Press; Gould, S. J., and Eldridge, N., 1972. "Punctuated Equilibrium: An Alternative to Phyletic Determinism," in *Models of Paleontology,* Schopf, T. M. J., ed. San Francisco: Freeman, pp. 82-115; Gould, S. J., and Eldridge, N., 1977. "Punctuated Equilibrium: The Tempo and Mode of Evolution Reconsidered," *Paleobiology 3:*115-151.
3. White, L. A., 1949. *The Science of Culture* New York: Grove.
4. Irsigler, F. J., 1984. "Qualitative Morphogenesis and Lateralization of the Human Brain," *Mankind Quarterly, 25:*3-46; Stephan, H., 1975. "Allocortex," in *Handbuch der Mikroskopischen Anatomie des Menschen,* Volume 4/9, Bargmann, W., ed. Berlin: Springer; Blinkov, S., and Glezer, I. I., 1968. *The Human Brain in Figures and Tables.* New York: Basic Books, 1968. (Thalamus volume has increased over chimpanzee as much as has cortex.)
5. Marshack, A., 1972. *The Roots of Civilization.* New York: McGraw-Hill.
6. Simpson, G. G., 1949. *The Meaning of Evolution.* New Haven: Yale University Press, pp. 130-159.
7. de Chardin, P. T., 1959. *The Phenomenon of Man.* New York: Harper and Brothers; Waddington, C. H., 1957. *The Strategy of the Genes.* London: George Allen and Unwin; Waddington, C. H., 1961. *The Nature of Life.* London: George Allen and Unwin; Russell, E. S., 1945. *The Directiveness of Organic Activities.* Cambridge: Cambridge University Press.
8. de Beer, G., 1958. *Embryos and Ancestors.* London: Oxford University Press; Gregory, W. K., 1937. "Supra-specific Variation in Nature and in Classification: A Few Examples from Mammalian Paleontology," *American Naturalist, 71:*268-276.

9. Morris, C., 1946. *Signs, Language, and Behavior.* New York: Prentice Hall.

10. Langer, S. K., 1957. *Philosophy in a New Key.* Cambridge: Harvard University Press, pp. 53-78.

11. Cassirer, E., 1944. *An Essay on Man.* New Haven: Yale University Press, pp. 27-41.

12. Lumsden, C. J., and Wilson, E. O., 1983. *Promethean Fire.* Cambridge: Harvard University Press.

13. Freedman, D. G., 1979. *Human Sociobiology.* New York: The Free Press, pp. 144-150.

14. The Hellenistic Ptolemies of Egypt, descendants of the Macedonian Greek conquerors of this land, were notorious. Cleopatra was a member of this clan.

15. Blum, H. F., 1951. *Time's Arrow and Evolution.* Princeton: Princeton University Press.

16. Wallace, A. R., 1889. *Darwinism.* London: Macmillan.

## Chapter VII
### Human Aggression: A Modest Clarification

1. Wynn-Edwards, V. C., 1962. *Animal Dispersion in Relation to Social Behavior.* Edinburgh: Oliver and Boyd; Chagnon, N., 1968. *The Yanomamo: The Fierce People.* New York: Holt, Rinehart, and Winston.

2. Lorenz, K., 1966. *On Aggression.* New York: Harcourt Brace, p. 275.

3. Quoted in Wilson, E. O., 1978. *On Human Nature.* Cambridge: Harvard University Press, p. 105; Sipes, R. G., 1973. "War, Sports, and Aggression: An Empirical Test of Two Rival Theories," *American Anthropologist,* 75:64-86.

4. Colinvaux, P., 1978. *Why Big Fierce Animals Are Rare.* Princeton, N. J.: Princeton University Press.

5. Hall, K. R. L., and DeVore, I., 1965. "Baboon Social Behavior," in *Primate Behavior,* DeVore, I., ed. New York: Holt, p. 53; Washburn, S. L., and DeVore, I., 1961. "The Social Life of Baboons," *Scientific American,* 204:62; Pilbeam, D., 1972. *The Ascent of Man.* New York: Macmillan, pp. 23-27.

6. Jolly, C., 1970. "The Large African Monkeys as an Adaptive Array," in *The Old World Monkeys,* Napier, J. R., and Napier, P. H., eds. New York: Academic Press, p. 139; Rowell, T. E., 1966. "Forest Living Baboons in Uganda," *J. Zool.,* 149:344.

7. Schwartz, J. H., 1983. "The Orangutan and Hominid Evolution," *Primates, 24:*231-240; Lewin, R., 1983. "Is the Orangutan a Living Fossil?" *Science, 222.* December 16; Andrews, P., and Cronin, J. F., 1982. "The Relationship of Sivapithecus and Ramapithecus and the Evolution of the Orangutan," *Nature, 297:*541-546.

8. Leakey, R. E., 1981. "The Making of Mankind," *The Listener,* Spring.

9. Campbell, B. G., 1966. *Human Evolution.* Chicago: Aldine.

10. Quoted in Leakey, R. E., and Lewin, R., 1977. *Origins.* New York: Dutton, pp. 197-198; see also Tobias, P. V., 1971. *The Brain in Hominid Evolution.* New York: Columbia University Press; Stephan, H., and Andy, O. J., 1970. "The Allocortex in Primates," in *The Primate Brain: Advances in Primatology,* Volume 1, Noback, C. R., Montagna, W., eds. New York: Appleton-Century-Crofts, pp. 109-135.

11. The work of Antonio Egas Moniz and Almeida Lima is discussed in Eysenck, H. J., and Eysenck, M., 1983. *Mindwatching.* Garden City, New York: Anchor, pp. 176-177; see also Halstead, W., 1947. *Brain and Intelligence.* Chicago: University of Chicago Press.

12. Stenhouse, D., 1974. *The Evolution of Intelligence.* New York: Harper; Halstead, W., 1951. "Biological Intelligence," *J. Pers., 20:*118-120.

13. Jakobson, R., 1971. *Studies on Child Language and Aphasia.* The Hague: Mouton.

14. See, for example, a basic textbook on the complexities of the genetic behavioral issue: Eccles, J. C., 1973. *The Understanding of the Brain.* New York: McGraw-Hill; Bodmer, W. F., and Cavalli-Sforza, L. L., 1976. *Genetics, Evolution, and Man.* San Francisco: Freeman; Lewontin, R. C., 1974. *The Genetic Basis of Evolutionary Change.* New York: Columbia University Press.

15. MacLean, P., 1961. "Psychosomatics," in *Handbook of Physiology and Neurophysiology III.;* Simeons, A. T., 1960. *Man's Presumptuous Brain.* New York: Dutton.

16. Bataille, G., 1962. *Death and Sensuality.* New York: Walker.

# Chapter VIII
### *The Biological Perspective*

1. Lewis, H., 1962. "Catastrophic Selection as a Factor in Speciation," *Evolution, 16:*262; Cain, A. J., 1954. *Animal Species and Their Evolution.* London: Hutchinson's University Library; Romer, A., 1953. *Man and the Vertebrates.* Chicago: University of Chicago Press.

2. Allee, W. C., 1958. *The Social Life of Animals.* Boston: Beacon; Scott, J. P., 1958. *Animal Behavior.* Chicago: University of Chicago Press.

3. Pilbeam, D., 1970. "Gigantophithecus and the Origins of the Hominidae," *Nature, 225:*516; Simons, E. L., 1964. "The Early Relatives of Man," *Scientific American, 211:*51; Browne, M. W., 1986. "Fossils Point to Giant Ape's Violent End," *New York Times,* November 11, C1, C7.

4. Bordes, F., ed., 1972. *The Origins of Homo Sapiens.* Paris: UNESCO; Clark G., 1967. *The Stone Age Hunters.* New York: McGraw-Hill; Bailey, G., ed., 1983. *Hunter-Gatherer Economy in Pre-History: A European Perspective.* New York: Cambridge University Press.

5. Binford, S. R., 1968. "Early Upper Pleistocene Adaptations in the Levant," *American Anthropologist, 70:*714; Pilbeam, D., 1972. *The Ascent of Man.* New York: Macmillan, p. 186; Pilbeam, D., 1972. "Adaptive Response of Hominids," *Social Biology, 19:*2.

6. See, for example, Harris, M., 1979. *Cultural Materialism: The Struggle for a Science of Culture.* New York: Random House; White, L., 1949. *The Science of Culture.* New York: Grove Press.

7. Smith, H., 1961. *From Fish to Philosopher.* Garden City, New York: Doubleday; Eiseley, L., 1957. *The Immense Journey.* New York: Random House, pp. 47-59.

8. Colbert, E. H., 1961. *Dinosaurs.* New York: E. P. Dutton; Colbert, E. H., 1958. *Evolution of the Vertebrates.* New York: John Wiley; Colbert, E. H., 1978. "The Ancestors of the Mammals," in *Evolution and the Fossil Record.* San Francisco: Freeman, pp. 142-145; Bakker, R. T., 1978. "Dinosaur Renaissance," in *Evolution and the Fossil Record.* San Francisco: Freeman, pp. 125-141.

9. Bram, C. K., 1981. *The Hunter and the Hunted.* Chicago: University of Chicago Press; Lovejoy, C. O., 1981. "The Origin of Man," *Science, 211:*341-350.

10. Itzkoff, S. W., 1985. *Triumph of the Intelligent.* Ashfield, Massachusetts: Paideia Publishers, pp. 79-85.

11. Baker, J. R., 1974. *Race.* New York: Oxford University Press; Coon, C. S., 1982. *Racial Adaptations.* Chicago: Nelson-Hall.

12. Colbert, E. H., 1975. "Mammoths and Man," in *Ants, Indians, and Little Dinosaurs.* Ternes, A., ed. New York: Charles Schuben and Sons, pp. 180-188; Coon, C. S., 1966. "The Taxonomy of Human Variation," *Annals of the New York Academy of Sciences, 134:*516-523.

13. Tattersall, I., and Delson, E., 1984. *Ancestors*. New York: Museum of Natural History; Coon. C. S., 1962. *The Origin of Races*. New York: Knopf, pp. 12-13.

14. Olivier, G., 1973. "Hominization and Cranial Capacity," in *Human Evolution*, Day, M. H., ed. New York: Barnes and Noble, pp. 87-101.

15. Simpson, G. G., 1949. *The Meaning of Evolution*. New Haven: Yale University Press, pp. 62-77; Rhodes, F. H. T., 1962. *The Evolution of Life*. Baltimore: Penguin, pp. 228-245.

## Chapter IX
### In Search of General Intelligence: I.Q.

1. Binet, A., and Simon, T., 1916 (1905). "Upon the Necessity of Establishing a Scientific Diagnosis of Inferior States of Intelligence," from *L'Annee Psychologique, XI:*163-190, in *The Development of Intelligence*. Kite, E. S., trans. Baltimore: Williams and Williams; Binet, A., and Simon, T., 1905. "Methodes nouvelles pour le diagnostic du niveau intellectual des anormaux," *L'Annee Psychologique, 11:*199-244; Binet, A., and Simon, T., 1905. "Application des methodes nouvelles au diagnostic du niveau intellectual chez des enfants normaux d'hospice et d'ecole primaire," *L'Annee Psychologique, 11:*245-336. Note: I am indebted for much of this historical analysis to Arthur R. Jensen's paper (in manuscript, 1986), "Individual Differences in Mental Ability."

2. Ebbinghaus, H., 1913 (1885). *Concerning Memory*. Ruger, H. A., and Bussenius, C. E., trans. New York: Teachers College, Columbia University; Wundt, W., 1904 (1873). *Principles of Physiological Psychology*. Titchener, E. B., trans. New York: Macmillan.

3. Cattell, J. Mc., 1885. "The Influence of the Intensity of the Stimulus on the Length of the Reaction Time," *Brain 8:*512-515; Cattell, J. Mc., 1886. "The Time It Takes To See and Name Objects," *Mind, 11:*63-65; Cattell, J. Mc., 1887. "Experiments on the Association of Ideas," *Mind, 12:*68-74; Wissler, C., 1901. "The Correlation of Mental and Physical Tests," *Psychological Review Monograph Supplement*, No. 6 (whole No. 16).

4. Terman, L. M., 1916. *The Measurement of Intelligence*. Boston: Houghton-Mifflin; Terman, L. M., 1921. "Intelligence and Its Measurement, Part II," *J. Educational Psychology, 12:*127-133; Goddard, H. H., 1920. *Human Efficiency and Levels of Intelligence*. Princeton: Princeton University Press.

5. Cattell, J. Mc., 1885, 1886, op. cit.

6. Galton, F., 1883. *Inquiries on Human Faculty and its Development.* London: Macmillan; Galton, F., 1888. "Co-Relations and Their Measurement, Chiefly from Anthropometric Data," *Proceedings of the Royal Society, 15:*135-145; Cattell, J. Mc., 1890. "Mental tests and Measurements," *Mind, 15:*373-380.

7. See Chapter X of *Why Humans Vary in Intelligence.*

8. Gillingham, A., and Stillman, R., 1966. *Remedial Training for Children with Specific Disabilities.* Cambridge, Massachusetts: Educators' Publishing Service; Wedell, K., 1970 "Perceptuo-Motor Factors," *J. Special Education 4,* Number 3; Montessori, M., 1964 (1912). *The Montessori Method.* George, A. E., trans. New York: Schocken Books.

9. Bateman, B., 1968. "The Efficacy of an Auditory and a Visual Method . . . ," in *Perception and Reading.* Smith, H. K., ed. Newark, Delaware: I. R. A., pp. 105-112; Robinson, H. M., 1972. "Perceptual Training—Does It Result in Reading Improvement?" in *Some Persistent Questions in Beginning Reading,* Aukerman, R. C., ed. Newark, Delaware: I. R. A., pp. 135-150; Waugh, R. P., 1973. "Relationship Between Modality Preference and Performance," *Exceptional Children, 39:*465-469.

10. Tuddenham, R. D., 1962. "The Nature and Measurement of Intelligence," in *Psychology in the Making: Histories of Selected Research Problems,* Postman, L., ed. New York: Knopf, pp. 469-525.

11. Ebbinghaus, E., 1902. *Grundzuge der Psychologie.* Leipzig. Von Veit.

12. Terman, L. M., and Merrill, M. A., 1937. *Measuring Intelligence.* Boston: Houghton-Mifflin; Stern, W., 1914. *Psychology of Early Childhood Up to the Sixth Year of Age.* Barwell, A., trans. New York.

13. Spencer, H., 1855. *Principles of Psychology.* London.

14. Fiske, J., 1884. *The Destiny of Man.* Boston: Houghton-Mifflin; Huxley, T. H., 1894. *Evolution and Ethics and Other Essays.* New York: The Humboldt Publishing Co.; Sumner, W. G., 1934. *Essays of William Graham Sumner.* Keller, A. G., and Davie, M. R., eds. New Haven: Yale University Press; Spencer, H., 1874. *The Study of Sociology.* New York: D. Appleton and Co.; Hofstadter, R., 1944. *Social Darwinism in American Thought.* Philadelphia. University of Pennsylvania Press.

15. Guilford, J. P., 1967. *The Nature of Human Intelligence.* New York: McGraw-Hill. Guilford states that both Cyril Burt and Charles Spearman attributed the bringing of the term "intelligence" into psychology to Herbert Spencer.

16. Galton, F., 1892 (1869). *Hereditary Genius.* London: Macmillan; Galton, F. *Natural Inheritance.* London: Macmillan.

17. Jensen, A. R., 1986. "Individual Differences in Mental Ability," *MS* pp. 17-27; Forrest, D. W., 1974. *Francis Galton: The Life and Work of a Victorian Genius.* New York: Taplinger.

18. Lombroso, C., 1891. *The Man of Genius.* London: Walter Scott; Ellis, H., 1904. *A Study of British Genius.* London: Hurst and Blackett.

19. Jensen, A. R., 1986. "Individual Differences," op. cit., p. 28.

20. Wechsler, D., 1958. *The Measurement and Appraisal of Adult Intelligence,* Fourth Edition. Baltimore: Williams and Wilkins; Wechsler, D., 1975. "Intelligence Defined and Undefined: A Relativistic Approach," *American Psychologist, 30:*135-139; Terman, L. M., and Merrill, M. A., 1960. *Stanford-Binet Intelligence Scale: Manual for the Third Revision.* Boston: Houghton-Mifflin; Matarazzo, J. D., 1974. *Wechsler's Measurement and Appraisal of Adult Intelligence,* Fifth Edition. Baltimore: Williams and Wilkins.

21. Spearman, C. E., 1904. "'General Intelligence' Objectively Determined and Measured," *American Journal of Psychology, 15:*201-293; Spearman, C. E., 1923. *The Nature of "Intelligence" and the Principles of Cognition.* London: Macmillan.

22. Jensen, A. R., 1986. "Individual Differences . . . ," op. cit.; Spearman, C. E., 1927. *The Abilities of Man.* New York: Macmillan.

23. Jensen, A. R., 1986. "Individual Differences . . . ," op. cit.

24. Spearman, C. E., 1930. *Creative Mind.* New York: Cambridge University Press; Spearman, C. E., and Jones, L. L. W., 1950. *Human Ability.* London: Macmillan.

25. Thorndike, E., and Woodworth, R. S., 1901. "The Influence of Improvement in One Mental Function upon the Efficiency of Other Functions," *Psychol. Review, 8:*247-261, 384-396, 553-564; Thorndike, E. L., *et. al.,* 1927. *The Measurement of Intelligence.* New York: Teachers College, Columbia University; Thorndike, E. L., 1931. *Human Learning.* New York: Appleton-Century-Crofts.

26. Thurstone, L. L., 1947. *Multiple Factor Analysis.* Chicago: University of Chicago Press; Thurstone, L. L., 1938. "Primary Mental Abilities," *Psychometric Monographs,* Volume 1. Chicago: University of Chicago Press; Guilford, J. P., 1967. *The Nature of Human Intelligence.* New York: McGraw-Hill; Cattell, R. B., 1963. "Theory of Fluid and Crystallized Intelligence: A Critical Experiment," *J. of Educational Psychology, 54:*1-22; Cattell, R. B., 1971. *Abilities: Their Structure, Growth, and Action.* Boston: Houghton-Mifflin.

27. Jensen, A. R., 1986. "Individual Differences . . . ," op. cit. pp. 44-45.

28. Butcher, H. J., 1968. *Human Intelligence: Its Nature and Development.* New York: Harper, pp. 226-231.

29. Jensen, A. R., 1980. *Bias in Mental Testing.* New York: The Free Press, pp. 61-123.

30. Sternberg, R. J., 1983. "How Much Gall is Too Much Gall?: A Review of Frames of the Mind: The Theory of Multiple Intelligence," *Contemporary Education Review,* 2:220-221; Thurstone, L. L., 1938. "Primary Mental Abilities," op. cit.; Guilford, J. P., 1967. *The Nature of Human Intelligence,* op. cit.; Guilford, J. P., 1982. "Cognitive Psychology's Ambiguities: Some Suggested Remedies," *Psychological Review,* 89:48-59.

31. Terman, L. M., 1925. *Genetic Studies of Genius Part I: Mental and Physical Traits of a Thousand Gifted Children.* Stanford: Stanford University Press.

32. Fincher, J., 1973. "The Terman Study Is Fifty Years Old . . . ," *Human Behavior,* 2:8-15.

33. Stanley, J. C., 1979. "The Study and Facilitation of Talent for Mathematics," in *The Gifted and the Talented,* Passow, A. H., ed. Chicago: National Society for the Study of Education; Stanley, J. C., and Benbow, C. P., 1983. "Educating Mathematically Precocious Youths: Twelve Policy Recommendations," *Education Researcher, 11:*4-9.

34. Lehman, H. C., 1953. *Age and Achievement.* Princeton: Princeton University Press; For contrasting views on the prime creative period of mathematics see: Hardy, G. H., 1941. *A Mathematician's Apology.* Cambridge: Cambridge University Press; Gruber, H. E., 1986. "The Self-Construction of the Extraordinary," in *Conceptions of Giftedness,* Sternberg, R. J., and Davidson, J. E., eds. Cambridge: Cambridge University Press, pp. 247-263.

35. Stanley, J. C., 1977. "Rationale of the Study of Mathematically Precocious Youth . . . ," in *The Gifted and the Creative,* Stanley, J. C., George, W. C., and Solano, C. H., eds. Baltimore: The Johns Hopkins University Press, pp. 78-82.

36. Albert, R. S., and Runco, M. A., 1986. "The Achievement of Eminence," in *Conceptions of Giftedness,* Sternberg, R. J., and Davidson, J. E., eds., op. cit., pp. 332-357.

37. Davis, G. A., and Rimm, S. B., 1985. *Education of the Gifted and Talented.* Englewood Cliffs, New Jersey: Prentice Hall. Davis and Rimm note that Terman rejected for inclusion in their study two boys who later won Nobel Prizes, William B. Shockley and Luis Alvarez. Their I.Q. scores were below 140. None of those included in the Terman study (over 1500 children) were so honored (p. 19). See also Hermann, K. E., and Stanley, J. C., 1983. "An Exchange: Thoughts on Non-Natural Precocity," *G/C/T,* Nov.-Dec., pp. 30-36.

## Chapter X
### *The Enigma of General Intelligence: The New Experimentalism*

1. Jensen, A. R., 1985. "The Nature of the Black-White Difference on Various Psychometric Tests: Spearman's Hypothesis," *The Behavioral and Brain Sciences, 8:*193-263. Included in this issue are twenty-six responses of professionals plus the author's reply; Burks, B. S., 1928. "The Relative Influences of Nature and Nurture upon Mental Development," in *National Society for the Study of Education, Part I.* Chicago: University of Chicago Press, pp. 219-224, 302-309, the first quantitative analysis of the heredity-environment conundrum. Eysenck, H. J., and Kamin, L., 1981. *The Intelligence Controversy.* New York: John Wiley and Sons; Lewontin, R. C., Rose, S., and Kamin, L., 1984. *Not in Our Genes.* New York: Pantheon, a contrasting position; Scarr, S., and Carter-Saltzmann, L., 1982. "Genetics and Intelligence," in *Handbook of Human Intelligence,* Sternberg, R. J., ed. Cambridge: Cambridge University Press, comprehensive and impartial.

2. Eysenck, H. J., 1982. "The Sociology of Psychological Knowledge, the Genetic Interpretation of the I. Q. and Marxist-Leninist Ideology," *Bulletin of the British Psychological Society, 35:*449-451; Eysenck, H. J., 1985. "The Nature and Measurement of Intelligence," in *The Psychology of Gifted Children.* New York: John Wiley and Sons, pp. 115-140.

3. Lehrke, R. G., 1978. "Sex Linkage: A Biological Basis for Greater Male Variability in Intelligence," in *Human Variation: The Biopsychology of Age, Race, and Sex.* Osborne, R. T., *et al.,* eds. New York: Academic Press, pp. 171-198.

4. Kennedy, W. A., *et. al.,* 1963. "A Normative Sample of Intelligence and Achievement of Negro Elementary School Children in the Southern United States," *Monographs of the Society for Research in Child Development 28,* Number 6; Weyl, N., 1978. "World Population Growth and the Geography of Intelligence," *Modern Age, 22:*64-71; Vining, D. R., Jr., 1983. "Fertility Differentials and the Status of Nations: A Speculative Essay on Japan and the West," in Cattell, R. B., ed. *Intelligence and National Achievement.* Washington, D. C.: The Cliveden Press, pp. 100-141.

5. Jensen, A. R., 1983. "The Effects of Inbreeding on Mental Ability Factors," *Personality and Individual Differences, 4:*71-87; Agrawal, N., *et al.,* 1984. "Effects of Inbreeding on Raven Matrices," *Behavioral Genetics, 14:*579-585.

6. Jensen, A. R. (1986) "Intelligence as a Fact of Nature," Lecture, Virginia Tech., Blacksburg, VA, 30 September 1986, in which Jensen states that "twelve published studies on the effects of inbreeding on I. Q. . . . are all highly consistent in their findings," (p. 19.); Bashi, J., 1977. "Effects of Inbreeding on Cognitive Performance of Israeli-Arab Children," *Nature, 266:*440-442.

7. Reed, T. E., and Reed, S. C., 1965. *Mental Retardation.* Philadelphia: Saunders; Eysenck, H. J., 1979. *The Structure and Measurement of Intelligence.* New York: Springer-Verlag, p. 122; Eysenck, H. J., and Kamin, L., 1981. *The Intelligence Controversy.* New York: John Wiley and Sons, pp. 62-66.

8. Cronback, L. J., 1957. "The Two Disciplines of Scientific Psychology," *American Psychologist, 12:*671-684.

9. Sternberg, R. J., 1977. *Intelligence, Information Processing, and Analogical Reasoning: The Componential Analysis of Human Abilities.* Hilldale, New Jersey: Erlbaum; Jensen, A. R., and Munro, E., 1974. "Reaction Time, Movement Time, and Intelligence," *Intelligence, 3:*121-126; Jensen, A. R., 1982. "Reaction Time and Psychometric *g,*" in Eysenck, H. J., ed., *A Model for Intelligence.* New York: Springer - Verlag, pp. 93-132.

10. Sternberg, S., 1966. "High Speed Scanning in Human Memory," *Science, 153:*652-654; Sternberg, S., 1969. "Memory-Scanning: Mental Processes Revealed by Reaction-Time Experiments," *American Scientist, 57:*421-457.

11. Goldberg, R. A., Schwartz, S., and Stewart, M., 1977. "Individual Differences in Cognitive Processes," *J. Educational Psychology, 69:*9-14.

12. Jensen, A. R., and Munro, E., 1979. "Reaction Time, Movement Time, and Intelligence," *Intelligence, 3:*121-126.

13. Carlson, J. S., and Jensen, C. M., 1982. "Reaction Time, Movement Time, and Intelligence: A Replication and Extension," *Intelligence, 6:*265-274.

14. Jensen, A. R., 1985. "The Nature of Black-White Differences . . . ," *Behavioral and Brain Sciences, 8:*208.

15. Sternberg, R. J., 1985. *Beyond I.Q..* New York: Cambridge University Press, p. 99; Vernon, P. A., and Jensen, A. R., 1984. "Individual and Group Differences in Intelligence and Speed of Information Processing," *Person. Individ. Diff., 5:*411-423, especially 422-423; Sternberg, R. J., and Gardiner, K., 1982. "A Componential Interpretation of the General Factor in Human Intelligence," in *A Model of Intelligence,* Eysenck, H. J., ed. New York: Springer-Verlag.

16. Jensen, A. R., 1985. "The Nature of Black-White Differences . . . ," *Behavioral and Brain Sciences,* op. cit., p. 212.

17. See Chapters by Eysenck, H. J., Berger, M., and White, P. O. in *A Model for Intelligence.* Eysenck, H. J., ed. New York: Springer-Verlag, pp. 1-90.

18. Jensen, A. R., 1985. "The Nature of Black-White Differences . . . ," *Behavioral and Brain Sciences, 8:*208.

19. Cohn, S. J., Carlson, J. S., and Jensen, A. R. (in press) "Speed of Information Processing in Academically Gifted Youth," *Personality and Individual Differences,* p. 16 of manuscript.

20. Hendrickson, A. E. and D. E., 1982. "The Psychophysiology of Intelligence," in *A Model of the Mind,* Eysenck, H. J., ed. New York: Springer-Verlag, pp. 151-228; Eysenck, H. J., 1986. *The Theory of Intelligence and the Psychophysiology of Cognition.* London: Institute of Psychiatry, University of London; Schafer, E. W. P., 1982. "Neural Adaptability: A Biological Determinant of Behavioral Intelligence," *International Journal of Neuroscience, 17:*183-191; Schafer, E. W. P., 1985. "Neural Adaptability: A Biological Determinant of 'G' Factor Intelligence," *The Behavioral and Brain Sciences, 8:*240-241.

21. Jensen, A. R., 1986. "Individual Differences in Mental Ability," manuscript. Berkeley: University of California, pp. 57-58.

22. Hendrickson, A. E., 1982. "The Biological Basis of Intelligence, Part I: Theory," in *A Model for Intelligence.* Eysenck, H. J., ed. New York: Springer-Verlag, pp. 195-196.

23. Hendrickson, A. E., 1982, op. cit., pp. 192-195.

24. Eysenck, H. J., ed., 1982. *A Model for Intelligence,* op. cit., pp. 8-9; Jensen, A. R., 1985. "The Nature of Black-White Differences . . . ," *Behavioral and Brain Sciences,* op. cit., p. 212.

## Chapter XI
### *The Executor: "P" Factor*

1. Laycock, F., 1979. *Gifted Children.* Chicago: Scott Foresman, pp. 40-48; Sears, P. S., and Barbee, A. H., 1977. "Career and Life Satisfaction Among Terman's Gifted Women," in *The Gifted and Creative: A Fifty-Year Perspective,* Stanley, J. C. *et al.,* eds. Baltimore: Johns Hopkins; Sears, R. R., 1977. "Sources of Life Satisfaction of the Terman Gifted Men," *American Psychologist, 32:*119-128; Fincher, J., 1973. "The Terman Study is Fifty Years Old . . . ," *Human Behavior, 2:*8-15.

2. Vernon, P. A., and Jensen, A. R., 1984. "Individual Differences in Intelligence and Speed of Information Processing," *Person. Individ. Diff., 5:*411-423; Vernon, P. A., 1983. "Speed of Information Processing and General Intelligence," *Intelligence, 7:*53-70.

3. Jensen, A. R., 1986. "Intelligence as a Fact of Nature," *Lecture at Virginia Tech.,* Blacksburg, VA, 30 September 1986.

4. Eysenck, H. J., ed., 1982. *A Model for Intelligence.* New York: Springer, chapters 1-3; Sternberg, R. J., and Gardner, M. K., 1982. "A Componential Interpretation of the General Factor in Human Intelligence," in *A Model for Intelligence,* Eysenck, H. J., ed., op. cit., pp. 231-254.

5. Hendrickson, A. E., 1982. "The Biological Basis of Intelligence, Part I: Theory," in *A Model for Intelligence,* Eysenck, H. J., ed. New York: Springer, pp. 151-196; Hendrickson, D. E., 1982. "The Biological Basis of Intelligence, Part II: Measurement," in *A Model for Intelligence,* Eysenck, H. J., ed. New York: Springer, pp. 197-228; Eysenck, H. J., 1986. "The Theory of Intelligence and the Psychophysiology of Cognition," London: *Institute of Psychiatry,* University of London, p. 27; Eysenck, H. J., 1985. "The Nature and Measurement of Intelligence," in *The Psychology of Gifted Children,* Freeman, J., ed. New York: John Wiley, pp. 127-131.

6. Jensen, A. R., 1985. "The Nature of Black-White Differences . . . ," *The Behavioral and Brain Sciences, 8:*206-210; Eysenck, H. J., 1986. "The Theory of Intelligence and the Psychophysiology of Cognition," op. cit. pp. 30-41.

7. Halstead, W. C., 1947. *Brain and Intelligence.* Chicago: University of Chicago Press.

8. Stenhouse, D., 1973. *The Evolution of Intelligence.* New York: Harper and Row.

9. Stenhouse, D., 1973, op. cit., 157f.; Goldstein, K., 1963 (1940). *Human Nature in the Light of Psychopathology.* New York: Schocken, pp. 34-68.

10. Holloway, R. L. (1980) "Within Species: Brain-Body Weight Variability," *American Journal of Physical Anthropology, 52:*109-121; Itzkoff, S. W., 1983. *The Form of Man.* Ashfield, Massachusetts: Paideia Publishers, pp. 264-265; Tobias, P. V., 1971. *The Brain in Hominid Evolution.* New York: Columbia University Press.

11. Phenice, T. W., 1972. *Hominid Fossils.* Dubuque, Iowa: William C. Brown, pp. 46-50.

12. Yerkes, R. M., and Dodson, J. D., 1908. "The Relation of Strength of Stimulus to Rapidity of Habit Formation," *Journal of Comparative Neurology, 18:*459-482.

13. Vernon, P. A., and Jensen, A. R., 1984. "Individual and Group Differences . . . ," op. cit., pp. 419-420.
14. Wernicke, C., 1874. *Der Aphasische Symptomen Complex.* Breslau: Franck and Weigert.
15. Jackson, J. H., 1958 (1860-1890) *Selected Writings.* New York; Head, H., 1915. "Hughlings Jackson on Aphasia and Kindred Affections of Speech," *Brain, 38:*1-190.
16. Head, H., 1926. *Aphasia and Kindred Disorders of Speech,* two volumes. Cambridge: Cambridge University Press.
17. Goldstein, K., 1948. *Language and Language Disturbances: Aphasic Symptoms and Complexes.* New York; Goldstein, K., 1927. *Ueber Aphasie.* Zurich: Orel Fuessli; Gelb, A., and Goldstein, K., 1920. *A Psychological Analysis of Neuropathological Cases.* Leipzig; Cassirer, E., 1957 (1923-1929). *The Philosophy of Symbolic Forms,* three volumes, Manheim, R., trans. New Haven: Yale University Press.
18. Goldstein, K., 1963 (1934). *The Organism.* Boston: Beacon Press; Goldstein, K., 1940. *Human Nature in the Light of Psychopathology.* Cambridge: Harvard University Press.
19. Eysenck, H. J., and Eysenck, M., 1983. *Mindwatching.* Garden City, New York: Anchor, pp. 176-177.
20. Jakobson, R., 1971. *Studies on Child Language and Aphasia.* The Hague: Mouton; Luria, A. R., 1958. "Brain Disorders and Language Analysis," *Language and Speech, 1:*14-34; Luria, A. R., and Yudovich, F. I., 1971 (1956) *Speech and the Development of Mental Processes in the Child.* Baltimore: Penguin.
21. Jakobson, R., 1971. *Studies on Child Language . . . ,* op. cit., pp. 44-48.
22. Jakobson, R., 1971. *Studies on Child Language . . . ,* op. cit., pp. 62-63, 67-73.
23. Jakobson, R., 1971. *Studies on Child Language . . . ,* op. cit., pp. 95-109.
24. Luria, A. R., 1959. "Disorders of 'Simultaneous Perception' in a Case of Bilateral Occipital Parietal Injury," *Brain, 82:*437-449.
25. Eysenck, H. J., 1979. *The Structure and Measurement of Intelligence.* New York: Springer, pp. 126-127; Jinks, J. L., and Fulker, D. W., 1970. "Comparison of the Biometrical, Genetical, MHVA, and Classical Approaches to the Analysis of Human Behavior," *Psychological Bulletin 73:*311-349.
26. Itzkoff, S. W., 1983. *The Form of Man.* Ashfield, Massachusetts: Paideia Publishers, pp. 271-273.

## Chapter XII
### Factors: Language and the Integrational System

1. See the discussion in Cassirer, E., 1957 (1929). *The Philosophy of Symbolic Forms,* Volume III, Manheim, R., trans. New Haven: Yale University Press, pp. 205-277; Jakobson, R., 1971. *Studies on Child Language and Aphasia.* The Hague: Mouton.

2. Dejerine, J ., 1892. "Contribution a L'Etude Anatomo-Pathologique et Clinique des Differentes Varietes de Cecite Verbal," *C. R., Soc. Bio* (Paris), *44:*61-90; Hinshelwood, J., 1917. *Congenital Word Blindness.* London: Lewis.

3. Wechsler, D., 1958. *The Measurement and Appraisal of Adult Intelligence.* Baltimore: Williams and Wilkins; Porteus, S. D., 1965. *Porteus Maze Test—Fifty Years' Application.* London: Harrap.

4. Chomsky, N., 1957. *Syntactic Structures.* The Hague. Mouton; Chomsky, N., 1965. *Aspects of the Theory of Syntax.* Cambridge: MIT Press; Miller, G. A., 1965. "Some Preliminaries to Psycholinguistics," *American Psychologist, 20:*15-20; Smith, F., and Miller, G. A., eds., 1966. *The Genesis of Language.* Cambridge: MIT Press.

5. Smith, F., 1971. *Understandi⸗ ʒ Reading.* New York: Holt, Rinehart, and Winston. This book cor ⸗ains a general discussion of the relationship of spoken language and its elements to reading and writing; Miller, G. A., 1964. "The Psycholinguistics," *Encounter, 23:*29-37.

6. Chomsky, N., 1968. *Language and Mind.* New York: Harcourt, Brace, and World; Chomsky, N., 1957. *Syntactic Structures,* op. cit.; Chomsky, N., 1965. *Aspects,* op. cit.

7. Bever, T., 1970. "The Cognitive Basis for Linguistic Structures," in *Cognition and the Development of Language,* Hayes, J. R., ed. New York: John Wiley, pp. 281-353.

8. Cromer, W., 1970. "The Difference Model: A New Explanation for Some Reading Difficulties," *Journal of Educational Psychology, 61:*471-483; Harris, A. J., and Sipay, E. R., 1980. *How to Increase Reading Ability,* seventh edition. New York: Longman, p. 472.

9. Critchley, M., 1970. *The Dyslexic Child.* London: Heinemann; Keeney, A. H. and V. T., eds., 1963. *Dyslexia.* St. Louis: C. V. Mosby.

10. Galaburda, N., and Kemper, T., 1979. "Cytoarchitectonic Abnormalities in Developmental Dyslexia . . . ," *Annals of Neurology, 6:*2.

11. Geschwind, N., and Behan, P., 1982. "Left-Handedness: Association with Immune Disease, Migraine, and Developmental Learning Disorder," *Proceedings of the National Academy of Sciences,* August; Durden-Smith, J., and de Simone, D., 1983. *Sex and the Brain.* New York: Arbor House, p. 167.

12. See the work of Paul Fleschsig (1847-1929) cited in Keeney, A. H. and V. T., eds., 1968. *Dyslexia,* op. cit., p. 15; Kinsbourne, M., and Warrington, E. K., 1962. "A Disorder of Simultaneous Form Perception," *Brain, 85:*461-486.

13. Wepman, J. M., 1964. "The Perceptual Basis for Learning," in *Reading and the Language Arts.* Chicago: University of Chicago Press, pp. 25-33.

14. See the work of Lloyd J. Thompson of the University of North Carolina cited in Clarke, L., 1973. *Can't Read, Can't Write . . . .* New York: Penguin, p. 36.

15. Wing, L., 1978. "The Autiology and Pathogenesis of Early Infant Autism," *Trends in Neuroscience,* July.

16. See the work of Dr. A. L. Hill of the New York State Institute for Basic Research in Developmental Disabilities on Staten Island, New York, and Dr. B. Rimland of the Institute for Child Behavior Research in San Diego cited in *The New York Times,* 12 July 1983, C2.

17. Lindsley, O. R., 1965. "Can Deficiency Produce Specific Superiority—The Challenge of the Idiot Savant," *Exceptional Children, 31:*226-231; Scheerer, M., Rothman, E., and Goldstein, K., 1945. "A Case of 'Idiot Savant': An Experimental Study of Personality Organization," *Psychological Monographs 58,* Number 4.

18. Springer, S. P., and Deutsch, G., 1981. *Left Brain, Right Brain.* San Francisco: Freeman.

19. Bever, T., and Chiarello, R. J., 1974. "Cerebral Dominance in Musicians and Nonmusicians," *Science, 184:*4150; See also Damasio, A. R. and H. "Musical Faculty and Cerebral Dominance," in Critchley, M., and Henson, R. A., eds., 1977. *Music and the Brain.* London: Heinemann, pp. 141-155.

20. Gillingham, A., and Stillman, B. W., 1966. *Remedial Training for Children with Specific Difficulty in Reading, Spelling, and Phonetics.* Cambridge, Massachusetts: Educators' Publishing Service; Wedell, K., 1970. "Perceptuo-Motor Factors," *Journal of Special Education 4,* number 3.

21. Robinson, H. M., 1972. "Perceptual Training—Does it Result in Reading Improvement?", and Klesius, S. E., 1972. "Perceptual-Motor Development and Reading—A Closer Look," both in Aukerman, R. C., 1972. *Some Persistent Questions on Beginning Reading.* Newark, Delaware: International Reading Association, pp. 135-150, 151-159.

22. Hildreth, G., 1950. *Readiness for School Beginners.* New York: Harcourt Brace.

23. Smith, F., 1982. *Understanding Reading.* New York: Holt, Rinehart, and Winston, pp. 110-119.

24. Money, J., ed., 1966. *The Disabled Reader: Education of the Dyslexic Child.* Baltimore: Johns Hopkins; Orton, S., 1937. *Reading, Writing, and Speech Problems in Children.* New York: Norton.

25. Epstein, H. T., 1978. "Growth Spurts During Brain Development: Implications for Educational Policy and Practice," in Chall, J. S., and Mirsky, A. F., *Education and the Brain,* N. S. S. E. Chicago: University of Chicago Press.

26. Stanley, J. C., 1973. "Accelerating the Educational Progress of Intellectually Gifted Youth," *Educational Psychology, 10:.*133-146; Stanley, J. C., George, W. C., and Solano, C. H., eds., 1977. *The Gifted and the Creative: A Fifty-Year Perspective.* Baltimore: Johns Hopkins University Press; Stanley, J. C., Keating, D. P., and Fox, L. H., eds., 1974. *Mathematical Talent: Discovery, Description, and Development.* Baltimore: Johns Hopkins University Press.

27. See a classic discussion of this mystery: Duhem, P., 1954 (1905). *The Aim and Structure of Physical Theory.* Weiner, P., trans. Princeton: Princeton University Press.

28. Keating, D. P., ed., 1976. *Intellectual Talent: Research and Development.* Baltimore: Johns Hopkins University Press, pp. 316-342; Laycock, F., 1979. *Gifted Children.* Chicago: Scott-Foresman, pp. 52-54, 76-77.

29. Geschwind, N., 1982. "Why Orton Was Right," *Annals of Dyslexia, 32:*13-30.

## Chapter XIII
### Our Psychic Inheritance

1. Szalay, F. S., and Delson, E., 1979. *Evolutionary History of the Primates.* New York: Academic Press; Ciochin, R., and Corracini, R. S., eds., 1983. *New Interpretations of Ape and Human Ancestors.* New York: Plenum; Eimerl, S., and DeVore, I., 1979. *The Primates.* New York: Time-Life, pp. 44-45.

2. Carter, G. S., 1954. *Animal Evolution.* London: Sidgewick and Jackson, 164f.; Simpson, G. G., 1953. *The Major Features of Evolution.* New York: Columbia, p. 199f.

3. Campbell, B. G., 1960. *Human Evolution.* Chicago, Aldine.

4. Simons, E., 1972. *Primate Evolution.* New York: Macmillan; Schultz, A. H., 1966. "Changing Views on the Nature and Interrelations of the Higher Primates," *Yerkes Newsletter, 3:*15; Clark, L. G., and Leakey, L. S. B., 1951. "The Miocene Hominidae of East Africa," *Fossil Mammals of Africa, Number Three,* British Museum of Natural History.

5. Lovejoy, C. O., 1981. "The Origin of Man," *Science, 211:*341-350.

6. Campbell, B. G., 1960. *Human Evolution,* op. cit.; Pilbeam, D., 1972. *The Ascent of Man.* New York: Macmillan.

7. Jolly, A., 1972. *The Evolution of Primate Behavior.* New York: Macmillan; Zuckerman, S., 1932. *The Social Life of Monkeys and Apes.* New York: Harcourt Brace; Carpenter, C. R., 1964. *Naturalistic Behavior of Nonhuman Primates.* State College, Pennsylvania: Pennsylvania State University Press.

8. Jerison, H., 1973. *Evolution of Brain and Intelligence.* New York: Academic Press.

9. Sagan, C., 1977. *The Dragons of Eden.* New York: Random House, 157f.; Gazzaniga, M., 1967. "The Split Brain in Man," *Scientific American, 217:*24-29.

10. Penfield, W., and Roberts, L., 1959. *Speech and Brain Mechanisms.* Princeton: Princeton University Press; LeMay, M., and Geschwind, N., 1975. "Hemisphere Differences in the Brains of Great Apes," *Brain, Behavior, and Evolution 11:*48-52; Holloway, R. L., 1972. "New Australopithecine Endocasts SK 1585 from Southern South Africa," *American Journal of Physical Anthropology 37:*173-186.

11. Sagan, C., 1977. *The Dragons of Eden,* op. cit., p. 173; Eccles, J. C., 1979. *The Human Mystery.* New York: Springer; Geschwind, N., 1972. "The Organization of Language and the Brain," in Washburn, S. L., and Dolhinow, P., eds., *Perspectives on Human Evolution II.* New York: Holt, Rinehart, and Winston, pp. 386-389; Robinson, B., 1972. "Anatomical and Physiological Contrasts Between Humans and other Primate Vocalizations," in *Perspectives on Human Evolution,* op. cit., pp. 438-443.

12. LaBarre, W., 1968. "Reply to Hockett and Ascher," in Ashley Montagu, M. F., ed., *Culture: Man's Adaptive Dimension.* New York: Oxford University Press, p. 55; Milne, L. J. and M., 1962. *The Senses of Animals and Men.* New York: Atheneum, pp. 40, 42-43.

13. Lovejoy, C. O., 1981. "The Origin of Man," op. cit.; Raff, R. A., and Kaufman, T. C., 1983. *Embryos, Genes, and Evolution.* New York: Macmillan; Gould, S. J., 1977. *Ontogeny and Phylogeny.* Cambridge: Harvard University Press; Carrington, R., 1963. *A Million Years of Man.* New York: Mentor.

14. Langer, S. K., 1962. *Philosophical Sketches.* Baltimore: Johns Hopkins University Press, pp. 26-53; Lieberman, P., 1968. "Primate Vocalizations and Human Linguistic Ability," *Journal of the Acoustical Society of America, 44:*1574-1584.

15. Lieberman, P., and Crelin, E., 1972. "On the Speech of Neanderthal Man," *Linguistic Inquiry, 11:*203-222; Lieberman, P., 1978. "More Talk on Neanderthal Speech," *Current Anthropology, 19:*407.

16. Spuhler, J. N., 1977. "Biology, Speech, and Language," *Annual Review of Anthropology, 6:*509-561.

17. von Frisch, K., 1950. *Bees, Their Vision, Chemical Senses, and Language.* Ithaca: Cornell University Press.

18. See the discussion in Chapter XI.

19. Goldstein, K., 1940. *Human Nature in the Light of Psychopathology.* Cambridge: Harvard University Press, pp. 67-68; Halstead, W., 1947. *Brain and Intelligence.* Chicago: University of Chicago Press, pp. 147-149.

20. The work of Antonio E. Moniz (Nobel Laureate 1949), Almeida Lima, and Walter Freeman is both famous and infamous for this now supplanted form of surgical therapy.

21. Halstead, W., 1947. *Brain and Intelligence,* op. cit., Part II, pp. 103-149; Cattell, R. B., 1963. "Theory of Fluid and Crystallized Intelligence: A Critical Experiment," *J. Educational Psychology, 54:*1-22; Luria, A. R., and Yudovich, F., 1971. *Speech and the Development of Mental Processes in the Child.* Baltimore: Penguin, pp. 19-38.

22. Stenhouse, D., 1973. *The Evolution of Intelligence.* New York: Harper; Halstead, W., 1947. *Brain and Intelligence,* op. cit.; See also the references to the work of A. R. Jensen and R. Sternberg with respect to the "Executor" component of psychometric intelligence; Langer, S. K., 1972. *Mind: An Essay on Human Feeling, Volume II.* Baltimore: Johns Hopkins University Press.

23. Washburn, S. L., and Strum, S. C., 1972, in *Perspectives on Human Evolution-2.* New York: Holt, Rinehart, and Winston, pp. 469-471.

24. Jakobson, R., 1971. *Studies on Child Language and Aphasia.* The Hague: Mouton; Luria, A. R., 1958. "Brain Disorders and Language Analysis," *Lang. Speech, 1:*14-34.

25. Clark, G., 1967. *The Stone Age Hunters.* New York: McGraw-Hill, pp. 43-66; Day, M. H., 1971. *Fossil Man.* New York: Bantam, pp. 132-135; von Koenigswald, G. H. R., 1962. *The Evolution of Man.* Ann Arbor: University of Michigan, figure 74.

26. Pfeiffer, J. E., 1983. *The Creative Explosion: An Inquiry into the Origins of Art and Religion.* New York: Harper and Row; Marshack, A., 1972. *The Roots of Civilization.* New York: McGraw-Hill.

27. Jerison, H., 1973. *Evolution of the Brain and Intelligence*. New York: Academic Press; Coon, C., 1962. *The Origin of Races*. New York: Knopf; Coon, C., 1982. *Racial Adaptations*. Chicago: Nelson-Hall, Chapter 9; See also Spitzka, E. A. (1907) "A Study of the Brains of Six Eminent Scientists and Scholars Belonging to the American Anthropometric Society," *Transactions of the American Philosophical Society, 2:*175-303. Spitzke compares these six with one hundred other "eminent" figures mostly from Paris and Philadelphia. His formula produced a mean of 200 cubic centimeters larger than the already high European mean.

28. Holloway, R., 1966. "Cranial Capacity and Neuron Number," *American Journal of Physical Anthropology, 25:*305-314; Tobias, P. V., 1971. *The Brain in Hominid Evolution*. New York: Columbia University Press, p. 104.

29. Day, M., 1968. *Guide to Fossil Man: A Handbook of Human Paleontology*. Cleveland: The World Publishing Co.; Bordes, F., 1968. *The Old Stone Age*. New York: McGraw-Hill; Phenice, T. W., 1972. *Hominid Fossils*. Dubuque, Iowa: William C. Brown.

30. Jinks, J. L., and Fulker, D. W., 1970. "Comparison of the Biometrical Genetical, MAVA, and Classical Approaches to the Analysis of Human Behavior," *Psychological Bulletin, 73:*311-349; Eccles, J. C., 1979. *The Human Mystery*. New York: Springer International, p. 148.

31. Budko, V. D., 1972. "The Paleolithic Period of Byelorussia," in *The Origin of Homo Sapiens*. Bordes, F., ed. Paris: UNESCO, pp. 187-198; Zvelebil, M., 1984. "Clues to Recent Evolution from Specialized Technologies," *Nature, 307:*314-315; Coon, C., 1982. *Racial Adaptations*. Chicago: Nelson-Hall, pp. 151-165.

32. Leakey, R. E., and Lewin, R., 1977. *Origins*. New York: E. P. Dutton, pp. 136-144; Campbell, B. G., 1982. *Humankind Emerging,* Third Edition. Boston: Little Brown, pp. 418-429.

33. Irsigler, F. J., 1983. "The Role of the Temporal Lobe on Morphogenesis and Lateralization of the Human Brain," *Speculations in Science and Technology, 6:*445-453; Irsigler, F. J., 1984. "Quantitative Morphogenesis and Lateralization of the Human Brain," *Mankind Quarterly, 25:*3-46.

34. Sanides, F., 1975. "Comparative Neurology of the Temporal Lobe in Primates Including Man, With Reference to Speech," *Brain and Language, 2:*396-419; Pribram, K. H., 1971. "What Makes Man Human," *James Arthur Lecture on the Evolution of the Human Brain*. New York: The American Museum of Natural History.

35. Coon, C. S., 1965. *The Living Races of Man*. New York: Knopf; Brues, A.M., 1977. *People and Races*. New York: Macmillan.

36. Cassirer, E., 1944. *An Essay on Man*. New Haven: Yale University Press, p. 24.
37. Shapiro, H. L., 1974. *Peking Man*. New York: Simon and Schuster, pp. 74-100; Eiseley, L., 1960. *The Firmament of Time*. New York: Atheneum.
38. Washburn, S. E., and Strum, S. C., 1972. "Concluding Comments," in Dolhinow, op. cit., p. 481; Ashley Montagu, M. F., 1968. "Brains, Genes, Culture, Gestation," in Ashley Montagu, M. F., ed., *Culture: Man's Adaptive Dimension*. New York: Oxford University Press, pp. 109-112.
39. See discussion in Chapter X.
40. See also Chapter X discussion. However, none of Terman's "geniuses" received universal honors for creative work. As noted earlier, two whose I.Q.s were not high enough (below 140) and thus were rejected, Luis Alvarez and William Shockley, became Nobel Prize winners.
41. Geschwind, N., and Behan, P., 1982. "Left-Handedness: Association with Immune Disease, Migraine, and Developmental Learning Disorder," *Proceedings of the National Academy of Sciences,* August.
42. Cajori, F., 1919. *History of Mathematics,* Second Edition. New York; Lehman, H. C., 1953. *Age and Achievement*. Princeton: Princeton University Press; For a contrasting view see Hardy, G. H., 1941. *A Mathematician's Apology*. Cambridge University Press; Gruber, H. E., 1986. "The Self-Construction of the Extraordinary," in Sternberg, R. J., and Davidson, J. E., *Conceptions of Giftedness*. New York: Cambridge University Press, pp. 247-263.

## Chapter XIV
### The Elements of Variable Intelligence

1. Thomas, E., 1959. *The Harmless People*. New York: Alfred Knopf.
2. Webster, H., 1940. *History of Civilization*. Boston: D. C. Heath, pp. 390-392.
3. On the work of Jakobson and Luria see Chapter XII and notes. See also Halstead, W., 1947. *Brain and Intelligence*. Chicago: University of Chicago Press, pp. 147-149. This is one of the first recognitions of the independence of psychometric intelligence from defects and lobectomies of the front areas of the brain.
4. Coon, C., 1982. *Racial Adaptations*. Chicago: Nelson-Hall, pp. 169-178.
5. Coon, C., 1982. *Racial Adaptations*. Chicago: Nelson-Hall, p. 124; Coon, C., 1962. *The Origin of Races*. New York: Knopf, p. 443.

6. See Chapter XI and notes.

7. Oden, M. H., 1968. "The Fulfillment of Promise: Forty Year Follow-Up of the Terman Gifted Group," *Genetic Psychology Monographs, 77*:3-93.

8. See Chapter XI and notes.

9. Gardner, H., 1983. *Frames of Mind.* New York: Basic Books. Gardner sees intelligence as multifaceted and separate, an extremely factor-oriented approach which in effect works out and eliminates the possibility of *g* comparisons. His book has not met with professional approbation.

10. Penfield, W., and Roberts, L., 1959. *Speech and Brain Mechanisms.* Princeton: Princeton University Press; Penfield, W., 1975. *The Mystery of the Mind.* Princeton: Princeton University Press. In this last book Penfield concludes that the parts and functions lead to a whole, a concept of mind as a reality distinct, if dependent on the body.

11. Geschwind, N., 1962. "The Anatomy of Acquired Disorders of Reading" in *Reading Disabilities,* Money, J., ed. Baltimore: Johns Hopkins University Press, pp. 115-129.

12. MacLean, P., 1973. *A Triune Conception of the Brain and Behavior.* Toronto: University of Toronto Press; Simeons, A. T. W., 1962. *Man's Presumptuous Brain.* New York: Dutton.

13. See Chapter XIII, note 33.

14. Hardin, G., 1959. *Nature and Man's Fate.* New York: Rineholt and Co., p. 188; Hamburger, J., 1978. *Discovering the Individual.* New York: W. W. Norton.

15. Eysenck, H. J., 1982. *Personality, Genetics, and Behavior.* New York: Praeger, pp. 1-99; Kagan, J., *et al.,* and Garcia-Coll, C., 1984. "Behavioral Inhibitions to the Unfamiliar," *Child Development, 55*:2212-2225.

16. Howells, W. W., 1973. *Cranial Variation in Man.* Cambridge, Massachusetts: Peabody Museum.

17. Geschwind, N., 1965. "Disconnection Syndromes in Animals and Man," *Brain, 88*:237-294, 585-644; Bogen, J. E. and G. M., 1969. "The Other Side of the Brain III: The Corpus Callosum and Creativity," *Bulletin of the Los Angeles Neurological Society, 34*:191-220.

18. Stephan, H., 1975. "Allocortex," in Bargmann, W., ed., *Handbuch der Mikroskopischen Anatomie des Menschen,* 4/9. Berlin: Springer.

19. Sperry, R. W., 1972. "Mental Unity Following Surgical Disconnection of the Cerebral Hemispheres," in Washburn, S. L., and Dolhinow, P., eds., *Perspectives on Human Evolution II.* New York: Holt, Rinehart, and Winston, pp. 416-417; Wertheim, N., 1977. "Is There an Anatomical Localisation for Musical Faculties?," in *Music and the Brain,* Critchley, M., and Henson, R. A., eds. London: William Heinemann Medical Books, pp. 282-297; MacLean, P., 1978. "A Mind of Three Minds," in Chall, J. S., and Mirsky, A. F., *Education and the Brain,* M. S. S. E. Chicago: University of Chicago Press, pp. 308-342; Henahan, D., 1979. "When Neurologists Study Song," *New York Times,* January 14.

## Chapter XV
### Male and Female Intelligence: The Evidence for Variability

1. World Almanac, 1982. Some of the differences have been attributed to a skewing of the statistics by the extreme longevity of a minority of females.

2. Wilson, J. Q., and Herrnstein, R., 1985. *Crime and Human Nature.* New York: Simon and Schuster; Holliday, L., 1978. *The Violent Sex.* Guernville, California: Bluestocking Books.

3. Flor-Henry, P., 1978. "Gender, Hemisphere Specialization, and Psychopathology," *Society, Science, and Medicine,* 1213; Flor-Henry, P., and Yeudall, L. T., 1979. "Neuropsychological Investigations of Schizophrenia and Manic-Depressive Psychoses," in Gruzelier, J., and Flor-Henry, P., eds., *Hemispheric Asymmetries of Function in Psychopathology.* Amsterdam: Elsevier.

4. Durden-Smith, M. J., and de Simone, D., 1983. *Sex and the Brain.* New York: Arbor House, p. 162.

5. Critchley, M., 1973. *The Dyslexic Child.* London: William Heinemann Medical Books, p. 91.

6. Goldberg, S., 1973. *The Inevitability of Patriarchy.* New York: Morrow.

7. Money, J., 1963. "Cytogenetic and Psychosocial Incongruities with a Note on Space-Form Blindness," *American Journal of Psychiatry,* 119:820-827; Money, J., and Ehrhardt, A. A., 1972. *Man and Woman, Boy and Girl.* Baltimore: Johns Hopkins University Press.

8. Velle, W., 1982. "Sex Hormones and Behavior in Animals and Man," *Perspectives in Biology and Medicine,* 25:2.

9. *New York Times,* 3 August 1986.

10. Lehrke, R. G., 1978. "Sex Linkage: A Biological Basis for Greater Male Variability in Intelligence," in Osborne, R. T., ed., *Human Variation.* New York: Academic Press, pp. 171-198.

11. Lehrke, R. G., 1978, "Sex Linkage . . . ," op. cit., pp. 186-187.

12. Lehrke, R. G., 1978, "Sex Linkage . . . ," op. cit., p. 176.

13. Lehrke, R. G., 1978, "Sex Linkage . . . ," op. cit., pp. 187-193; Bayley, N., 1966. "Developmental Problems of the Mentally Retarded Child," Philips, I., ed., *Prevention and Treatment of Mental Retardation.* New York: Basic Books, pp. 85-110; Jensen, A. R., 1980. *Bias in Mental Testing.* New York: The Free Press, pp. 427-428.

14. Lehrke, R. G., 1978. "Sex Linkage . . . ," op. cit. pp. 187-193; Lehrke, R. G., 1974. "X-Linked Mental Retardation and Verbal Disability," in *National Foundation of the March of Dimes, Birth Defects Original Article Series,* Volume 10, Number 1. Miami, Florida: Symposium Specialists; Outhut, M. C., 1933. "A Study of the Resemblance of Parents and Children in General Intelligence," *Archive of Psychology, 149:*1-60; Kamin, L., 1981. *The Intelligence Controversy (versus Eysenck, H. J.).* New York: John Wiley, pp. 173-176. A contrasting perspective.

15. *Hendrickson, D. E., 1982.* "The Biological Basis of Intelligence, Part II: Measurement," in Eysenck, H. J., ed., *A Model for Intelligence.* New York: Springer-Verlag, pp. 197-228; Hendrickson, D. E. and A. E., 1980. "The Biological Basis for Individual Differences in Intelligence," *Person. Indiv. Diff., 1:*3-33.

16. Hendrickson, D. E., 1982, "The Biological Basis of Intelligence . . . ," op. cit., pp. 207-208.

17. Hendrickson, D. E., 1982, "The Biological Basis of Intelligence . . . ," op. cit., p. 208.

18. Bayley, N., 1966, "Developmental Problems of the Mentally Retarded Child . . . ," op. cit.; Outhit, M. C., 1933, "A Study of the Resemblance of Parents . . . ," op. cit.

19. Eysenck, H. J., and Kamin, L., 1981. *The Intelligence Controversy.* New York: John Wiley, pp. 43-44.

20. Lehrke, R. G., 1978, "Sex Linkage . . . ," op. cit., p. 188; Reed, E. W. and S. C., 1965. *Mental Retardation: A Family Study.* Philadelphia: Saunders; Wright, W. S., Tarjan, G., and Fyer, L., 1959. "Investigation of Families with Two or More Mentally Defective Siblings," *American Journal of Diseases of Children, 97:*445-463.

21. Stanley, J. C., 1977. "Rationale for the Study of Mathematically Precocious Youth (SMPY)," in Stanley, J. C., *et al.,* eds., *The Gifted and the Creative: A Fifty Year Perspective.* Baltimore: Johns Hopkins University Press.

22. Kolata, G. B., 1980. "Math and Sex: Are Girls Born With Less Ability?", *Science, 210:*1234-1235; Benbow, C. P., and Stanley, J. C., 1980. "Sex Differences in Mathematical Ability: Fact or Artifact?", *Science, 210:*1262-1264; Benbow, C. P., and Stanley, J. C., 1981. "Mathematical Ability: Is Sex a Factor?", *Science, 212:*4491.

23. Hendrickson, D. E., 1982, "The Biological Basis of Intelligence . . . ," op. cit., p. 208; Benbow, C. P., and Stanley, J. C., 1983. "Sex Differences in Mathematical Reasoning Ability: More Facts," *Science, 222:*1029-1031.

24. Hendrickson, D. E., 1982, "The Biological Basis of Intelligence . . . ," op. cit.

25. Page, E. B., 1976. "A Historical Step Beyond Terman," in Keating, D. P., ed., *Intellectual Talent.* Baltimore: Johns Hopkins University Press, pp. 295-307; Lehrke, R. G., 1978, "Sex Linkage . . . ," op. cit.; Bock, R. D., and Kolakowski, D., 1973. "Further Evidence of Sex-Linked Major Gene Influence on Human Spatial Ability," *American Journal of Human Genetics, 25:*1-14.

26. Page, E. B., 1976, "A Historical Step Beyond Terman," op. cit., pp. 303-304; Jensen, A. R., 1982. "Changing Conceptions of Intelligence," *American Educational Research Association,* New York, April; Davis, G. A., and Rimm, S. B., 1985. *Education of the Gifted and Talented.* Englewood, New Jersey: Prentice-Hall, pp. 302-321.

27. Armstrong, J., 1980. "Education Commission of the United States-Denver," *Science, 210:*1235.

28. Kolata, G., 1983. "Math Genius May Have a Hormonal Basis," *Science, 222:*1312.

29. Marx, J. L. 1982. "Auto-Immunity in Left-Handers," *Science, 217:*144; Geschwind, N., and Behan, P., 1982. "Left-Handedness: Association with Immune Disease, Migraine, and Developmental Learning Disorder," *Proceedings of the National Academy of Sciences,* August.

30. Benbow, C. P., and Stanley, J. C., 1983. "Sex Differences in Mathematical Reasoning Ability . . . ," op. cit., p. 1031.

31. Kolata, G., 1983. "Math Genius May Have a Hormonal Basis," op. cit.

32. Hildreth, G. H., Griffith, N. C., and McGauvian, M. E., 1969. *Metropolitan Readiness Tests.* New York: Harcourt, Brace, and World. Manual of directions.

33. Kolata, G. B., 1980. "Math and Sex: Are Girls Born with Less Ability?", *Science, 210:*1234-1235. Aside from much anecdotal reportage of feminist anger with the Johns Hopkins SMPY and the female research participants, the following lists much research from the standpoint of an environmentalist explanation: Davis, G. A., and Rimm, S. B., 1985. *Educating the Gifted and Talented.* Englewood, New Jersey: Prentice-Hall, 321-331.

## Chapter XVI
### *The Meaning of Male/Female Intellectual Differences*

1. Brace, C. L., and Ashley Montagu, M. F., 1977. *Human Evolution.* New York: Macmillan, pp. 278-282.
2. Campbell, B. G., 1966. *Human Evolution.* Chicago, Aldine, p. 256.
3. Lewin, R., 1985. "Tooth Enamel Tells a Complex Story," *Science, 228:*707.
4. Ellefson, J. O., 1968. "Territorial Behavior in Common White-Handed Gibbon Hylobates Lar Linn," in Jay, P. C., ed. *Primates.* New York: Holt; Schultz, A. H., 1966. "Changing Views on the Nature and Interrelation of the Higher Primates," *Yerkes Newsletter, 3:*15.
5. Jolly, A., 1972. *The Evolution of Primate Behavior.* New York: Macmillan; Lancaster, J. B., 1975. *Primate Behavior and the Evolution of Human Culture.* New York: Holt, Rinehart, and Winston.
6. Fischer, H. E., 1982. *The Sex Contract.* New York: Morrow, p. 100.
7. Itzkoff, S. W., 1983. *The Form of Man.* Ashfield, Massachusetts: Paideia Publishers, pp. 77-81.
8. Goodall, J., 1986. *The Chimpanzees of Gombe.* Cambridge: Belknap Harvard University Press.
9. Most scientists have not as yet put down on paper the probable genocide of the australopithecines. They were perfectly well-adapted creatures, at least as powerful as the gorillas or chimpanzees, but unfortunately too close to *Homo* in behavior and ecology. Itzkoff, S. W., 1985. *Triumph of the Intelligent.* Ashfield, Massachusetts: Paideia Publishers, pp. 63-69; Browne, M. W., 1986. "Fossils Point to Giant Ape's Violent End," *New York Times,* 11 November.
10. Eiseley, L., 1957. *The Immense Journey.* New York: Random House, pp. 127-141; Itzkoff, S. W., 1985. *Triumph of the Intelligent,* op. cit., pp. 133-140.
11. Coon, C. S., 1962. *The Origin of Races.* New York: Knopf, pp. 636-639, 645-649; Baker, J. R., 1974. *Race.* New York: Oxford University Press, pp. 305-306.

12. Fischer, H. E., 1982. *The Sex Contract*. New York: Morrow, pp. 34-36.
13. Clark, G., 1967. *The Stone Age Hunters*. New York: McGraw Hill, pp. 55-61.
14. Solecki, R. S., 1960. "Three Adult Neanderthal Skeletons from the Shanidar Cave in Northern Iraq," *Smithsonian Report Publication for 1959*, Number 4414, pp. 603-635; Solecki, R. S., 1975. "Shanidar IV, A Neanderthal Flower Burial in Northern Iraq," *Science, 190:*880-881.
15. See Chapter XV text and notes for a general overview of the evidence.
16. Page, E. B., 1976, and Lehrke, R. G., 1978, text and notes on Chapter XV for specific contributions to this problem.
17. Lehrke, R. G., 1978, op. cit. Chapter XV.
18. Suojasen, W. W., and Bassinger, R. C., eds., 1984. *Management and the Brain*.
19. Hendrickson, A. E., 1982. "The Biological Basis of Intelligence, Part I: Theory," in Eysenck, H. J., ed. *A Model for Intelligence*. New York: Springer-Verlag, p. 188.
20. Hendrickson, A. E., 1982. "The Biological Basis of Intelligence, Part I: Theory," op. cit., pp. 188-189.
21. Coon, C. S., 1982. *Racial Adaptations*. Chicago: Nelson-Hall, pp. 172-173.
22. Marshack, A., 1972. *The Roots of Civilization*. New York: McGraw-Hill.

## Chapter XVII
### *The Irrelevance of Race*

1. Bouchard, T. J., Jr., and McGue, M., 1981. "Familial Studies of Intelligence: A Review," *Science, 212:*1055-1059. A summary of 111 worldwide studies.
2. Eysenck, H. J., and Kamin, L., 1981. *The Intelligence Controversy*. New York: John Wiley, pp. 82-83; McGurk, F. C. J., 1975. "Race Differences—Twenty Years Later," *Homo, 26:*219-239; Flynn, J. R., 1984. "The Mean I. Q. of Americans: Massive Gains, 1932-1978," *Psychological Bulletin, 95:*29-51; Jensen, A. R., 1977. "Cumulative Deficit in I. Q. of Blacks in the Rural South," *Developmental Psychology, 13:*184-191; Jensen, A. R., 1980. *Bias in Mental Testing*. New York: The Free Press, pp. 98-99; Kennedy, W. A., *et al.*, 1963. "A Normative Sample of Intelligence and Achievement of Negro Elementary School Children in the Southeastern United States," *Monographs of the Society for Research on Child Development*, Volume 28, Number 6. A mean I. Q. of 80.7 is reported for the 1800 black children tested.

3. As reported in the media in 1986.

4. Lynn, R., 1978. "Ethnic and Racial Differences in Intelligence: International Comparisons," in Osborne, R. T., *et al., eds. Human Variation*. New York: Academic Press, pp. 272-273; Lynn, R., 1982. "I. Q. in Japan and the United States Shows a Growing Disparity," *Nature, 297:*222-223; Lynn shows a Japanese mean of 111; Anderson, A. A., 1982. "The Great Japanese I. Q. Increase," *Nature, 297:*180-181; Lynn, R., and Hampson, S., 1986. "The Structure of Japanese Abilities . . . ," *Current Psychological Research and Reviews,* Winter, 1985-1986, 309-322. Lynn here shows a Japanese mean I. Q. slightly higher than that of the United States.

5. Vining, D. R., Jr., 1983. "Mean I. Q. Differences in Japan and the United States," *Nature, 30:*738; Weyl, N., 1978. "World Population Growth and the Geography of Intelligence," *Modern Age, 22:*64-71; Jensen, A. R., 1980. *Bias in Mental Testing,* op. cit., pp. 100-105; this is a general discussion of the nature of standard deviation; Cattell, R. B., and Brennan, J., 1981. "Population Intelligence and National Syntality Dimensions," *Mankind Quarterly, 21:*327-340; Vining, D. R, Jr., 1983. "Fertility Differentials and the Status of Nations," in Cattell, R. B., ed. *Intelligence and National Achievement*. Washington, D. C.: The Institute for the Study of Man, pp. 118-122.

6. Charles Robb to national symposium of democratic party leaders as reported in the national press.

7. Eysenck, H. J., and Kamin, L., 1981. *The Intelligence Controversy.,* op. cit., pp. 74-76; Jensen, A. R., 1980. *Bias in Mental Testing,* op. cit., pp. 87-92.

8. The situation in the Horn of Africa, Ethiopia, Somalia, even Sudan amidst potential plenty is an aspect of a continent sinking. The quiet evidence is that the French are back in their old West African colonies such as Senegal, the Ivory Coast, the Belgians in Zaire, the Russians and Cubans in Angola and Mozamique.

9. Jensen, A. R., 1985. "The Nature of the Black-White Difference on Various Psychometric Tests: Spearman's Hypothesis," *The Behavioral and Brain Sciences, 8:*193-263 (203-206).

10. The vilification of psychologists, evolutionists, and anthropologists who have argued the question of variability of intelligence and achievement from a genetic or hereditarian standpoint led to a now well-known resolution on intelligence from fifty scientists affirming the right of scholars to pursue such studies in the light of strong evidence for their position. Page, E. B., 1972. "Behavior and Heredity," *American Psychologist,* July:660-661.

11. Coon, C. S., 1966. "The Taxonomy of Human Variation," *Annals of the New York Academy of Sciences, 134:*516-523; Yablakov, A. V., 1974. *Variability of Mammals.* New Delhi: Amerind.

12. Weidenreich, F., 1946. *Apes, Giants, and Man.* Chicago, University of Chicago Press.

13. Coon, C. S., 1962. *The Origin of Races.* New York: Knopf, pp. 458-460; Itzkoff, S. W., 1983. *The Form of Man.* Ashfield, Massachusetts: Paideia Publishers, pp. 150-180. A general discussion of variability.

14. Coon, C. S., 1962. *The Origin of Races,* op. cit., especially pp. 371-663.

15. Roberts, D. F., 1963. "Review of *Origin of Races* by Carleton Coon" *Human Biology, 35:*443-445; Hulse, F., 1963. "Review of *Origin of Races* by Carleton Coon," *American Anthropologist, 65:*685-687.

16. Coon, C. S., 1966. "The Taxonomy of Human Variation," op. cit.; Coon, C. S., 1967. "Reply to Buethner-Janusch," *American Journal of Physical Anthropology, 26:*359-360.

17. Lewontin, R. C., 1974. "The Analysis of Variance and the Analysis of Causes," *American Journal of Human Genetics, 26:*400-411; Lewontin, R. C., 1972. "The Apportionment of Human Diversity," in Dobzhansky, T., *et al.,* eds. *Evolutionary Biology, Volume 6.* New York: Appleton-Century-Crofts, pp. 381-398.

18. Coon, C. S., 1962. *The Origin of Races,* op. cit., pp. 630-636; Baker, J. R., 1974. *Race.* New York: Oxford University Press, pp. 160, 174-176.

19. Itzkoff, S. W., 1985. *Triumph of the Intelligent.* Ashfield, Massachusetts: Paideia Publishers, pp. 159-176.

20. Coon, C. S., 1962. *The Origin of Races,* op. cit., p. 489; Coon, C. S., 1965. *The Living Races of Man.* New York: Knopf, pp. 149, 234.

21. Coon, C. S., 1962. *The Origin of Races,* op. cit. The basic argument of Coon has held up. This is that largely internal selective factors, for each of the geographical races, were responsible for the variable progress toward the *sapiens* grade. That the races can be traced back to geographically distinctive forms of *Homo erectus* is now part of the accepted canon of anthropological and evolutionary knowledge.

22. Itzkoff, S. W., 1985. *Triumph of the Intelligent,* op. cit., Part 3, Chapters XIV, XV, and XVI; de Laubenfels, D., 1983. "The Upper Paleolithic Revolution," *Mankind Quarterly, 23:*329-356.

23. Kennedy, G., 1980. "The Emergence of Modern Man," *Nature, 284:*11; Day, M. H., and Leakey, R. E., 1980. "A New Hominid Fossil Skull (L. H. 18) from the Ngaloba Beds, Laetoli, Northern Tanzania," *Nature, 284:*55-60.

24. Day, M. H., 1977. *Guide to Fossil Man.* Chicago: University of Chicago Press, pp. 310-312; Phenice, T. W., 1972. *Hominid Fossils.* Dubuque, Iowa: William Brown Co., p. 152.

25. Howell, F. C., 1957. "The Evolutionary Significance of Variation and Varieties of 'Neanderthal' Man," *Quarterly Review of Biology, 32:*330; Higgs, F. S., 1961. "Some Pleistocene Faunas of the Mediterranean Coastal Areas," *Proceedings of the Prehistorical Society, 27:*144.

26. Baker, J. R., 1974. *Race,* op. cit., pp. 95-98. Baker advances the very surprising argument that on the basis of a long and separated history, Hottentots of South Africa and Europeans could not be thought of as belonging to one species. Their very different body structures and social patterns would ordinarily preclude this. But like other forms of life, under special conditions they *have* interbred. However, Baker suspects that much of the success has been in the form of a backcross to the parental and advanced type. See also Brace, C. L., and Ashley Montagu, M. F., 1977. *Human Evolution.* New York: Macmillan. A series of photographs of Bushman-Caucasoid hybridity would tend to confirm Baker's speculation. pp. 400-401.

27. Baker, J. R., 1974. *Race,* op. cit., pp. 174-177.

28. Coon, C. S., 1966. "The Taxonomy of Human Variation," op. cit. Coon would modify this claim by stating that "like" would prefer "like" if the choice were available.

29. Coon, C. S., 1982. *Racial Adaptations.* Chicago: Nelson-Hall, pp. 85-112.

30. Freedman, D. G., 1979. *Human Sociobiology.* New York: The Free Press; Freedman, D. G., 1974. *Human Infancy: An Evolutionary Perspective.* New York: Wiley; Freedman, D. G., 1976. "Infancy, Biology, and Culture," in Lipsitt, L. P., ed., *Developmental Psychobiology.* New York: Wiley.

31. Freedman, D. G., 1979. *Human Sociobiology,* op. cit., pp. 141-162.

32. The following books present the vital statistics linking morphological development, accompanying tool kit finds, as well as approximate datings, for each fossil skull: Coon, C. S., 1962. *The Origin of Races,* op. cit.; Day, M. H., 1977. *Guide to Fossil Man.* op. cit.; Phenice, T. W., 1972. *Hominid Fossils,* op. cit.

33. Howell, F. C., 1965. *Early Man.* New York: Time, Inc., pp. 83-100.

34. Tattersall, I., and Delson, E., 1984. *Ancestors.* New York: American Museum of Natural History.

35. Pilbeam, D., 1972. *The Ascent of Man.* New York: Macmillan.

36. See the illustration in Phenice, T. W., 1972. *Hominid Fossils,* op. cit., p. 45.

37. Pilbeam, D., 1972. *The Ascent of Man,* op. cit., pp. 176-178; Pearson, R., 1974. *Introduction to Anthropology.* New York: Holt, Rinehart, and Winston, pp. 103-104.

38. Russell, I. S., 1979. "Brain Size and Intelligence: A Comparative Perspective," in Oakley, D. A., and Plotkin, H. C., eds. *Brain, Behavior, and Evolution.* London: Methuen, (pp. 126-153) p. 151.

39. If indeed the modern races can be traced to their erectine progenitors in a variety of slowly-evolving nonselective structures—teeth, bone, etc., then it is highly likely that in a rapidly-evolving and complex structure, the brain, there will exist numerous differences, rooted in ancient patterns that have been "dragged" into the present as the cortex has expanded, through the process of gene linkages.

40. Oakley, K. P., *et al.,* 1971. *Catalogue of Fossil Hominids, Part 2: Europe.* London: British Museum of Natural History. It will be seen that there is a gap, both chronologically and morphologically, between the erectine-like group, which includes Swanscombe, Fontechevade, Steinheim, and Vértesszőllős; the Neanderthals; and Cro-Magnons *(Homo sapiens sapiens).* This gap argues for the development of a tiny break-away group undergoing radical heterochronic development. It must have taken at least 100,000 years for this paedomorph (Cro-Magnon) to reach a critical adaptive Rubicon. At that point the expansion into Europe and the rest of the world became a flood of powerfully selective genes for intelligent cultural behavior.

41. Coon, C. S., 1965. *The Living Races of Man.* New York: Knopf, pp. 155-162.

42. Brues, A., 1977. *People and Races.* New York: Macmillan, pp. 258-259; Coon, C. S., 1965. *The Living Races of Man,* op. cit., pp. 150-152. Coon describes the Ainu as Caucasoids.

43. Howells, W., 1963. *Back of History.* New York: Doubleday-Anchor, p. 90.

44. Coon, C. S., 1965. *The Living Races of Man,* op. cit., Plate 43b.

45. Brues, A., 1977. *People and Races,* op. cit., p. 295.

46. Brues, A., 1977. *People and Races,* op. cit., pp. 297, 300. Brues sees an Ainu and thus a possible Caucasoid element in the Maidu. However, she does note that the Eastern Indians, who look quite different from the Maidu, are very Caucasoid in appearance.

47. Pearson, R., 1974. *Introduction to Anthropology,* op. cit., p. 553; Murdock, G. P., 1964. "Genetic Classification of the Austronesian Languages: A Key to Oceanic Cultural History," *Ethnology,* 3:117-126.

48. Darlington, C. D., 1969. *The Evolution of Man and Society.* London: George Allen and Unwin, pp. 613-618.

49. Both Brues, 1977, op. cit., and Coon, 1962 and 1965, op. cit., illustrate this argument with photographs showing the Japanese aristocratic aquiline profile reminiscent of the Turkic or Kazahk facial patterns. Both also show a long-faced northern Chinese type with prominent brow ridges that may reflect the hypothesized Neanderthal (Caucasoid) infusion of genes to this area from the west and their Mousterian flint tools found in the Fen River Valley, a tributary of the Yellow River, southwest of Peking. See Thoma, A., 1964. "Die Enstehung der Mongoliden," *Homo, 15:*1-12; Coon, C. S., 1982. *Racial Adaptations.* Chicago: Nelson-Hall, pp. 156-157.

50. von Wissman, H., 1956. "The Dry Belt of Asia . . . ," in Thomas, W. L., *et al.,* eds. *Man's Role in Changing the Face of the Earth.* Chicago: University of Chicago Press-Wenner Gren Symposium; Littleton, C. S., 1985. "The Indo-European Strain in Japanese Mythology," *Mankind Quarterly, 26:*152-174; Obayashi, T., 1984. "Japanese Myths of Descent from Heaven and Their Korean Parallels," *Asian Folklore Studies, 43:*171-184; Yoshida, A., 1977. "Japanese Mythology and the Indo-European Trifunctional System," *Diogenes, 98:*93-116.

51. Pearson, R., 1974. *Introduction to Anthropology,* op. cit., pp. 485-486.

52. Darlington, C. D., 1969. *The Evolution of Man and Society.* London: George Allen and Unwin, p. 618.

53. Brues, A., 1977. *People and Races,* op. cit., pp. 292-302.

54. Brues, A., 1977. *People and Races,* op. cit., pp. 265-271.

55. Coon, C. S., 1965. *The Living Races of Man,* op. cit., p. 95.

56. Coon, C. S., 1965. *The Living Races of Man,* op. cit., pp. 150-152.

57. Brues, A., 1977. *People and Races,* op. cit., p. 260.

58. Eichhorn, W., 1969. *Chinese Civilization.* New York: Praeger; Latourette, K. S., 1934. *The Chinese.* New York: Macmillan, pp. 40-42; Pearson, R., 1974. *Introduction to Anthropology,* op. cit., pp. 485-488.

59. Pearson, R., 1974. *Introduction to Anthropology,* op. cit., p. 486; Polome, E., ed., 1985. "Recent Russian Papers on the Indo-European Problem," *Journal of Indo-European Studies, 13:*1-2. The entire issue is devoted to the origin of the Indo-Europeans and the relationship of the various branches, including Tokharian, to proto-Indo-European.

60. Day, M. H., 1977. *Guide to Fossil Man.* Chicago: University of Chicago Press, pp. 207-214; Day dates this fossil to 40,000 B. P. even though much earlier dates have recently been suggested; Coon, C. S., 1982. *Racial Adaptations,* op. cit., pp. 129-131. Coon originally argued for a date of about 26,000 B. P. Taking all the new studies into consideration, he now opts for a date more recent than 62,000 B. P.

61. Coon, C. S., 1965. *The Living Races of Man,* op. cit., pp. 122-125.
62. Coon, C. S., 1962. *The Origin of Races,* op. cit., pp. 645-649; Baker, J. R., 1974. *Race,* op. cit., p. 306.
63. Coon, C. S., 1982. *Racial Adaptations,* op. cit., p. 156.
64. Coon, C. S., 1962. *The Origin of Races,* op. cit., pp. 651-656.
65. Coon, C. S., 1962. *The Origin of Races,* op. cit., pp. 654-655; Brues, A., 1977. *People and Races,* op. cit., pp. 286-291.
66. Coon, C. S., 1962. *The Origin of Races,* op. cit., pp. 655-656.
67. Brues, A., 1977. *People and Races,* op. cit., p. 291.
68. Coon, C. S., 1962. *The Origin of Races,* op. cit., p. 656; Coon, C. S., 1965. *The Living Races of Man,* op. cit., pp. 101-102, 123-124.
69. Coon, C. S., 1965. *The Living Races of Man,* op. cit., Plates 122-124.
70. Brues, A., 1977. *People and Races,* op. cit., pp. 13, 285-286; Coon, C. S., 1965. *The Living Races of Man,* op. cit., pp. 84-125.
71. Coon, C. S., 1965. *The Living Races of Man,* op. cit., Plate 96b, c.
72. Baker, J. R., 1974. *Race,* op. cit., pp. 303-324.
73. Baker, J. R., 1974. *Race,* op. cit., pp. 311, 315.

## Chapter XVIII
*"Every Nation Needs a Southern Neighbor"*

1. Leakey, R. E., and Lewin, R., 1977. *Origins.* New York: Dutton, pp. 120-124.
2. Campbell, B. G., 1982. *Humankind Emerging.* Boston: Little Brown, 291-293.
3. Shapiro, H. L., 1974. *Peking Man.* New York: Simon and Schuster.
4. Leakey, R. E., 1981. "The Making of Mankind," *The Listener,* Spring, Part 7.
5. Pilbeam, D., 1972. *The Ascent of Man.* New York: Macmillan, p. 183; Day, M. H., 1973. *Human Evolution.* New York: Barnes and Noble.
6. Hemmer, H., 1972. "The Evolutionary Significance . . . ," in Bordes, F., ed. *The Origin of Homo Sapiens.* Paris: UNESCO, pp. 65-71.
7. Coon, C. S., 1982. *Racial Adaptations.* Chicago: Nelson-Hall, pp. 151-165; Macintosh, N. S. W., 1967. "Recent Discoveries of Early Australian Men," *Annals of the Australian College of Dental Surgery,* p. 1104; Coon, C. S., 1962. *The Origin of Races.* New York: Knopf, pp. 410-411.
8. Coon, C. S., 1962. *The Origin of Races,* op. cit., p. 427; Itzkoff, S. W., 1983. *The Form of Man.* Ashfield, Massachusetts: Paideia Publishers, pp. 150-180.

9. Mayr, E., 1963. *Animal Species and Evolution.* Cambridge: Harvard University Press-Belknap, p. 214; Simpson, G. G., 1953. *The Major Features of Evolution.* New York: Columbia University Press, pp. 135-136, 287-288.

10. Dinnell, R., 1983. "A New Chronology for the Mousterian," *Nature, 301:*199; Howells, W. W., 1974. "Neanderthals: Names, Hypotheses, Scientific Method," *American Anthropologist, 76:*24-38; Howells, W. W., 1975. "Neanderthal Man: Facts and Figures," in Tuttle, R. H., ed., *Paleoanthropology, Morphology, and Paleoecology.* The Hague: Mouton, pp. 390-407.

11. Clark, G., and Piggott, S., 1967. *Prehistoric Societies.* New York: Knopf, pp. 58-63.

12. Pfeiffer, J. E., 1983. *The Creative Explosion.* New York: Harper and Row; Marshack, A., 1979. "Upper Paleolithic Symbol Systems of the Russian Plain: Cognitive and Comparative Analysis," *Current Anthropology, 20:*271-311; Bahn, P. G., 1983. "A Paleolithic Treasure House in the Pyrenees," *Nature, 302,* April 14.

13. de Beer, G., 1958. *Embryos and Ancestors.* London: Oxford University Press; Hardy, A. C., 1954. "Escape from Specialization," in *Evolution as a Process.* London.

14. Weiner, J. S., and Campbell, B. G., 1964. "The Taxonomic Status of the Swanscombe Skull," in Ovey, C. D., ed. *The Swanscombe Skull.* Great Britain: The Royal Anthropological Society.

15. Itzkoff, S. W., 1985. *Triumph of the Intelligent.* Ashfield, Massachusetts: Paideia Publishers, pp. 150-176; Gould, S. J., and Eldridge, N., 1977. "Punctuated Equilibrium . . . ," *Paleobiology, 3:*115-151.

16. Lovejoy, C. O., 1981. "The Origin of Man," *Science, 211:*341-350.

17. von Koenigswald, G. H. R., 1962. *The Evolution of Man.* Ann Arbor: University of Michigan Press, p. 124.

18. Carrington, R., 1964. *A Million Years of Man.* New York: Mentor, pp. 113-114.

19. Pearson, R., 1974. *Introduction to Anthropology.* New York: Holt, Rinehart, and Winston, pp. 491-492.

20. Coon, C. S., 1962. *The Origin of Races,* op. cit., pp. 426-427, 485-486.

21. Marshack, A., 1972. *The Roots of Civilization.* New York: McGraw-Hill; Marshack, A., 1972. "Cognitive Aspects of Upper Paleolithic Engraving," *Current Anthropology, 13:*445-477.

22. Coon, C. S., 1982. *Racial Adaptations.* Chicago: Nelson-Hall, pp. 153-154; Coon, C. S., 1962. *The Origin of Races,* op. cit., pp. 636-639, 645-649.

23. Darlington, C. D., 1969. *The Evolution of Man and Society*. London: George Allen and Unwin, pp. 613-618.
24. Oakley, K. P., 1957. *Man as the Tool-Maker*. Chicago: University of Chicago Press, pp. 92-109.
25. Baker, J. R., 1974. *Race*. New York: Oxford University Press, pp. 243-247; Coon, C. S., 1965. *The Living Races of Man*. New York: Knopf, pp. 72-75, Plates 86-99; Coon, C. S., 1939. *The Races of Europe*. New York: Macmillan.
26. Moorehead, A., 1966. *The Fatal Impact*. New York: Harper and Row, pp. 99-176; Coon, C. S., 1965. *The Living Races of Man, op. cit.*, pp. 155-185.
27. Oakley, K. P., 1957. *Man as the Tool-Maker, op. cit.*, p. 109; Marshack, A., 1972. *The Roots of Civilization. op. cit.*, p. 136.
28. Tylor, E. B., 1865. *Researches into the Early History of Mankind and the Development of Civilization*. London: Murray; Morgan, L. H., 1877. *Ancient Society*. London: Macmillan.
29. Boas, F., 1932. *Anthropology and Modern Life*. New York; Boas, F., 1940. *Race, Language, and Culture*. New York: The Free Press.

## Chapter XIX
### *The Ethnic Membrane*

1. White, L. A., 1949. *The Concept of Culture*. New York: Grove Press; Kluckhohn, C., 1949. *Mirror for Man*. New York: McGraw-Hill; Harris, M., 1977. *Cannibals and Kings: The Origin of Cultures*. New York: Random House.
2. The American philosopher John Dewey (1859-1952) gave impetus to the so-called reconstructionist movement which saw the role of schools and other institutions as building a more rational, secular, and liberal scientific society. See: Dewey, J., 1935. *Liberalism and Social Action*. New York: Putnam; Kilpatrick, W. H., ed., 1933. *The Educational Frontier*. New York: Appleton; Brameld, T., 1965. *Education as Power*. New York: Holt, Rinehart, and Winston.
3. Gould, S. J., 1981. *The Mismeasure of Man*. New York: Norton; Kamin, L. J., 1974. *The Science and Politics of I. Q.*. Potomac, Maryland: Erlbaum; Lewontin, R. C., Rose, S., and Kamin, L., 1984. *Not in Our Genes*. New York: Pantheon.

4. On ethnicity and its explosive force in human culture see: Isaacs, H. R., 1975. *Idols of the Tribe.* New York: Harper: Isaacs, H. R. 1979. *Power and Identity.* New York: Foreign Policy Association; van den Berghe, P. L., 1981. *The Ethnic Phenomenon.* New York: Elsevier; Horowitz, D. L., 1985. *Ethnic Groups in Conflict.* Berkeley: University of California Press.

5. "History itself is a real part of natural history—of nature developing with man. Natural science will in time incorporate into itself the science of man, just as the science of man will incorporate into itself natural science: there will be one science." Marx, K., 1844. *The Paris Manuscripts.*

6. Brace, C. L., and Ashley Montagu, M. F., 1977. *Human Evolution.* New York: Macmillan, pp. 333-338.

7. Oakley, K. P., 1957. *Man the Tool-Maker.* Chicago: University of Chicago Press, pp. 92-109.

8. See Itzkoff, S. W., 1983. *The Form of Man.* Ashfield, Massachusetts: Paideia Publishers, pp. 181-209, "Culture as a Biological Activity," Chapter 8.

9. A traditional sociobiological, theoretical perspective is given in Lumsden, C. J., and Wilson, E. O., 1981. *Genes, Mind, and Culture.* Cambridge: Harvard University Press. An agnostic perspective on this relationship can be seen in a now classic book, Cassirer, E., 1944. *An Essay on Man.* New Haven: Yale University Press.

10. Langer, S. K., 1942. *Philosophy in a New Key.* Cambridge: Harvard University Press, pp. 103-143; Langer, S. K., 1972. *Mind: An Essay on Human Feeling, Volume II.* Baltimore: Johns Hopkins University Press, pp. 317-355.

11. The Bengalis of Bangladesh (formerly East Pakistan) shared a common Islamic religious identity with their West Pakistani overlords (they were supposedly one nation formed out of the colonial Indian subcontinent). Ethnically, however, they were quite different. They speak Bengali, an Indo-European dialect related to Hindi, while their West Pakistani co-nationals over a thousand miles west speak Urdu, a Persian dialect also derived from the Indo-European family. In 1971 they fought and won their independence, enduring frightful slaughter by the Pakistani armies.

12. See Chapter XII and notes (Irsigler, Holloway, *et al.)* on the ancient rooting of the language areas of the brain to the allocortical connections with the limbic system. The several millions of years of growth of the cortical brain while absorbing language into the mass of neurological tissue has yet allowed for the ancient connection to transmit the midbrain energies and affect to our cortical behavior.

13. Howell, F. C., 1965. *Early Man.* New York: Time, pp. 144-163; Clark, G., 1967. *The Stone Age Hunters.* New York: McGraw-Hill, pp. 43-90.

14. From Cassirer, E., 1944. *An Essay on Man.* New Haven: Yale University Press: ". . . man does not live in a world of hard facts, or according to his immediate needs and desires. He lives rather in the midst of imaginary emotions, in hopes and fears, in illusions and disillusions, in his fantasies and dreams." p. 25.

15. As we have documented in the first two volumes of this series and in Part 1 of this book, as *Homo's* brain and competency grew throughout the Pliocene and early Pleistocene, the adaptive demands of plains living turned the defensive proto-*Homo* into a typically far-ranging and aggressive anthropoid mainly concerned with eliminating his weaker competitors from his new ecological niche.

16. van den Berghe, P. L., 1975. *Man and Society.* New York: Elsevier, pp. 65-89.

17. Weber, M., 1958 (1915). "The Protestant Ethic and the Spirit of Capitalism," in Gerth, H. H., and Mills, C. W., eds. *From Max Weber: Essays in Sociology.* New York: Galaxy, pp. 302-322; Tawney, R. H., 1938 (1922). *Religion and the Rise of Capitalism.* Harmondsworth, England: Penguin.

18. Neale, J. E., 1962 (1943). *The Age of Catherine de Medici.* New York: Harper Torchbook.

19. Jamieson, J. W., 1983. "Familial Charisma," *Mankind Quarterly, 23:*357-364.

20. Both Earl Browder and William Foster, leaders of the American Communist Party during the 1940s and 1950s, came from good, Protestant, midwestern families. For an analysis of the backgrounds of radical youth, see Rothman, S., and Lichter, R. S., 1982. *Roots of Radicalism.* New York: Oxford University Press.

21. Hooton, E. A., 1940. *Why Men behave Like Apes and Vice Versa.* Princeton: Princeton University Press; Hooton, E. A., 1937. *Apes, Men, and Morons.* New York: G. P., Putnam and Co.

## Chapter XX
### Ideology, Egalitarianism, and Genocide

1. Cassirer, E., 1944. *An Essay on Man.* New Haven: Yale University Press, chapters 2 and 3.

2. Fossey, D., 1984. *Gorillas in the Mist.* Boston: Houghton-Mifflin.

3. Tobias, P. V., 1971. *The Brain in Hominid Evolution.* New York: Columbia University Press, p. 88.

4. Barnhart, C. L., ed., 1956. *American College Dictionary.* New York: Random House, p. 599.

5. Gould, S. J., 1981. *The Mismeasure of Man.* New York: W. W., Norton; Lewontin, R. C., Rose, S., and Kamin, L., 1984. *Not in Our Genes.* New York: Pantheon.

6. Moorehead, A., 1966. *The Fatal Impact.* New York: Harper and Row, pp. 101-104.

7. Rousseau, J. J., 1950 (1762). *The Social Contract.* New York: E. P. Dutton, book 4, chapter 2.

8. Nisbet, R. A., 1953. *The Quest for Community.* New York: Oxford University Press, pp. 189-211.

9. Mannheim, K., 1936. *Ideology and Utopia.* Wirth, L., and Shils, E., trans. New York: International Library of Psychology, Philosophy, and Scientific Method, pp. 97-136. Here is one of the most interesting discussions of the relationship of irrationalism in politics to the types of ideological social structures which have existed in the last several hundred years, including communism and fascism.

10. Cassirer, E., 1946. *The Myth of the State.* New Haven: Yale University Press. Cassirer demonstrates in this book, written at the close of World War II, how the state has spawned a series of myths about human nature that has enveloped its citizens and caused them to accept the will of the leadership even as it carries the state to the abyss.

11. Tocqueville, A. de, 1945 (1840). *Democracy in America.* New York. de Tocqueville was one of the first to warn against the "tutelary power" of the state. See also Nisbet, R. A., 1953. *A Quest for Community* op. cit.

12. Gay, P., 1966. *The Enlightenment: An Interpretation.* New York: Knopf, pp. 126, 325-326.

13. Jefferson, T., 1779. "A Bill for the More General Diffusion of Knowledge," and "Notes on the State of Virginia," in Lee, G. C., ed., 1961. *Crusade Against Ignorance.* New York: Teachers College Press, pp. 83-97.

14. Hegel, G. W. F., 1820. *Philosophy of Right,* and 1822-25. *Philosophy of History,* in Jones, W. T., 1952. *A History of Western Philosophy.* New York: Harcourt Brace; for a discussion of the relationship of Hegel's view of the state, the deterministic nature of historical process to Marx's elaboration of those views, see pp. 882-889, 915-920.

15. Tashjian, J. H., "Genocide, the United Nations and the Armenians," in Porter, J. N., ed., *Genocide and Human Rights*. Washington, D. C.: University Press of America, p. 131; Morgenthau, H., Sr., 1918. *Ambassador Morgenthau's Story*. Garden City, New York: Doubleday; Toynbee, A. J., 1916. *The Treatment of Armenians in the Ottoman Empire, 1915-1916*. London: His Majesty's Stationery Office (also by Bryce, Viscount J.); Kuper, L., 1981. *Genocide: Its Political Use in the Twentieth Century*. New Haven: Yale University Press; a general survey of the various atrocities.

16. Conquest, R., 1968. *The Great Terror: Stalin's Purge of the Thirties*. New York: Macmillan; Conquest, R., 1970. *The Nation Killers: Soviet Deportation of Nationalities*. New York: Macmillan.

17. Conquest, R., 1986. *The Harvest of Sorrow: Soviet Collectivization and the Terror-Famine*. New York: Oxford University Press; Solzhenitsyn, A. I., 1974-78. *The Gulag Archipelago, Volumes 1-3*. New York: Harper and Row.

18. Dawidowicz, L., 1975. *The War Against the Jews, 1933-1945*. New York: Holt, Rinehart, and Winston; Hilberg, R., 1967. *The Destruction of the European Jews*. Chicago: Quadrangle; Levin, N., 1973. *The Destruction of European Jewry, 1933-1945*. New York: Schocken; Reitlinger, G., 1961. *The Final Solution*. New York: A. S. Barnes.

19. Thucydides (420-411 B. C.) *The Peloponnesian War*, book 5, chapter 7.

20. Campbell-Johnson, A., 1951. *Mission with Mountbatten*. London: Hale; Collins, L., and Lapierre, D., 1975. *Freedom at Midnight*. New York: Simon and Schuster; Moon, P., 1962. *Divide and Quit*. Berkeley: University of California Press; Chaudhuri, K., 1972. *Genocide in Bangladesh*. Bombay: Orient Longman; International Commission of the Jurists, 1971. *The Events in East Pakistan: A Legal Study*. Geneva.

21. Wertheim, W. F., 1966. "Indonesia Before and After the Untung Coup," *Pacific Affairs 39*:115-127; Amnesty International, 1977. *Indonesia: An Amnesty International Report*. London.

22. MacBride, S., 1979. "The 1979 Sean MacBride Human Rights Lecture. London: Amnesty International; Kamm, H., 1981. "The Silent Suffering of East Timor," *The New York Times Magazine*, 15 February, pp. 34-35.

23. Meisner, M., 1977. *Mao's China: A History of the People's Republic*, p. 107.

24. Kuper, L., 1981. *Genocide*. op. cit., p. 153; Horowitz, D. L., 1985. *Ethnic Groups in Conflict*. Berkeley: University of California Press, pp. 118-122.

25. Kuper, L., 1977. *The Pity of it All.* Minneapolis: University of Minnesota Press, pp. 145-170.

26. Le Marchand, R., and Martin, D., 1974. *Selective Genocide in Burundi.* London: Minority Rights Groups Report, Number 20; DuBois, V., 1972. *To Die in Burundi.* New York: American University Field Staff Reports, Volume 16, Number 4.

27. de St. Jorre, J., 1972. *The Brothers' War: Biafra and Nigeria.* Boston: Houghton-Mifflin; Perham, M., 1970. "Reflections on the Nigerian Civil War," *International Affairs 46:*231-246; Jacobs, D., 1987. *The Brutality of Nations.* New York: Knopf.

28. Barron, J., and Paul, A., 1977. *Murder of a Gentle Land.* New York: Crowell; Shawcross, W., 1978. "Cambodia: Nightmare Without End," *Far Eastern Economic Review 100:*32-34; Tan, L. H., 1978. "Cambodia's Total Revolution," *Index on Censorship.* January-February, pp. 3-10; Wallace, J. N., 1977. "The Death of a Million Cambodians," *U. S. News and World Report,* 8 August, p. 33.

29. Chiera, E., 1938. *They Wrote on clay.* Chicago: University of Chicago Press; Kramer, S. N., 1959. *History Begins at Sumer.* New York: Doubleday-Anchor.

30. Pfeiffer, J. E., 1983. *The Creative Explosion: An Inquiry into the Origins of Art and Religion.* New York: Harper and Row.

31. Weber, M., 1930 (1904-5) *The Protestant Ethic and the Spirit of Capitalism.* Parsons, T., trans. London; Tawney, R. W., 1938 (1922). *Religion and the Rise of Capitalism.* London: Penguin.

32. Feuer, L., ed., 1959. *Marx and Engels: Basic Writings on Politics and Philosophy.* New York: Doubleday Anchor, p. 119, from Karl Marx's "Critique of the Gotha Program," 1875.

33. Sartre, J. P., 1968. "On Genocide," *Ramparts,* February, pp. 37-42; Dadrian, V. N., 1980. "A Theoretical Model of Genocide," *Sociology International,* January; Lemkin, R., 1946. "Genocide," *The American Scholar, 15:*2, pp. 227-230.

34. Conquest, R., 1968. *The Great Terror: Stalin's Purge of the Thirties,* op. cit.

35. Mosse, G., 1978. *Toward the Final Solution.* New York: Howard Fertig. It must be emphasized in the strongest terms that Nazi propaganda cannot be accepted on face value. It was a tissue of hallucinations and lies. It is sad that George Mosse accepts the racial propaganda as a serious argument. Oddly, he documents the numerous Jewish scientists—Lombroso, Nordau, etc.—who were converts to eugenicism and the biological point of view and thus who supposedly undergirded Nazi "scientific racism."

36. The only book on the cultural history of Austria, 1900-1938, or Germany during the same period, that, to my knowledge, does not mention the contributions of the Jews as an ethnic group was written by an emigre Jewish historian: Gay, P., 1968. *Weimar Culture: The Outsider as Insider.* New York: Harper and Row.

37. For a picture of the musical scene in Weimar Germany, see Itzkoff, S. W., 1979. *Emanuel Feuermann: Virtuoso.* University: University of Alabama Press.

38. Living in Vienna in 1983 and speaking with the few aged survivors of the Holocaust still living in that tragically beautiful city, one is deeply moved by the remembrances of musicians scrubbing the streets with lye solutions while the "brown shirts" laughed, of Sigmund Freud's aged sisters, left behind while the ransomed master was dying in London, being brutally shipped off to a concentration camp and to inevitable death. The barbarism was everywhere, from the Channel to the plains before the Volga. Here in the city of the waltz king the testimony was devastating.

39. Feuer, L., ed., *Marx and Engels.* op. cit., pp. 118-119.

40. Heer, F., 1969. *The Medieval World.* New York: Praeger, pp. 114-115, 254-260; Thomas, H., 1979. *A History of the World.* New York: Harper and Row, pp. 492-494.

41. Feuer, L., 1986. *Imperialism and the Anti-Imperialist Mind.* Buffalo, New York: Prometheus.

42. I have reference here to the conscious and systematic opening of the gates in Britain under socialist governments during the sixties and into the seventies, giving permanent homes to former colonists from South Asia, Africa, the West Indies, even at a time of economic decline, unemployment, and overpopulation.

43. Bruckner, P., 1986. *The Tears of the White Man.* New York: The Free Press.

44. Guthke, J., 1978. *Ist Intelligenz Messbar?* Berlin (East): Deutscher Verlag der Wissenschaften; Eysenck, H. J. *Personality, Genetics, and Behavior.* New York: Praeger, p. 258. Eysenck cites the Guthke book as representing a Marxist tradition in East Germany and the Soviet Union in general that accepts the reality of intellectual differences and the usefulness of I. Q. testing.

45. Teilhard de Chardin, P., 1959 (1938). *The Phenomenon of Man.* New York: Harper and Brothers, p. 282.

46. Lehmann-Haupt, C., 1985. *New York Times,* 23 May.

47. Hooton, E. A., 1946. *Up From the Ape.* New York: Macmillan, pp. 660-661.

# Index

mar, 164; human specialization, 47, 182; talents, 202, 227-228; thought, 160-161; vocalization, 178-179, 231-232; writing, 168-169. *See also* Reading.

Leadership, 318-323.

Leakey, Louis, 274.

Leakey, Mary, 119.

Leakey, Richard, 64.

Learning: 42-46; disabilities, 225-227, 229.

Lehmann-Haupt, Christopher, 330.

Lehrke, Robert G., 220, 240.

Lenin, 20, 312, 316.

Leonardo, 205-207.

Lewontin, R., 254.

Liberalism, 327-331.

Life: origin, 38; thermodynamics, 95-96.

Limbic system, 107-108, 110, 203-205, 209, 301.

Lobotomization, 109, 157-158, 181, 196.

Locke, J., 111.

Lombards, 267.

Lombroso, Cesare, 130, 190.

Lorenz, Konrad, 100.

Lovejoy, Owen, 54.

Lumsden, Charles, 79-81.

Luria, A. R., 110, 158, 182, 195.

**M**

Maclean, P., 111.

*Making of the Civilized Mind, The,* 34.

Male: aggression, 106, 216-217, 233-237; fragility, 213-216, 220, 241; human intelligence, 190-191, 240; size, 244.

Mammals: aggression in, 103, 105-106; bonding of, 295-297, 301; expansion of, 32, 117; human inheritance, 203-205; interfertility of, 59, 253; origins of, 52-53.

Maoism, 18, 325.

Maori, 264.

Marx, Karl, 16, 17, 24, 34, 72, 310, 315, 326.

Marxism, 15-17, 72, 83, 84, 313, 315, 316, 322, 324, 326.

Mathematics: ability in, 222-227; intelligence, 218, 226-227; precocity, 138-139, 170-171; reading and, 167-169.

Memory, 199.

Mental illness: 214; retardation, 222.

Michelangelo, 205-207.

Minoans, 66.

Miocene, 59, 90, 92, 104, 186, 231-232, 236.

Mongoloids: hybridizations of, 264-268; intelligence, 250; migrations of, 255, 264-265, 279-280; origins of, 253-254, 255-256; progressive, 284, 287; uniqueness, 253, 255-256.

Monkey, 53.

Monogamy, 232.

Monotheism, 14.

Morality: 283-285; of state, 318, 333.

Morgan, L. H., 71, 284.

Mortality rates, 214-215.

Moullians, 66, 268.

Movement time, 144.

Mozart, W. A., 111.